# The Learning Society

# Adult Learners, Education and Training 2

**THE OPEN UNIVERSITY MA IN EDUCATION**

This Reader, *The Learning Society: Challenges and Trends,* and its companion volume, *Boundaries of Adult Learning,* are both part of a course, *Adult Learners, Education and Training,* that is itself part of the Open University MA in Education programme.

The Open University MA in Education is now firmly established as the most popular postgraduate degree for education professionals in Europe, with over 3,500 students registering each year. The MA in Education is designed particularly for those with experience of teaching, the advisory service, educational administration or allied fields.

**Structure of the MA**

The MA is a modular degree, and students are therefore free to select from a range of options the programme which best fits in with their interests and professional goals. Specialist lines in management and primary education are also available. Study in the Open University's Advanced Diploma and Certificate Programmes can also be counted towards the MA, and successful study in the MA programme entitles students to apply for entry into the Open University Doctorate in Education programme.

---

COURSES CURRENTLY AVAILABLE:
• Management • Child Development • Primary Education
• Curriculum, Learning and Assessment • Special Needs
• Language and Literacy • Mentoring • Classroom Studies
• Education, Training and Employment • Gender
• Educational Research • Science Education
• Adult Learners • Maths Education

---

**OU supported open learning**

The MA in Education programme provides great flexibility. Students study at their own pace, in their own time, anywhere in the European Union. They receive specially prepared study materials, supported by tutorials, thus offering the chance to work with other students.

**How to apply**

If you would like to register for this programme, or simply to find out more information, please write for the *Professional Development in Education* prospectus to the Central Enquiry Service, PO Box 200, The Open University, Walton Hall, Milton Keynes, MK7 6YZ, UK (Telephone 01908 653231).

Adult Learners, Education and Training 2

# The Learning Society

## Challenges and Trends

Edited by Peter Raggatt, Richard
Edwards and Nick Small at
The Open University

London and New York in association with
The Open University

First published 1996
by Routledge
11 New Fetter Lane, London EC4P 4EE

Simultaneously published in the USA and Canada
by Routledge
29 West 35th Street, New York, NY 10001

Reprinted 2000

*Routledge is an imprint of the Taylor & Francis Group*

Typeset in Garamond by Datix International Limited, Bungay, Suffolk
Printed and bound in Great Britain by Biddles Ltd, www.Biddles.co.uk

*British Library Cataloguing in Publication Data*
A catalogue record for this book is available from the British Library

*Library of Congress Cataloguing in Publication Data*
A catalogue record for this book has been requested

ISBN 0–415–13615–6

# Contents

# Illustrations

## FIGURES

## TABLES

# Acknowledgements

Acknowledgement is gratefully expressed for material from the following publications:

1 Stock, A. (1993) *Lifelong Learning: Thirty Years of Educational Change*, Association for Lifelong Learning.

2 Tuijnman, A. (1992) 'The expansion of adult education and training in Europe', *International Review of Education*, vol. 38, no. 6: 673–92. © 1992 UNESCO Institute for Education, © 1992 Kluwer Academic Publishing. Reprinted by permission of Kluwer Academic Publishers.

5 Schuller, T. and Bostyn, A.M. (1993) 'Learners of the future: preparing a policy for the third age', *Journal of Education Policy*, vol. 8, no. 5: 365–79. Reprinted by permission.

6 Hart, M. (1992) *Working and Educating for Life*, London: Routledge.

7 Worpole, K. (1991) 'The age of leisure' in J. Corner and S. Harvey (eds) *Enterprise and Heritage: Crosscurrents of a National Culture*, London: Routledge.

8 Jansen, T. and van der Veen, R. (1992) 'Adult education in the light of the risk society', *International Journal of Lifelong Education*, vol. 11, no. 4: 275–86. Reprinted by permission.

9 Field, J. (1994) 'Open learning and consumer culture', *Open Learning*, vol. 9, no. 2: 3–11. Reprinted by permission of Longman Group Ltd.

10 Tett, L. (1993) 'Education and the marketplace', *Scottish Educational Review*, vol. 25, no. 2: 123–31. Reprinted by permission.

11 van der Zee, H. (1991) 'The learning society', *International Journal of Lifelong Education*, vol. 10, no. 3: 213–30. Reprinted by permission.

12 Commission on Social Justice/Institute for Public Policy Research (1991) 'Investment: adding life through lifelong learning' in *Strategies for National Renewal*, London: Vintage. Reprinted by permission.

13 Waterman, R.H. Jr., Waterman J.A. and Collard, B.A. (1994) 'Towards a career-resilient workforce', *Harvard Business Review*, July–August: 87–9. Reprinted by permission of *Harvard Business Review*. © 1994 by the President and Fellows of Harvard College; all rights reserved.

15 Scott, P. (1993,)'The idea of the university in the 21st century: a British perspecctive', *British Journal of Educational Studies*, vol. 41: 4–25. © 1993 Blackwell Publishers Ltd and SCSE.

While the publishers have made every effort to contact copyright holders of material used in this volume, they would be grateful to hear from any they were unable to contact.

# Introduction

## From adult education to a learning society?

*Peter Raggatt, Richard Edwards and Nick Small*

Thirty years ago adult education resounded to the merits of permanent education, lifelong education and recurrent education. Each had their champions, drawn in the main from adult educators and think tanks such as Unesco. Careful distinctions were made between these concepts but two overriding characteristics united them. First, all directed their attention to education, to the providers and provision and, second, all agreed that it was principally the responsibility of the state to create the institutions and provide the resources to deliver the preferred policy.

Today the vocabulary is different. It speaks of lifelong learning, learning organizations and a learning society. The debate is enriched and enlivened by contributions from employers, policy-makers, active politicians, academics from different disciplines and research studies. Each has a range of perspectives. The centrepoint of discussion is learning and there is a general and widespread recognition and acceptance that it takes place in many different settings – in the workplace, the home, in groups or alone – and not only, or primarily, in formal educational settings. This has produced new practices and a new challenge has arisen as how best to accredit learning which takes place in these non-formal settings. But by focusing on learning, in contrast to education or training, attention has been directed to the individual. It is the individual who has to take responsibility for learning and for selecting what, where and how to learn. Although not absolving the state from responsibility it shifts the balance of responsibility, acts to redefine boundaries and is used to legitimize selective withdrawal.

We therefore witness a central paradox: a shift in the responsibility for developing learning opportunities for adults from the state to individuals and employers is taking place at the very same time that there is growing recognition of the need to move towards the notion of lifelong learning as we move towards the 21st century. The origins for the surge in interest in lifelong learning and the learning society lie in the constellation of technological, economic, cultural and demographic forces that surround and affect adults. Running through each of these forces and providing a common strand of analysis in the chapters of this book is the concept of change. Both institutions and individuals are being encouraged, even required, to respond to changes elsewhere in the system. Most obvious, perhaps, are the new technologies which are continuously reconstructing the world we live in, how we cook, communicate with each other, how we choose our entertainment and where, how and whether we can work and learn. Whether we want it or not we need to learn how to use new technology in order to function in society whatever our age.

Change is also a fact of life for employment with the new technologies changing the ways in which work is organized, the modes of production and the skills required by workers. An important and pervasive argument is that employers need workers who are more highly skilled and more multi-skilled than in the past. These labour market skills have increasingly been provided through post-school organizations, which have accordingly attracted much more attention from policy-makers and employers than in the past, and through the workplace as human resource development (HRD) has become a strategic issue for many employers. The content of these learning opportunities is also changing with a wider recognition that technological skills are not enough if an organization is to respond effectively and speedily to changes in its environment. Softer skills, such as creativity, the ability to take initiatives, to solve problems, to identify where improvements can be made in production and openings for new products and services, are also needed. In some cases organizations have gone further, providing opportunities for individuals to develop their full potential and encouraging workers to identify with and participate in the formation of the company goals. This goes beyond HRD; the organization itself is engaged in the process of learning and developing its potential by developing its workers. It becomes a 'learning organization'.

It is, of course, no coincidence that the concepts of lifelong learning, the learning society and learning organizations should have emerged at a time when the European Union (EU), individual member states and nations around the globe have been preoccupied with ways of improving economic competitiveness and raising the skill levels of workers. But to regard this as a satisfactory characterization of lifelong learning or of a learning society is to overlook most of the population and the much broader base on which these concepts are founded. Moreover, it is an invitation to concentrate attention and resources on the better off, on those who are economically active and those who are most likely to have access to education and training.

Technological and economic changes are important touchstones for proponents of lifelong learning but cultural changes are also important. Of particular consequence are changes in lifestyles manifested in the growth of a range of recreational activities, personal development pursuits (such as assertiveness training and consciousness raising), health and personal services ranging through aerobics and step classes to advice on aromatherapy, colour and fashion. Each provides evidence of the interest in learning and finds its expression through new forms of opportunity developed by public and private providers operating within what is often termed 'a consumer culture'. To these can be added new learning opportunities which have developed around environmental, feminist, conservation and self-help groups, forms of social activism aimed at shaping change in particular ways.

The chapters that follow explore the challenges confronting people today. The concept and trends towards a learning society in which lifelong learning may contribute not only to economic and labour market objectives but also to wider cultural, social and equitable goals. Thirty years ago the tension between these differing goals was largely resolved in favour of the latter. In Britain adult education was a particular form of bounded provision which, and as Stock (Chapter 1) points out, operated within a liberal paradigm in which adult educators saw themselves as engaged in the transformation of the social condition. This period of uncritical romanticism was supplanted from the 1970s by more instrumental programmes supported by targeted funding. The growth of opportunities for adult learners through the 1980s and into the 1990s, frequently justified in terms of economic benefits flowing from a more highly educated and skilled society, led to a further relative and absolute decline in traditional adult education. Britain was not alone in this for, as Tuijnman (Chapter 2) explains, a similar experience is evident in other European countries where there has been an expansion of continuing vocational education and a consolidation, or decline, of liberal adult education.

These changes in the distribution of opportunities for adult learners have been made easier because adult education has never featured as a significant component of social policy and has has only a weak statutory legislative base, particularly in Britain. Paradoxically, recent changes (notably the *Further and Higher Education Act* of 1992) have brought greater coherence to adult education but at the cost of restricting public funding to programmes which lead to particular qualifications. As Tuckett (Chapter 3) argues, despite creative curriculum design by practitioners one consequence of the 1992 *Act* has been a massive decline in participation of older people even as opportunities have grown for younger adults.

Drawing on empirical studies in Scotland, Tett (Chapter 10) also focuses on changing opportunities and participation by different groups of adults. She cites the low levels of participation by the older age group, minority ethnic groups, long-term unemployed, those in semiskilled and unskilled occupations, women with dependent children and people living in rural areas. Tett argues that collaboration between providers has been a key factor in helping such adults engage in education and training for the first time and is also an important factor in sustaining participation by providing information and advice on progression. She argues that the adoption of market-inspired policies will undermine collaboration and reduce disinterested advice, ultimately disadvantaging potential participants.

The reconstruction of adult education as part of industrial and economic policy can also be seen in EU initiatives to improve competitiveness through the effective use of new technologies. The many and varied effects of these on employment, job content and work organization are examined by Clarke (Chapter 4), who also identifies evidence of differences between national and company cultures which affect the ways in which work is organized and the form and distribution of skills which are required. These differences have important implications for worker participation, company skill profiles at all levels and training programmes in different countries.

Concentration on opportunities for adult learners may obscure the broader social consequences of economic change. The increasingly precarious employment for many people and the feminization of poverty which accompanies the rise in part-time casual and temporary work, primarily among women, provides the focus for Hart's (Chapter 6) contribution. From her perspective it is not the shortfall in skills that is the problem but the direction of economic policy itself. Even if we accept the current direction of economic policy Hart's analysis is an important reminder of the psychological consequences of living with instability which bear most heavily on the least skilled and most vulnerable adults. Here, too, there is a challenge for social and educational policy for adults which is not touched by skills development initiatives aimed solely at upskilling and multi-skilling.

The concentration on adult learners as part of economic policy therefore raises serious questions about whether the distribution of opportunities for adult learners is equitable. If most opportunities are determined by occupational relevance it limits them to those who are, or could be, economically active. Age and gender become important influences affecting access to learning. Opportunities for people of retirement age and those approaching it have been in decline despite an increasing population of third-agers (over 50), whereas empirical studies have demonstrated significant differences in participation rates in occupational continuing education with women having much lower rates. Who controls opportunities for adult learners then becomes a key issue. As Tuijnman (Chapter 2) argues, 'The question of the social distribution of educational opportunities is far too important both for countries as a whole and for individuals to be decided exclusively by representatives of the world of work.'

Schuller and Bostyn (Chapter 5) focus on the absence of any initiative at national level to produce a coherent policy to meet the educational needs of older people despite the rapid increase in the numbers of older people in the population. The lack of a serious political movement pressing for more opportunities for third-agers despite their large numbers may be a consequence of their limited experience of initial education – many studies have shown that a 'virtuous circle' exists, that participation in learning after school is greatest among those who have already enjoyed a lengthy educational experience. Older people who have received the least initial education have been infrequent users of opportunities available in later life. In the long term there is likely to be increased demand for education as younger generations, who have enjoyed more initial education, age. There is none the less a powerful case for reversing the current decline in participation by older adults and for seeking an improvement in opportunities for third-agers as part of social policy. Governments, both national and local, and institutions need to tackle this issue and develop clear policy statements about access for older learners if the concept of a learning society is to be an inclusive one; they cannot omit groups that lack economic power.

Changes in the learning opportunities available to adults and their distribution have been affected by two factors. First, by a shift in language with vocational activities justified as 'investment' whereas non--vocational activities are rejected as 'consumption', a matter for individual decisions and choices. Second, in some countries they are weakened by the lack of any history of adult education as part of social policy. In different ways these issues are addressed by Tuckett, Schuller and Bostyn, Worpole and Field. Worpole (Chapter 7) argues that non-vocational adult education has been intentionally reconstructed as 'leisure' which provides a justification for removing local authority funding and subjecting it to charges. Whether this can be interpreted as government policy intended to ensure that the private leisure industry will prosper, as suggested by Worpole, or is a casual consequence of public expenditure cuts is a matter for debate. The challenge now is to find some way of filling the gaps developing in civic culture as the state withdraws support.

Field (Chapter 9) explores how changes in consumer culture are reflected in developments in both adult education and open learning. Noting that supply and demand for open learning have burgeoned over the last two decades, he focuses on the rapid growth in the consumption of open learning by individuals, much of which is for use in the home. This creates new links between the educational and domestic worlds. He suggests that the popularity of open learning is indicative of an interest in personal change, an interest which can be pursued and new identities explored and new skills developed through 'furtive learning'. The analysis is challenging in the view it offers of consumption patterns of adult learners, and how decisions about preferred forms of learning relate to, for example, styles of life, the motivation to learn as an individual or with close friends and to levels of disposable income. In other words, cultural capital as well as economic capital plays a central role both in the forms of lifelong learning that develop and in who becomes a lifelong learner.

The nature and intensity of change and uncertainty about its direction have produced contending theories about the future characteristics of society. Each implies different arrangements and challenges for lifelong learning. Jansen and van der Veen (Chapter 8) explore the notion of the risk society which is characterized by the uncontrolled and unpredictable influences of scientific and technological innovation which threaten the quality of life and reform the organization of social life in unforeseen ways. These 'uncertainties' are universal, crossing traditional boundaries of class, sex, age and race and producing new alliances. Thus, for them, although the redistribution of societal goods and wealth remains a relevant objective it must be reconfigured. Jansen and van der Veen expect adult education to become more an instrument of broad cultural policy than an instrument of social policy. As such it is likely to be 'more modest about its contribution to social problems'. Problem-solving networks in which practitioners act as brokers, for example, between a company and its workers or the local community, the use of experiential learning as a learning resource in heterogeneous workshop groups, and new forms of community education offer ways forward.

The realization of a learning society is therefore likely to be a slow, fragmentary and contested process. By use of the metaphor of a musical score, which provides a common inspiration around which a number of (jazz or classical) arrangements are possible, van der Zee (Chapter 11) argues that five strategic issues should guide the development of a learning society. There are echoes in the analysis of the traditional commitments of adult education to matters such as personal growth, fostering autonomous learning, but the core value of such a society is that learning is a right, not a privilege available to the few, and, as Tett suggested, there must be doubts about this where educational opportunity is left to market forces.

The issue of education as a human right is at the heart of the arguments presented by the Commission on Social Justice (Chapter 12) which maintains that governments are responsible for ensuring that learning throughout life is available to all. However, the Commission's report moves away from traditional notions of state provision or support to a more individualized conception of personal investment. The key proposal is for a Learning Bank funded by individuals, employers and government combined with a modular system of credits. The system would be driven by individuals who would draw on the bank to pay public and private providers for education and training. A radical reform such as this might promote the realization of a learning society, but would need to be supported by an effective accreditation system and highly competent quality assurance procedures. It also relies on individuals viewing personal investment as a realistic choice.

Government policies may create the framework for the development of a learning society, but its realization will be a result of fragmentary development in individual organizations, influenced to a greater rather than a lesser extent by self-interest, whose policies contribute coincidentally. These include both formal providers of education and training (for example, universities) and employers. Drawing on experience with high-tech industries in Silicon Valley, California, Waterman *et al.* (Chapter 13) start from the position that lifetime employment with an employer is a thing of the past and argue the need for a new covenant between employee and employer, based on employability rather than employment. The reciprocal obligation would be for the employer to provide individuals with the opportunity to develop their skills and enhance their employability, inside and outside the workplace, in exchange for improved productivity and commitment to success of the organization. Continuous learning of new technologies and their application, flexibility in working practices and responsiveness to customer needs would be the responsibility of workers as well as management. Such an approach would have to be supported by a change in attitudes and values in many workplaces, in particular in a more open approach to information and worker participation, as well as practical measures, such as confidential skills audits and counselling for employees. In this way, Waterman *et al.* suggest, workplaces will become learning organizations able to respond rapidly and effectively to unpredictable changes.

Similar ideas lie behind support for employee development (ED) schemes. These are education and training initiatives which support the personal development of employees; they are entirely voluntary and extend over a period of time. Although EDs are much broader in their objectives than training schemes – and have a much smaller budget – they are still regarded in most cases as the prerogative of management and are associated with human resource development. Where employers give priority to workers who have had little or no education after school there is an encouraging level of participation. However, as Payne (Chapter 14) observes, employer support for those in employment needs to be matched by public support for those excluded (for whatever reason) from the labour market.

As pragmatic institutions, universities have a long and varied history of successful adaptation to economic and cultural change. However, contemporary challenges are more far-reaching, particularly where universities are opened up to a mass clientele, and support for lifelong learning becomes part of their mission. Addressing the role of UK universities in this new age, Scott (Chapter 15) argues that their intellectual environment has been destabilized as they adjust to massification and commodification of knowledge. As a consequence, universities in the 21st century may have unfamiliar forms and less coherence in their value systems as they continue to adapt the pattern and the content of their courses and provide new forms of teaching and learning opportunities for their new and more heterogeneous clientele.

Shifting values and a loss of coherence can be seen across the range of post-school education and training. It is also apparent in the workplace where the rate of change, the transformation of work, the ending of the covenant of lifetime employment in many countries and areas of employment and changes in learning opportunities add to uncertainty. Necessarily, individuals (as Cooper (Chapter 16), drawing on experience in the UK, points out) will face frequent and often difficult choices about how to enhance or to ensure their career. The variety of educational pathways and the availability of new forms of learning will make these choices more complex and will need to be supported by provision for educational guidance both in educational institutions and in workplaces. However, as Cooper also notes, with the development of portfolio careers many people will be beyond the scope of institutional guidance systems and local community-based independent guidance systems will be necessary.

One of the most ubiquitous assumptions about the provision of learning methods in a learning society is that open and distance learning (ODL) will play a central role. There seems little doubt that this will be so but it needs further scrutiny. This is provided in Chapter 17 by Kirkup and Jones. They argue that while ODL has clearly brought new opportunities to many adult learners it also has a number of weaknesses which are less frequently discussed by politicians and policy-makers seeking to deliver more education and training more cheaply. Some, but by no means all, of these may be overcome by the new information and communication technologies which offer the potential to communicate across time and space and which link the delivery of education and training to notions of the learning society. However, the problem, as ever, is that these new technologies are unevenly distributed across social groups and this will limit their potential or it will sustain historic and contemporary inequities in the opportunities available for adult learners.

The learning society is thus not likely to be a Utopian society in which learning opportunities are available to all without restriction but one in which fresh challenges and new opportunities will be presented to those concerned with adult learners and lifelong learning alongside older questions of justice and equity.

# Chapter 1

# Lifelong learning
## Thirty years of educational change†

*Arthur Stock*

## INTRODUCTION

This chapter began life as part of the 1991 Centenary Lecture Programme celebrating the 100th Anniversary of the founding of the University of Manchester's School of Education. [. . .]

In presenting the lecture, I attempted to identify significant elements of recent and contemporary history which had contributed to the present paradoxical situation in which education for adults finds itself today, a situation where there is growing endorsement for and take-up of formal, often work-related, always *instrumental* education for adults; but where the accessible, joyful, neighbourhood-based, 'cultural' adult education is either being closed down entirely or operated as very high priced private or public enterprise aimed at the upper socio-economic segments. [. . .]

The empirical evidence of enrolment statistics indicates that the academic year 1975/76 was the apogee of numbers of people participating in locally available, general education for adults. Never, since that year, have there been as many of those 'community' adult education students, nor even as many when the several special-programme target-group members are added in. There is assumed to be an increase in systematic adult vocational education and training, at least as far as can be gathered from the quite inadequate statistical information available. However, it could be argued that the attraction of many traditional non-participants to tailor-made adult learning programmes has substantially improved the profile of participation; and that although the total numbers are lower than they should be, the distribution is better.

Whatever the judgement on current levels and types of participation, we may be certain that the present picture is very different from that of the early to mid 1970s. Whether the service is better or worse in terms

---

† This chapter is an edited version of a paper published by the *Association for Lifelong Learning*, 1993.

of what is needed for individuals, groups and a nation-state at this point in history we may defer for later arguments. From the analysis attempted in this chapter, we may infer that it is hardly good enough; and international comparative perspectives suggest that other near neighbours in Europe as well as countries further afield are investing much more in education and training for adults, often from a diversity of sources.

## ROMANTICISM

Clive James, the well-known broadcaster and critic, has claimed (*Clive James Interview*, BBC2, 17 February 1991), 'You have to have been a romantic to be a realist.' And certainly most of us engaged in education for adults, whether part-time or full-time, during the 1950s, 1960s and early 1970s were romantics in the best cultural sense of the term. We believed we were doing something 'worthwhile', in the immortal, question begging words of educational philosopher Hurst. As many of us had come from more rigid and traditional sectors of education, we recognized stimulating trends towards equity and democracy in the conduct and even the organization of parts of adult education; we were aware of universalist – even populist – claims for adult education which harmonized with our socio-ethical perspectives; and moreover, during the 1960s we were encouraged by the governing political ethos and even administrative fiat, to be aware of and relate to 'neighbourhood', 'community', 'the disadvantaged', 'individual and group needs'. Not only were we in an expanding service, we were on the side of the angels too! In a sense we had inherited the 'social consciousness' of previous generations of adult educators, such as Albert Mansbridge, founder of so many adult education institutions as well as the Workers' Educational Association (WEA), who believed fervently that a rigorous voluntary education by and for 'workers' would be a major engine of social and political change. The difference was that we were busy marketing its programmes and classes in a hyperactive but undiscriminating way to a larger audience than that envisaged in the latter-day notion of 'Workers' Education'. The change is symbolized in mirror-image form in Raymond Williams' 1983 *Tony McLean Memorial Lecture* (Williams 1983) when he recalls G. D. H. Cole's outburst at a 1950s meeting of the Oxford Delegacy for Extra-Mural Studies. 'I don't give a damn about Adult Education, I am only interested in Workers' Education', said Cole; and, although this was undoubtedly a throwback to an older tradition, unaware of the new demands and new horizons, impatient perhaps of the new 'respectability' demanded of the trade, it harmonizes with the romanticist belief of many adult educators: that their work was part of 'social transformation'. Williams again, in the same lecture, puts his finger unerringly upon the source of this in-built credo of three post-war decades, when he says:

> the impulse to Adult Education was not only a matter of remedying deficit, making up for inadequate educational resources in the wider society, nor only a case of meeting new needs in the society, though those things contributed. The deepest impulse was the desire to make learning part of the process of social change itself.
>
> (Williams 1983)

To much of this 'wider' adult education especially as promulgated in the universities, a pre-existing label was attached, namely liberal education which, in spite of a vast nineteenth-century and twentieth-century literature expounding or merely using the term, has never to my mind been satisfactorily defined. As a concept label, however vague, it received reinforcement from two quite disparate sources: on the one hand the long-running traditional liberal/vocational antithesis (or rather the tedious arguments surrounding it); and on the other from the so-called Responsible Body (RB) grant regulations which resulted, on occasions, in university extra-mural departments studiously committed to teaching foreign cultures, but studiously avoiding teaching foreign languages.

A further strengthening of this ethically based romantic period of education for adults, notably in the 1950s and early 1960s, was achieved by the vast outpouring in the relevant journals of the time about the Great Tradition: albeit that this was mostly confined to university adult education – though not entirely. The Great Tradition centred upon a partnership between WEA Districts and appropriate regional universities whereby the WEA identified programme elements and also recruited students for the classes, and the local friendly university provided, for the most part, the teaching staff. In addition, as Professor Harold Wiltshire noted:

> the only selection used is self-selection, and it is assumed that if you are interested enough to attend the course and competent enough to meet its demands then you are a suitable student.
>
> (Wiltshire 1956)

What a marvellously romantic statement, exuding liberation as well as liberality; but the now-understood barriers implied by the phrase 'competent enough to meet its demands' . . . indicate its limitations as a principle for the present day. It certainly seems unlikely that Professor Wiltshire would have wished to enter upon the competency-based education and training of the National Council for Vocational Qualifications which is a constant (though many would say inadequate) stimulus to much professional thinking and course development in the 1990s.

Even for the then newly re-invented university extension programmes of the 1950s – the forerunners of so much continuing education of the

1980s – a romantic liberality was frequently claimed, as J. W. Saunders exemplified about such courses:

> They are liberal, because even with courses established with vocational groups it is now generally recognized by the leaders of various professions that the best vocational asset that a man can have is a non-vocational liberal education.
>
> (Saunders 1959)

The sheer romantic arrogance of this statement – apart from its period sexism – quite takes one's breath away, especially the, at least in my experience, totally unwarranted assumption about the liberal education beliefs of 'leaders of various professions'.

However, throughout the 1950s and well into the 1960s there emerged increasingly the view that the only paradigm in which 'proper' adult education could be judged was the liberal paradigm. Norman Jepson [. . .] noted the growth in local authority promoted education for adults, in the following terms:

> Likewise, with the tremendous increase in the provision of social and recreational courses, there was the challenge to re-examine the precise function and value of such courses within the framework of liberal adult education.
>
> (Jepson 1959)

Looking back at that era from the broken glass and dereliction of the 1990s it appears like a garden of Eden, without even a wicked serpent but with merely a pompous, slow-moving lizard irritatingly denigrating the jungle-like growth and development of local education authority (LEA) provision.

Perhaps the reality of my romantic era of adult education was what Raymond Williams identifies as the paramount malaise of the nineteenth-century Oxford and Cambridge Extension Movement, when he says:

> they believed they were taking understanding to people. Not taking the tools of understanding; not taking the results of certain organised learning; not putting these into a process which would then be an interaction with what was often very solid experience in areas in which the learned were in fact ignorant; but rather a taking of learning itself, humanity itself. It is surprising how often in the writings of that period people whose individual lives we can respect, talk about 'humanising' or 'refining' people – of course mostly poor people. But the fact is that the real situation was never of that kind.
>
> (Williams 1983)

Of course, it was all done kindly and with good intent; but it is clear that the approach and the style were based on at best a blurred image through romantic spectacles, and at worst pure ignorance. The grand romantic assumptions of liberal educators or even those of the Great Tradition frequently did not accord and interrelate successfully with the real world of ordinary working people.

There was, nevertheless, for most adult educators a powerful synthesis of ethic, capability and faith which carried over from the university and WEA activists to many of the growing number of full-time professionals working in the LEA sector. And that is where the growth was occurring: rapidly accelerating growth in the 1960s. Nationally, between 1961 and 1968, the average rate of growth was around nine per cent a year. LEAs assumed that all the elements of further and adult education – including the financial resource – would constantly expand. There was a compliant expectation in many authorities of mid-year over-spending of budgets, with any criticism being countered by the claim that there would be inevitable under-spending when course closures or amalgamations through 'drop-out' occurred. For almost fifteen years (with only one major 'cuts' hiatus in 1968/70) a balmy climate of acceptance prevailed: that what was identified in further and adult education as needed would, more or less, be provided

Of course, when one peers back through the nostalgia and selective memories of that time, the blemishes and limitations emerge. For example, the staff training and development, particularly for the growing army of part-time tutors (probably 150,000 in England and Wales by 1970), was, in most authorities and institutions, either grossly inadequate or non-existent. Even in the most strongly defended university redoubts of the Great Tradition, there appeared to be consistent if not universal rejection of a requirement and provision for the competence of teaching staff, in educational if not academic terms. The University of Manchester and, indeed, some authorities in the North West, East Midlands and Yorkshire regions were unusual in offering in-service part-time and full-time courses for adult education teachers and organizers. But these were largely ignored or avoided by the rank and file in university extra-mural departments and the WEA even though the headquarters managers of those bodies frequently offered cooperation in promotion and development. [. . .]

It is fair to say that the authorities and institutions of the region now have a totally different mind-set to staff training and development, which is seen as a key instrumental necessity for quality provision.

Generally speaking, the 'romantic' era generated rather cavalier attitudes and assumptions – especially in administrators – about tutors of adults. These were partly a product of the marginality of that sector of the educational service and partly an historic inheritance of the styles of teaching and organization in the late nineteenth and early twentieth centuries, continued between the two world wars. The basic assumption was that, if tutors were reasonably well qualified in 'subject' terms, they would be able to teach 'their subject' to the untutored students who signed up for the essentially subject-based courses. Subsequent research related to tutor-training indicated that many tutors recruited on this basis and encouraged to venture into classrooms presented their material in a fashion modelled on a favourite teacher or lecturer of their own formal education experience. 'Presentation' was the dominant mode, although 'interactive' mode and some 'search' mode, especially in certain Responsible Body classes, were introduced. Indeed, many student groups were conditioned to expect hefty loads of straight lecturing-type presentation. I well remember the 1960s wise warning of a senior colleague at Manchester University on his receiving my highly active (and interactive) prescription for handling a fill-in class (because of the tutor's illness) at a local WEA branch. 'If you don't lecture for at least the first fifty minutes,' he said, 'they will not consider they've had their money's worth, especially as you're an unknown substitute.' His insight into the expectations of the group was only too accurate and I modified my plan accordingly. [. . .]

Amidst all this waywardness and occasional gross ineptitude there was, nevertheless, an acceptance in this country that a range of locally available and reasonably accessible educational provision for adults was a justifiable expectation in all communities. Whilst other countries, in the late 1960s and early 1970s, were incorporating 'rights' and 'quotas' and 'ratios' into new legislation for adult education, the British formula whereby most local authorities accepted broad catchment area responsibilities to provide education for adults within a loose framework law was much admired by many Continental neighbours. Our 'decentralized' system was seen as more democratic, more responsive than their over-centralized, if pluralistic, provision; and their local or municipal commitment was often small or non-existent.

The British apprehensions about the already emerging gross disparities of range, levels, resources and staffing, as between local education authorities up and down the country, were frequently brushed aside by Continental colleagues. [. . .]

In January 1970, Her Majesty's Inspectorate invited a group of interested academics, local authority inspectors, staff trainers, broadcasters and representatives of voluntary bodies to a New Year 'retreat' at Sydney Sussex College in Cambridge. One major purpose of the exercise was to explore what knowledge, insights and competences might be expected of a professional adult educator. The report which appeared (never officially published by the DES) was rather grandly titled *Explorations*. It offered a variety of useful insights, not least that a competent professional adult educator needed to understand about community networks, about their nature, strengths, frequency and importance, and how needs-based programmes could be related to or even help to build such networks.

In many ways, such critical analysis marked a break with the liberal romantic tradition. The 'social motives' of programme planning and recruitment were frequently based at best on the predilections of a group such as a WEA branch or at worst on the qualifications or subject preferences of an organizing tutor.

The ultimate moral imperatives of the romantic era had actually been encapsulated long before in the convinced prose of the *1919 Report*:

> The adult educational movement is inextricably interwoven with the whole organised life of the community. Whilst on the one hand it originates in a desire amongst individuals for adequate opportunities for self-expression and the cultivation of their personal powers and interests, it is, on the other hand, rooted in the social aspirations of the democratic movements of the country. In other words it rests upon the twin principles of personal development and social service. It aims at satisfying the needs of the individual and at the attainment of new standards of citizenship and a better social order. In some cases the personal motive predominates. In perhaps the greater majority of cases the dynamic character of adult education is due to its social motive.
>
> (Report of the Adult Education Committee to the Ministry of Reconstruction 1919)

Thus the generalized 'social motive' – idealistic and essentially rather vague, but nevertheless purposive and inspirational – was a core element, almost the leitmotiv, in liberal education for adults for almost exactly 100 years. Nor is the spirit dead today, although official recognition and endorsement of its value has diminished rapidly [. . .], threatening and often extinguishing organizations and institutions. The recent tragic demise of the long-cherished and purpose-built College of Adult Education in the city of Manchester is a case in point; and the wholesale butchery of local, community adult education, with the changes in emphasis in university extra-mural departments, is a current manifestation of governments' – local and central – lack of commitment to general/liberal education for adults.

Even in the academic world of professional philosophers a sinister version of liberalism and liberal education known in the trade as deontological liberalism has appeared. Rawls and Nozick, writing in the 1970s, provided a rationale derived in part from Locke and Kant for the ultra individualism of the 1980s. As Lawson has noted:

[Deontological liberalism] is a philosophy suited to a society which has no vision . . . where monetary values define worthwhileness.

(Lawson 1985)

It may be worth asking ourselves whether liberal adult educators have exacerbated the situation by apparently avoiding educational value questions. It is fashionable to say that adult education is about *process* not content. This is an eminently deontological view!

## MODERNISM

*not said why change*

What then do governments support, if anything? And when and how did the change take place? Taking the 'when' and 'how' first, one can identify a period during the mid-1970s when the Russell Report, essentially a social-purpose, liberal document which appeared in 1973, was effectively rejected by two different administrations of central government, even though some of its findings were implemented by local government. An adult literacy campaign, coordinated by the British Association of Settlements and supported by many voluntary bodies, the National Institute of Adult Education and the Association of Teachers in Technical Institutions, culminated in political and financial endorsement by central government of *special* adult literacy programmes in summer 1974, and the setting up in 1975 under the auspices of the National Institute of a special-purpose but narrowly framed Adult Literacy Resource Agency (ALRA). Furthermore, there appeared in 1976 the *Venables Report on Continuing Education*, ostensibly addressed to its instigators and sponsors, the Open University. More than half of it, however, was addressed to central and local government, to industry and to the country at large. The *Venables Report* defined in detail a comprehensive view of *continuing education* which gave as much kudos and emphasis to vocational education and role education as it did to 'balancing education', which was more-or-less 'liberal'.

At that time, as Director of the National Institute of Adult Continuing Education, I visited the corridors of power in Westminster and Elizabeth House (the then Department of Education and Science). I became increasingly aware that a combination of the demonstrable success in its field of a highly focused social policy-related agency such as ALRA, plus the growing awareness of the *utility* of focused continuing education in a number of departments of government *besides* the DES, was resulting in a very different perspective on education for adults. The idealistic but nevertheless holistic view of education for adults which had prevailed in the Education Ministry for some long time was changing to an alternative instrumental, targeted form. [. . .]

Thus, in answering the 'when' and 'how' questions referred to above, we may be certain that there was a sea change in the perception of both central and local government as to what constituted 'useful' education for adults; and for most this meant basic education, i.e. for full literate and numerate capability and participation, plus:

- English language capability for immigrants;
- vocational and pre-vocational education and training;
- some instrumental education to cope with life-changes, such as retirement, unemployment, and re-training.

Furthermore, as the finance for *general* adult education in the 1970s and 1980s was reduced, the informing criterion-linked adjective became 'justifiable' rather than 'useful'.

This is not to say that all locally available general education for adults had disappeared during these latter difficult years. For many authorities, institutions and individual college principals or centre heads, the answer was, in part or in whole, to turn to market forces. Fees, once regarded as necessarily minimal, in many cases soared from an average of about 25p per student hour in the mid-1970s to a [1993] average of around 120p per student hour. Moreover, the exercise of what is politely called 'virement' whereby well-patronized, high-fee courses supplement or subsidize less popular courses, or in some cases contribute towards discretionary fees for low-income students, became fashionable.

This, whilst weakening the public financial base of general/liberal education for adults, has also contributed to the wilful diversity of the service, and its costs, from one authority to another. It has also led to the virtually total breakdown of inter-authority transfer of adult students, except for rare or high-cost vocational courses.

Into this melancholy twilight of general adult education was injected a further element of policy, causing the ultimate dilemma for committed adult education workers. I refer to the ever-proliferating number of special social and economic oriented adult learning programmes backed by many departments of government: Department of Employment; Manpower Services Commission; subsequently Training Agency, now Training, Enterprise and Education Directorate (TEED); Department of Health; Home Office; Department of the Environment; Department of Energy; Department of Trade and Industry, and *even* the Department of Education and Science, all specifically financed, sometimes specifically staffed. Many of these programmes addressed *needs* close to the hearts of adult education professionals. Yet they were limited and narrow and often short term. What was a concerned adult educator to do?

Thus, the 'modernist' reality of a majority of endorsed and funded education for adults is wholesale fragmentation. During the 'romantic era', as I have called it, there was, at least, some degree of holism in the concepts and precepts which informed the work of adult educators, even though organizational cooperation and collaboration was never easy.

Nowadays, in its most extreme form the fragmentation can produce, in some English and Welsh authorities, a 'private army' syndrome, where the quite numerous educators of adults are marshalled into separately named and organized cohorts, such as health educators, neighbourhood workers, basic education workers, rehabilitation workers, ethnic minority specialists etc. etc. etc.; and, perhaps the saddest thing of all, in several of these same authorities, they hardly ever communicate from one 'army' to another. In the worst case actual hostilities break out. The 'fragmentation' may be further encouraged by the 'divided responsibility' nature of the 1992 *Further and Higher Education Act*, which places most education for adults with the Colleges of Further Education, but leaves certain important areas of provision with the local authorities. [. . .]

In public education for adults there was a further body-blow which was a product of sins of omission and commission. In spite of hundreds of representations about the importance of a coherent service of education for adults, there was little comprehension or consequent amendment demonstrated by the Government in its steam-rollering of the 1988 *Education Reform Act* through the Houses of Parliament. The result was a woefully weak legislative position of education for adults. When this weakness encountered the lethal fall-out of actual or threatened poll-tax capping (and rate-capping before it and Council Tax capping after it) the results were catastrophic. Formerly sound, active purveyors of good services of community adult education were savaged by elected members desperate to avoid central government's 'capping' axe poised over their heads. It was an appalling comment on our times when an almost totally discredited local tax legislation was able to assault and ruin so many worthwhile features of local life and community.

The inevitable casualties were the life-enhancing, equity-related, enriching, satisfying, supporting forms of job-unrelated, neighbourhood-available general adult education. But more, too, was made to suffer because many of the special-purpose, endorsed continuing education programmes of the recent past, plus the priorities of the immediate future, have been carried on the emaciated frame of the general adult education service. If this service is finally starved to death, or summarily despatched to the knacker's yard, then many of the glamorous special programmes are in great danger.

Thus, 'modernism' in many of its manifestations brings us to the supreme irony of our present adult educational times: when there has been more instrumental acceptance of the societal importance of education for adults than ever in history, as exemplified by all the disparate promotions of the many departments of government; but when the essential and basic educational structure is falling to pieces around us, like the broken windows of abandoned buildings. In this respect, as other commentators have noted, education for adults replicates the totally fragmented cultural landscape of this country following the devastation of the 1980s.

This *Götterdämmerung* scenario is neither total nor inevitable. There has been some good news in the trade in recent years, and the HM Inspectorate Review, *Education for Adults* (HM Inspectorate 1991), puts a brave face on current difficulties. The Review praises the highly motivated adult students, the dedicated teaching force, the high incidence of good-quality teaching and learning, quick response to identified needs, a wide variety of course provision at different levels, a range of local delivery points.

In spite of well-bred inhibitions in HMI reporting, the Review does emphasize a number of the current ailments in the service.

- *A failure to clarify aims and objectives*; for this one could substitute: 'weakening of local responsibilities and resources and superimposition of transitory national political objectives – often purely cosmetic'.
- *Wide variation in the amount of provision made by different LEAs*; there's no arguing with that.
- *Inadequate machinery to identify local needs and to plan, monitor and evaluate provision*; the *Further and Higher Education Act* of 1992 must weaken the LEAs' duty to do those things.
- *Barely adequate accommodation and equipment*; that must be either an averaged or plainly generous assessment.
- *Management deficiencies due to the low ratio of full-time to part-time staff*; and the ratio has deteriorated drastically in many LEAs following the transfer of nearly all 'Schedule 2' work to the Colleges of Further Education.

I should further wish to emphasize a number of other bright spots in the otherwise darkening landscape.

- *Open learning systems* of a varied, responsive and sophisticated character are attracting many individuals and groups (including employers/employees) to systematic learning with a high degree of flexibility offered to the student.
- More *adults* are enrolling in rather better produced and better accessed *further and higher education*; the skilled design and management of adult-friendly part-time and/or modular courses in institutions of further and higher education is a major contribution to this welcome trend. We should note the growth of Assessment of Prior Learning, too, in this connection.
- *Educational guidance and counselling for adults* has achieved a moral and intellectual victory – after fifteen years of report, demonstration and exhortation by ACACE, and particularly the Unit for the Development of Adult Continuing Education (UDACE). [Educational guid-

ance services for adults] are still very financially fragile.

- Focused, social-purpose education for specific adult *target groups* has often been very successful within the confines of the respective groups; but, with the possible exceptions of Adult Basic Education and, temporarily, the REPLAN programme [for unemployed adults], this strategy has not yet proved itself in a societal improvement or societal transformation way.
- More systematic and purposeful *staff development*, including the conceptual and operational development beyond mere 'training'.
- The development of open offers of supported general education for adults by the Ford Motor Company, through its Employee Development and Assistance Programme (EDAP), in the UK, by Motorola, General Motors and many other companies in the USA and other private sector organizations in Germany, Switzerland and Japan.

## THE FUTURE

There has always been a tendency when adult educators get together to bemoan the alleged lack of coherent theory which would not only underpin our thinking about the work but would convince the many doubting purse-holders and power-brokers.

Theory there certainly is; but like the provision itself this theory is rather fragmented, or even compartmentalized within the several academic disciplines which feed into the study of education for adults.

This is not the right circumstance to derive splendid, insightful, theoretical paradigms for this purpose in this present chapter. Suffice to say that part of the original semi-articulated model of the liberal educators of old, of the seeking, searching individual learning to understand and change a hostile social milieu, has received some reinforcement by recent research.

For example, Kelly's Personal Construct Theory of Learning which – put rather simply – stresses the reality of individuals trying to make sense of a complex world, and then *constructing their own knowledge and understanding of it*, is of paramount importance. It reinforces the long-held belief among many of us that education and training regimes, programmes and courses which do *not* contribute to this constant effort of 'personal construction' will not do very well. Or to put it another way, the insistence by course sponsors or purchasers upon what will be often perceived as arbitrary or irrelevant externally imposed learning goals and objectives (frequently somebody else's interpretations of the economic, manpower or social-conformity notions of the power people of our society) will only achieve minority success, as indicated by high drop-out rates, failures in required competency and loss of confidence.

This idiographic or personal side of the model interacts with the nomothetic or societal/institutional/political/managerial factors on the other side which so much influence the present-day patterns of our educational institutions, as also to a considerable extent their curricula. In passing, one should note there are still some colleges so dominated by these purely nomothetic elements that the individuality, the personal growth, the construction of usable knowledge which are intrinsic to the idiographic side are non-existent in the working of their organizations. In short, you then have an education/training factory which, no matter what apparent success is achieved as judged by external assessment, will have poor real and usable learning productivity. Such may well contribute to the frequently diagnosed malaise in British industry and society.

Even with the wholesale realization, indeed acceptance, of the current inadequacies, the necessary wholesale reforms needed to achieve a proper learning society in the UK are unlikely to be achieved within this century, although the recently published National Education and Training Targets may be a contribution to this. It may need a decade of the next century before radically different international social, political and economic comparisons and indicators will stimulate the required reappraisal and ultimate 'real' change. In the meantime there will probably be constant tinkering, mostly with the formal school system, and a continuation of the adoption of limited policy or programme learning projects outside the schools.

But we should still plan and organize for the necessary reforms, whether for the near or medium term. The following trends may take place in the not-too-distant future, partly because the usual motors of social policy development – demography, technology, economics and culture, in particular gender and multi-ethnic factors – will put pressure on people and establishments to undertake and underwrite them. The other increasingly powerful factor, ideology, may impinge upon the same for good or ill.

- The incorporation of the National Curriculum into the schools, with much-enhanced attainment testing, plus continuing research evidence of declining standards in some elements of basic education, may lead to the development of the notion of a *right* for all persons to achieve certain agreed attainment levels of basic education. In turn, this could result in further *much more evenly distributed* commitments of resource into adult basic education, in contrast to the very uneven distribution of the present time, including, in some cases, to the woefully inadequate.
- The present small beginnings of *workplace*-based adult education provision could easily develop very rapidly, as understanding grows of the essential necessary educational foundations and thresholds for satisfactory job training and re-training. This is happening already on

a very large scale in the USA. UK companies, factories and commercial employers may then decide to offer more in-house basic and follow-up education themselves, especially if the public sector remains so debilitated.

- *Open learning systems* will probably continue to be a major growth area, but with improved user-friendly packages marketed from many more points of sale including local/neighbourhood centres.
- The several active, *campaigning special-interest groups* and pressure groups may also discover the study-circle materials system – or open-learning packages – as a way to inform and stimulate scattered memberships.
- The success of the many *social-support or self-help* forms of education for adults, e.g. women's focused adult education or ethnic minorities' provision, may be recognized generically as being of major societal, as well as purely educational, significance, and could result in wider application throughout the community.
- There may well be a long-overdue resurgence in *political or quasi-political education* associated, for example, with gradually growing demands for proportional representation and/or a bill of rights, or other fundamental, but presently lacking, aspects of a modern democracy.
- The several pre-retirement, ageing-oriented, trips-for-the elderly, U3A, 'grey-power' organizations may be persuaded to federate (or at least confederate); and jointly to support a new dynamic curriculum stressing the great opportunities of third-age living.
- Multicultural education for adults may become more *positive* in its emphasis instead of producing essentially negative curricula, i.e *anti*-racism, and anti-sexism; not much anti-ageism yet! This whole crucial area of learning and development is finely balanced, and could easily be sabotaged by the combined forces of ignorance, oppression and fundamentalism.
- It seems likely that a whole reappraisal of the notions of *family and parent education,* i.e. education in and in relation to the family, will be necessary particularly in light of the ever-increasing proportions of single-parent and other non-traditional family structures. The consequential societal, group and individual adjustments may require much new thinking and new learning to make them work.
- *Euro-factors* are going to impinge even more on education for adults as the inevitable trend towards Euro-integration proceeds; and unless the formal educational system makes huge leaps forward in necessary transformation, there will be a great deal of demand upon post-initial education to try to counter the educational, linguistic and cultural deficiencies which many Britons will carry into European work and lifestyles.

However, I do forecast an early 21st century re-appraisal of *all* education which should proceed from a life-long learning or *education permanente* perspective. Thus:

- *A learning to enjoy learning stage*, for 3- to 6-year-olds; non-compulsory and fully financed.
- *A basic education stage*, for 7- to 14-year-olds; compulsory, but in a curricular sense, and with appropriate methodology, and available throughout life.
- *A further education stage*, for 15- to 18-year-olds; *not* compulsory 'schooling', but compulsory registration for varying options of education, training, work experience, assessed personal learning projects.
- *A higher education stage*, for 18- to 21-year-olds (and beyond), much of it 'sandwich', a large proportion modular, with credit accumulation and transfer inherent throughout. Access based on need, interest and experience in previous education and in life (Assessment of Prior Learning would be intrinsic).
- *Continuing education*; not really a stage, available throughout life on an 'entitlement' basis and financed by a mixture of compulsory personal insurance, payroll tax and personal contributions, these latter to vary in bands according to income. Clearly identifiable day and evening adult-oriented delivery points would be distributed throughout communities on, say, a 1:50,000 of population basis: but other educational institutions would also contribute. *All* would be points of delivery for approved distance and open learning; all would have guidance and counselling, also personal or group tutoring facilities.

Curricula would be perceived in whole-life terms, for example:

- life-enhancing education – cultural, physical, social, civic;
- special needs education;
- earnings-related education;
- life-stage changing education, including role education.

The whole reform would be approached with a reawakened sense of the priority and necessary coherence of education, for the health, happiness and growth of the people and the nation-state.

This would be 'post-modernism', or, in our terms, a truly Learning Society, informed, perhaps, by a new ethic of sharp environmental consciousness.

We must begin again to work for it; although it may be only our children who will see it.

# REFERENCES

HM Inspectorate (1991) *Education for Adults*, Education Observed series. Department of Education and Science, London: HMSO.

Jepson, N. A. (1959) 'The local authorities and adult education', in Raybould, S. G. (ed.), *Trends in English Adult Education*, London: Heinemann.

Lawson, K. (1985): 'Deontological liberalism: the political philosophy of liberal adult education', *International Journal of Life-long Education* 4 (3).

Saunders, J. W. (1959) 'University extension renascent', in Raybould, S. G. (ed.). *Trends in English Adult Education*, London: Heinemann.

Williams, R. (1983) 'Adult education and social purpose', in his retrospective anthology *What I Came Here to Say* (1990), London.

Wiltshire, H. C. (1956) 'The Great Tradition in university adult education', *Adult Education*, Autumn.

# Chapter 2

# The expansion of adult education and training in Europe

## Trends and issues†

*Albert C. Tuijnman*

## GROWTH AND DECLINE IN EUROPEAN ADULT EDUCATION

The guiding premise is that organized adult education expanded in Europe during the 1980s. But was this true of all countries and sectors of provision? These two questions ought to be answered before discussing the productive factors that are implicated in the process of expansion. The following statement by the Ministry of National Education of Turkey provides an illustration:

> The non-formal education will gain a greater significance during the current plan period with the development of international relations, the innovations in science and technology, the improvement of communication capabilities, the advent of the 'information society' age, the rapid changes in the structures of professions and the occurrence of sudden demands in the labor market. The resources allocated to the non-formal education will be increased during the period under study to ensure that the non-formal education is pursued together with the apprenticeship training in close collaboration of public and private sectors and not less than 7.5 per cent of the investment allocations earmarked for education will be diverted to the non-formal education of adults.
>
> (Ministry of National Education of Turkey 1990: 7)

There is an abundance of statistical evidence that adult education expanded in quantitative terms in Finland during the 1980s. It is stated in the report Finland (Finland, Ministry of Education 1990: 94) prepared for the IBE International Conference on Education that 'the rapid growth in the provision of vocational adult education has given it a status equal to other educational sectors. On the other hand, adult

† This chapter is an edited version of an article which appeared in the *International Review of Education*, 38 (6), 1992.

education lags behind in resource allocation.' According to the Finnish Advisory Council for Educational Planning, public demand for adult education will double in the 1990s.

The data available on Poland (Poland, Ministry of National Education 1990) suggest that from 1988 to 1990 there was a decrease of about 10 per cent in the enrolment of adults in schools providing vocational education. As in Norway, this may have been due to economic constraints. However, significant increases in the level of participation in non-formal education, mostly in job training programmes provided by enterprises and unions, have been recorded in recent years. Overall, therefore, participation would appear to have increased.

In Norway, adult and lifelong education are explicit and central elements of educational provision. A survey found that 25 per cent of the adult population took part in organized programmes at the beginning of the 1980s. Contrary to the development observed in most other countries, the overall level of participation in adult education apparently fell to 18 per cent in 1988 (Norway, Ministry of Education and Research 1989: 40). According to the Norwegian Ministry, this decrease was due to cuts in public expenditure. However, a survey conducted in 1989 among the employees of 1,050 enterprises and public sector establishments showed that about a third of the men and women in the sample reported that they had received some formal training in the form of a course offered in the organization during the past year. Employer-sponsored training in Norway seems to have expanded compared with the early 1980s (Torp and Skollerud 1990).

## General trends

The reports prepared by ministries of education for the 42nd Session of the International Conference on Education, which was held in Geneva in September 1990, show that nearly all governments are pursuing policies to expand provision and facilitate participation, in particular in vocational programmes. The conclusion that significant growth and even a 'silent enrolment explosion' occurred during the 1980s is supported, at least at a general level, by observations made in a recent Organisation for Economic Co-operation and Development (OECD) report (OECD 1991a). Further evidence that rhetoric about the value of adult education is reflected in real changes in investment, provision and the patterns of participation is offered in two reports presenting syntheses of a large number of country reviews and especially commissioned research studies (OECD 1991b; Clement et al. 1991). Although it has not been possible to conduct time series analyses of data on provision and participation a report presenting a survey carried out under the auspices of the European Communities (EC) (EC 1990a) testifies to the increasing significance of continuing education in the European region today.

This new significance is reflected by trends in expenditure. Total expenditure on adult education and training appears to have increased in many western European countries during the 1980s. This applies to both public and private expenditure. In fact, the rise in public expenditure generally lagged behind the growth rate of private investment (OECD 1991a). It can be seen from Table 2.1 that the financial share of employers in job training exceeds that of the government in countries such as Germany, The Netherlands and the UK. That France deviates from the pattern can possibly be explained as a consequence of the French training laws. [. . .]

*Table 2.1* Sources of finance for job training (%)

| Country | Government | Employers | Employees |
| --- | --- | --- | --- |
| Federal Republic of Germany | 25 | 50 | 25 |
| France | 53 | 43 | 4 |
| The Netherlands | 39 | 50 | 11 |
| UK | 20 | 51 | 29 |

*Source*: CEDEFOP (1990)

 It is probable that the level of private expenditure has surpassed that of total public outlays for both adult education and further training. Table 2.2 illustrates that this is true of Sweden, a country known for its achievements in adult education and its generous funding of active labour market policies, of which human resource development forms the central part.

*Table 2.2* Expenditure on adult education and job training (rough estimates, per cent of Gross Domestic Product (GDP))

| Country | Private investment in training | Public investment in adult education | Public investment in labour market training |
| --- | --- | --- | --- |
| Austria | 0.6 | 0.6 | 0.01 |
| Finland | 1.0 | 0.5 | 0.27 |
| Norway | n.a.* | 0.2 | 0.07 |
| Sweden | 2.2 | 1.0 | 0.51 |
| Switzerland | n.a. | 1.0 | 0.01 |

*Source*: Arvidson and Rubenson (1991)
*Note*: * n.a.: data not available

*Table 2.3* Public expenditure[a] on adult education in the Netherlands (1 million florins)

|  | 1985 | 1987 | 1989 | 1990[b] |
|---|---|---|---|---|
| Continuing vocational education[c] | 717 | 805 | 1,389 | 1,466 |
| Liberal adult education | 396 | 462 | 63 | 57 |
| Adult basic education | 7 | 156 | 145 | 140 |
| Adult secondary education | 164 | 182 | 175 | 175 |
| Part-time higher education | 45 | 80 | 76 | 83 |
| Others | 40 | 29 | 32 | 5 |
| Total[d] | 1,367 | 1,644 | 1,880 | 1,926 |

*Source*: Cramer and Van der Kamp (1991: 41)
*Notes*: [a] Expenditure of the Ministry of Education and Sciences; Ministry of Social Affairs and Manpower; Ministry of Well-being, Health and Culture
[b] Forecast
[c] Excluding industrial training sponsored by employers
[d] Rounded figures

Table 2.3 shows in more detail how the different sectors have developed in The Netherlands from 1985 to 1990. It is interesting to note the trend: public expenditure on continuing vocational education and part-time higher education more than doubled, whereas adult basic education actually decreased after 1987, which was the first year it was fully implemented. Liberal adult education was the really big loser, however. The total cost amounted to 1.5 per cent of Gross Domestic Product (GDP) in 1988.

[. . .] Not shown in Table 2.3 is the training effort by employers. Expenditure as a percentage of the payroll varied between 0.5 and 2.9 per cent in 1986, depending on firm size. This sum increased year by year until 1990 – although total employer outlays did not quite reach the levels recorded in Germany (2.9 per cent), France (3.0 per cent) and Sweden (3.3 per cent). It can be inferred that the growth rate of industrial training apparently differs not only between labour market segments but also between countries. This may partly be due to the differences in resource allocation.

Particularly where one-fifth or more of the adult population takes part in organized adult education, such as in the Nordic countries and The Netherlands, growth in the 1980s was largely accounted for by the expansion of continuing vocational education, especially industrial training. Growth in general adult education in Sweden, for example, seems to have halted about a decade ago, the social demand having been increasingly satisfied. The crisis of public financing may have also been a contributing factor. By contrast, the further education and training of the labour force continued to expand during the 1980s

(SCB 1990). [. . .] This shows that general and occupational adult education are not necessarily developing in the same direction at the same time.

Despite the fact that there are differences among the countries considered, the question of whether there has been growth in European adult education during the 1980s [. . .] can be answered affirmatively. Yet that growth has been mainly reflected in the volume of training provision in internal and external labour markets. In Belgium, The Netherlands, Norway and Sweden there appears to be no firm statistical evidence pointing at a substantial increase in liberal types of adult education (Houtkoop and Felix 1990). Naturally, there have been innovations, such as the Dutch Open University, although the increase represented by that institution is small in proportion to the total adult population (Netherlands, Ministry of Education and Sciences 1989). Changes in liberal adult education have mostly been of this kind. Some institutions have disappeared and others have emerged. Similarly, some programmes have declined while others have expanded. Accordingly, the overall picture is one of expansion in continuing vocational education, especially job training, and consolidation – or in some cases decline – in liberal adult education.

## FACTORS EXPLAINING RECENT CHANGES

The conclusion that European adult education is not necessarily moving in the same direction in all countries, despite the apparent similarities, has two implications. The first is that its development can be described only in broad and general terms and that any explanations of its expansion must be hypothetical and tentative. Second, even though many factors influencing change can be identified, only a limited number can be considered here, especially as empirical evidence concerning the relationship between macro-level societal trends and the expansion of adult education is scarce (Bengtsson and Wurzburg 1992).

Given the large number of explanations for the recent upsurge of interest in adult education and training, it is useful to group them in a few inclusive categories. One possibility is to perceive adult education and training institutions in three dimensions: (1) public and private delivery systems; (2) external and internal control; (3) public and private financing. Another possibility is to consider the impact on adult education of demographic, economic, political, social and cultural forces. Within each of these, a distinction can then be made between supply and demand. It is the latter approach that will be adopted here, even though the distinction between the public and private provision will also be taken into account.

## THE IMPACT OF DEMOGRAPHIC CHANGE

Most observers are agreed that adult education has risen in priorities of governments, particularly since the latter half of the 1980s. The actual or anticipated effects of demographic change on the health of the economy and the functioning of segmented labour markets provide a partial explanation. The following demographic trends are particularly salient.

The share of young people in the labour force is decreasing in most countries in western Europe. For example, in England and Wales the population forecast shows an expected annual rate of minus 1.9 per cent for the decade. The rate is as low as minus 3.2 per cent in The Netherlands. The same trend can be observed in Belgium, the Federal Republic of Germany, Finland, France, Italy, Norway and Sweden (OECD 1990a). Thus there will be a fall in the supply of labour market entrants in most western European countries [. . .] which may well have serious consequences, given that this age group brings new and up-to-date skills into the labour force (Dahlberg and Tuijnman 1991).

In Germany, The Netherlands, France, Switzerland, Denmark and Sweden there is also concern about the consequences of an ageing population for the ratio of working to non-working adults. The share of older people in the population is increasing rapidly. This has implications not only for the state of public finance but also for educational demand. With increased longevity and health, and increased formal education, there is likely to be a demand for adult education among the retired population. Special consideration will have to be given to the educational needs of older workers and those already in retirement.

The social demand for adult education and training is also influenced by immigration patterns and the continuing process of migration from rural to urban areas, which creates tensions between values anchored in different cultures, and by consequences of urbanization such as the demise of the traditional family household and the rise of individualism with people seeking to satisfy their own personal goals. In due course the demand for liberal adult education seems bound to increase in central and eastern European countries as they progress towards market capitalism.

## THE IMPACT OF ECONOMIC FACTORS

Another explanation for the recent growth in European adult education is that demands on the competencies and skills of the workforce increase as a result of the introduction of new technologies and the transformation of occupations. The premise guiding the extension of adult education provision in industrial societies is that, as technology, production systems and organizational structures become more complicated, there is a parallel increase in the need to augment experiences of education and work. This is so because the skill level, technical expertise and flexibility of the workforce are generally considered important elements in determining the speed and success of implementing new technologies and adapting organizations to rapidly changing demands in a highly competitive international environment (OECD 1988; Mincer 1989; OECD 1990b).

In future, national economies will rely on the competitiveness of industry and services. The skills of the workforce, whether acquired in earlier or later years of life, will become even more important for production. Investments in machinery, robots and other technologies do not necessarily bring about by themselves the expected economic returns in the form of decreased input, increased productivity and high profits. Rather, the competencies and flexibility of the workforce may well be the principal mediating factors behind production gains and other benefits accruing from capital rationalization.

## CHANGES IN POLITICAL AND SOCIAL GEOGRAPHY

The economies of nation-states are becoming increasingly interdependent. The intensifying competitiveness of international trade draws attention to the importance of adult education and training as instruments for raising the quality of the workforce. The transformation of European economies not only imposes specific demands on the skills and competencies of the workforce but also requires that adults, in their role as citizens in pluralist democracies, take part actively in the cultural and political processes that shape the future (EC 1990b). The current emphasis on European integration, the goals, means and ends of which are spelled out in the Draft Treaty Establishing the European Union, the White Paper on Completing the Internal Market, and the Single European Act, can be interpreted, to no small extent, as providing an answer by western European countries to the economic challenges presented by their worldwide competitors. As will be seen, adult education and vocational training are affected by the turn of events.

The Asian countries on the Pacific Rim are generally regarded as the main competitors of European industry. The balance of gains and losses in export shares among the EC member states, the USA and Japan over the period from 1979 to 1989 shows that both the European countries and the USA lost significant market shares to Japan. Japan has been particularly successful in sectors such as electrical equipment, cars, optical precision instruments and robots designed for industry and agriculture. There is some ground for arguing that the high economic performance of the high-flying Asian countries can be partly explained by effective training and the positive approach to human resource development (Charmes and Salome 1987).

The data presented above have been used to argue that industry in Europe is declining, and economies are becoming service- rather than production-oriented. The following facts provide a part of the background (EC 1990b: 32). In Greece, 75 per cent of workers have received only an elementary initial education. In France, 50 per cent of the workforce lacks a vocational qualification, as against 30 per cent in the (former) Federal Republic of Germany. In Portugal, at least 8 per cent of the workforce may be considered illiterate, 74 per cent being without qualifications. In Spain, 26 per cent of the youth between 16 and 24 years of age enter the labour market having obtained no more than a primary school leaving certificate.

Whether the plight of European industry is being overstated remains to be seen. Yet the data have been used to argue that the economic well-being of the region depends on maintaining a competitive 'high tech' industry. Moreover, they have led to the claim that European countries are faced with the harmful effects of underinvestment in vocational education and job training and the interrelated process of under- and de-skilling. This forceful argument has triggered off economic cooperation, and has had significant consequences for the development of adult education and training in the 1980s. Both decision-makers and employers seem to have taken heed of the evidence accumulated by labour economists, that the skills of the labour force are a key determinant of economic success. In view of the problems sketched above, it does not come as a surprise that most European countries are currently putting a heavy emphasis on policies to improve job training (e.g. see EC 1990c).

Repercussions of the economic integration process in Europe on educational systems are most easily recognized at the level of higher education. However, the pursuit of the largely economic goals of European integration as set out in the Single European Act may well be expected to produce a 'knock-on' effect with respect to adult education. The supply-side 'shock' administered to the European economy by market integration will have implications for monetary, industrial, labour market policy and social policies. Adult education is implicated in these dimensions. It can therefore be anticipated that changes affecting both the former and the latter are in the offing. The EC declares:

> The process of completing the Community's internal market will accentuate existing trends in the employment world. However, the difficulties which could emerge in the countdown to 1992 will be considerably attenuated by policies to promote economic and social cohesiveness. From this viewpoint, investment in training is indispensable for individuals, enterprises and regions alike. It is one of the constructive responses which the Community can give to the momentous challenges awaiting it, in the economic, technological and demographic

arenas, in terms of employment and, ultimately, of the cohesion of the Community itself. The Community's efforts in this connection have given rise to numerous programmes to promote training. The Community has, moreover, stated its desire to see continuing training recognized as a basic right of all European citizens. Vocational training offers the best means of creating a pool of skills in the Community which can be tapped to boost the positive effects of the internal market, while moderating the risks of imbalance.

(EC 1990b: 22–23)

Spectacular changes have not only taken place within the EC. Free communication and mobility across national borders have now been facilitated in central and eastern Europe. Any further removal of physical, technical and financial barriers, as foreseen in the *Single European Act*, may well have major implications for migration flows and labour mobility throughout the entire European region. There will be a need for the mutual recognition among countries of educational qualifications, including professional degrees and the various certificates awarded by institutions specializing in adult education and vocational training. Acceleration of the integration process will stimulate the demand for language courses. Yet another factor of importance for adult education is the intensification of technological cooperation among countries.

Estimates of standardized unemployment in eleven European countries are presented in Table 2.4 (OECD 1990a). [. . .]The opening up of frontiers may lead to a situation where unemployment will become a pan-European phenomenon. Providing adult education for migrants and the unemployed may therefore have to become an all-European responsibility, transcending the provincial confines of adult education strategies developed within the limited context of traditional nation-states.

It can be assumed that change will be particularly profound in central and eastern European countries. Once major political, economic and social changes are under way, they acquire a momentum that is difficult to control. The Ministry of National Education of Poland (1990: 30), for example, writes that the profound changes taking place in the social and political geography of the nation evidently require parallel changes in the system of education. Adult education and training are referred to in the Polish report as constituting elements in a strategy aimed at preparing the transition to a market economy and facilitating the close cooperation between Poland and the EC as well as with the other Member States of the Council of Europe. However, reference is made not only to the economic but also to the social function of adult education. The development of new attitudes is an example of the latter.

A partial convergence of the goals and content of adult education in eastern and western Europe can be anticipated as an outcome of forces

*Table 2.4* Standardized unemployment rate in European countries (per cent of labour force)

| Country | 1985 | 1987 | 1989 |
|---|---|---|---|
| Belgium | 11.3 | 11.0 | 8.1 |
| France | 10.2 | 10.5 | 9.6 |
| Germany | 7.2 | 6.2 | 5.5 |
| The Netherlands | 10.6 | 9.6 | 8.3 |
| UK | 11.2 | 10.3 | 6.9 |
| Italy | 9.6 | 10.9 | 10.9 |
| Portugal | 8.5 | 7.0 | 5.0 |
| Spain | 21.4 | 20.1 | 16.9 |
| Finland | 5.0 | 5.0 | 3.4 |
| Norway | 2.6 | 2.1 | 4.9 |
| Sweden | 2.8 | 1.9 | 1.4 |

*Source*: OECD (1990a)

seeking to increase social, economic and political interdependence among countries. If adult education practices are increasingly matched by those of the workplace, as has been the trend over the past decade, then common definitions of goals for long-term adult education policy are likely to be sought by politicians and, not least, agreed by employers. However, this is not the case with respect to legal and structural matters. At present, convergence in adult education and training is still a long way off. Examples of the inertia of educational institutions and their general resistance to change can be easily found in all countries. Another factor working against convergence is that the traditions of adult education are tied strongly to the rich diversity of European cultures. The governments of nation-states are bound to adhere to the legitimate goal of safeguarding this cultural diversity and maintaining traditions.

Emerging optimism about the opportunities created by the re-entry of central and eastern European countries into a pan-European market can be observed among certain groups. Adult education is faced with the challenge of helping to promote international tolerance, mutual respect and democracy. A unique chance has been presented of merging the best practices and achievements of adult education in the different cultures that collectively make up the identity of Europe.

Yet it is clear that Europe cannot be regarded as an entity in economic and cultural respects. Its increasing significance as an entire region raises difficult questions about the distribution of wealth and the consolidation of power. It also raises questions about the responsibility of a wealthy Europe *vis-à-vis* the needs of developing countries. Within Europe, the principal challenge is how to reduce and eventually close the development gap between countries, notably the gap between the relatively poor countries in eastern Europe and the rich countries in the northern and western parts. It is faced with the task of helping to create an atmosphere of friendship, trust and willingness to cooperate in pursuit of the common good, rather than for the competitive advantage of a single country or social élite. Adult education ought to contribute to the creation of a new ethic of responsibility and trusteeship for the whole of Europe.

## A PARADIGM SHIFT: MARKET PRINCIPLES IN ADULT EDUCATION

The new belief in the positive outcomes of education stands in sharp contrast with the generally pessimistic view of the value of formal education of the 1970s and early 1980s. Today, education is no longer seen only in terms of a social cost that has to be minimized but also as a strategic investment. The skills of the workforce are elements in a strategy for promoting the economic and social well-being of nations. This explains why the economic and labour-market functions of adult education are being so much emphasized. Even though it is easy to find parallels between the situation at present and two decades ago, there are some major differences. One of these is that there is a general distrust of the capacity of the public educational system to realize many of the goals sought by governments and employers. Accordingly, attention has shifted from adult education to training in enterprises. The concept of an adult education market has been introduced into the policy debate and seems to be making headway. The basic idea is that the matching of demand and supply of adult education and training should be left to the play of market forces. It is claimed that wastage would thereby decrease, and that the quality, internal efficiency and cost-effectiveness of adult education and training would improve (Ritzen 1989; Boot 1990).

The rising costs of education were perceived in the 1970s and 1980s as a problem in the rich countries of Europe, where an increasing share of the public budget for education went to salaries. In a situation in which educational budgets were generally not allowed to rise, increases in salaries led to cut-backs in other areas of expenditure. Thus, the problem of rising costs in education was, to an extent, also a problem of making choices among the various categories of public spending. The fundamental question asked particularly in the early 1980s was whether countries and citizens were getting value for money spent on formal education. Another was whether public funds should be employed to finance the desired expansion of the adult education system.

That the market principle of free competition was welcomed in the 1980s as an effective means of promoting the quality and flexibility of state-dominated educational systems in European countries can possibly be interpreted as a generally unfavourable answer to the questions raised above. This provides a powerful explanation of change in adult education in the 1980s. It was seen as presenting an attractive means of making the educational system flexible and responsive to the changes in social demand. Moreover, it was felt that the expansion of adult education could be achieved, by and large, without substantially increasing the recurrent public budget for education, as in most countries the additional funds needed for expansion would be borne by employers and individuals. The data presented previously in Table 2.1 indicate that this is exactly what happened in countries such as Germany, France, The Netherlands and the UK.

It can be inferred that the quantitative expansion of adult education and job training during the 1980s has been accompanied by some remarkable qualitative changes, particularly with respect to control, financing and management. Whereas it was common in European countries during the 1960s and 1970s to adhere to a strategy of implementing change by means of planning at the central level, the trend emerging in the 1980s was to decentralize, i.e. to leave the matching of supply and demand to market forces. This approach was accompanied by a tendency to increase the scope for 'third parties' to assume responsibility for the financing of adult education. With it came a call for effective leadership, which in some countries has led to a marked decrease in control by central governments and a concomitant increase in the autonomy of adult education institutions. These institutions, in turn, were increasingly held accountable for performance and quality, not by public inspectorates as was formerly often the case, but by the consumers of adult education. Interest groups, such as labour unions and employers, have tended to intervene in adult education policy-making and practice as a result.

## CHALLENGES AND OPPORTUNITIES

There is a revival of interest in the development of a 'learning society' as evinced by the current interest in theories of lifelong, continuing and recurrent education. For example, adherence to the principle of recurrent education, which refers to a system organized around a cyclical strategy, implies that school curricula should be broad and general in character, and that differentiation and specialization in secondary education should take place as late as possible (Tuijnman 1990a). It is clear that the role of the school in imparting knowledge and skills for employment and citizenship is diminishing relative to the influence of other educative agents operating in European society (Husén et al. 1991). Adult education, formerly considered the preserve of local communities and national ministries of education, is now being brought into the economic arena, and even the political realm, of the social partners.

The increased importance of skilled intelligence in production makes it imperative that high priority be given to the development of systems of recurrent or continuing education. The very notion of a system implies orderly planning. It is apparent that the process of decision-making requires a concerted effort on the part of all three responsible parties – governments, employers and employees (EC 1989; BIAC 1991). Not only is a measure of political consensus needed in order to achieve a balance between different, perhaps conflicting, interests, but policies in education must also be balanced with responsible and just social, economic and labour market policies. Dilemmas to be solved concern the trade-off between equality and efficiency, quality and quantity, and between the redistributive and economic growth objectives of education in working life.

Adult education has a role to fulfil in reducing the opportunity gap between the well-educated and resourceful 'two-thirds' and the under-educated and sometimes disadvantaged 'one-third' of the labour force. As the data in Table 2.5 suggest, the task of reducing disparities in the level and quality of participation in industry training, which some parties are bent to pursue, is not an easy one. One may wonder whether this objective, if it can be achieved, is in fact desirable under all circumstances.

Another challenge may be noted here. Higher levels of formal educa-

*Table 2.5* Variation in industrial training according to occupational level (per cent receiving training, notes) [a]

| Country | Occupational categories [b] | | | | |
|---|---|---|---|---|---|
| | High | M + | M | M − | Low |
| Germany [c] | 31 | 38 | 26 | 15 | 3 |
| France [c] | 46 | 49 | 27 | 22 | 12 |
| The Netherlands [c] | 34 | 32 | 26 | 11 | 5 |
| Sweden [d] | 37 | 39 | 27 | 18 | 12 |

[a] As the training definitions vary the estimates are not comparable in a strict sense.
[b] Socio-economic categories are defined as follows: High = professionals, managers and administrators; M + = lower-grade professionals, technicians, and supervisors of non-manual workers; M = routine non-manual workers in sales, commerce and administration, including rank-and-file service workers; M − = lower-grade technicians, supervisors of manual workers and skilled manual workers; Low = semi- and unskilled manual workers
[c] 1985–1987 data, EC labour force surveys, participation in job training schemes in the last 12 months. Source: CEDEFOP (1990)
[d] Quality of living survey, ULF 1986/1987, employer-sponsored training course in the last 12 months. Source of data: SCB (1990)

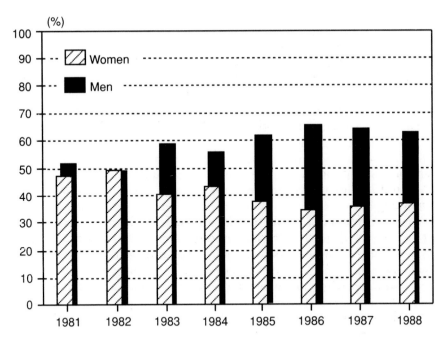

*Figure 2.1* Share of men and women in total participation (The Netherlands) adult education and training, excluding industrial training)
*Source*: Dutch Central Bureau of Statistics; and Cramer and Van der Kamp (1991)

tional attainment are consistently associated with lower unemployment incidence, better employment opportunities and higher-paying jobs. Education is for this reason seen as an economic variable. However, education also plays a role as a sorting and screening device. Cross-cutting these two perspectives is the issue of sex differences in the labour market outcomes of education. These differences cannot, in general, be attributed to 'human capital' variables such as cognitive ability, educational attainment, perseverance and health. Sex disparities in the labour market have a parallel in continuing education and training.

Figure 2.1 presents the position in The Netherlands. It can be seen that the *share* of women in total participation has decreased since the early 1980s. It can be recalled that *overall* participation increased over the same period. Thus, while the number of women in adult education increased, the number of men grew even more rapidly. The expansion of continuing vocational education since the early 1980s provides the explanation. Compared with women, men have a much higher probability of taking part in occupational adult education. It needs to be emphasized that employer-sponsored industrial training is not included in the data on which Figure 2.1 is based. If comparable time-series were available and job training included, then sex differences in participation would probably be even more dramatic.

The central message this conveys is that there are both qualitative and quantitative differences between men and women in adult education. Although The Netherlands has a comparatively low female labour force participation rate, the country is not atypical with respect to sex disparities in adult education. In many countries women are over-represented in liberal adult education but under-represented in occupational education. The disparities are generally largest in industrial training, where women not only have a lower overall participation rate than men but also tend to take part in programmes of brief duration. An accumulation of evidence shows that literacy, continuing vocational education and particularly job training are important determinants of career and life income (Tuijnman 1990b; Benton and Noyelle 1991). Mincer (1991), for example, reviews studies indicating that the rate of return on job training investments for men in the USA may be between 8 and 32 per cent, depending on variables such as assumed depreciation, age and labour market characteristics. This makes it very clear: sex bias in participation works to the disadvantage of women. Since training may well become even more decisive in determining opportunity and success in future labour markets, the reduction of such bias is a high priority. [. . .]

## WHO IS RESPONSIBLE?

PFI

Potential disagreement exists in most European countries about the desirability of increasing the role of private initiatives in adult education without simultaneously safeguarding and extending the mandate of the public sector. Indeed, the major change is that adult education is increasingly becoming part and parcel of the commodity market, to be developed, bought and sold under conditions of competitiveness and profitability. As we have seen, this development has contributed to creating a situation in some countries in which the expenditure on education, training and staff development programmes by industry and commerce exceeds total public funds allocated to adult education. At the same time, there is a shift in emphasis from time off from work for purposes of study to time for learning as an integral part of the occupational task, as in the Nordic countries, where the social partners and governments are involved in tripartite negotiations in an attempt to solve problems relating to the financing and distribution of adult education and training.

Whereas representatives of the social partners, political parties and government officials are in general agreement about the overall objectives of developing a system of continuing education, significant interpretative differences emerge when it comes to formulating specific policies and implementing them (cf. CEDEFOP 1987). Differences between countries in their approach to continuing education and, thus, in the way training systems are organized at ground level can in part be explained by national styles of policy-making and by prerequisite action demanded as a result of previous policy commitments. Labour economists generally agree that the degree of a state's involvement in the economy and the labour market influences its structural competitiveness – for better or for worse. A case is at present being argued by certain groups that state intervention in the domain of continuing education and training is undesirable, as any constraint on free competition is potentially harmful to the flexibility, efficiency and effectiveness of the 'market' where adult education is being sold and bought. In countries with a long tradition of public adult education, notably the Nordic group, the role of the state in determining adult education policy has, until fairly recently, not been called into question in any significant way – attempts on the part of the state to control popular adult education excepted. However, as the development of continuing education is rapidly emerging as one of the principal issues of the reform of working life in the Nordic countries, questions about the role of the state in influencing policy, decisions about objectives and the distribution of further education and training are being urgently asked and becoming increasingly controversial.

It is generally recognized that policies to encourage investment in adult education and job training are urgently needed in the context of a changing European economy. New ways of distributing learning opportunities over the entire life span and in different life settings are also required. However, the design of policies with this aim in view is no easy task. It is difficult for example to define and anticipate the kind of skills and knowledge needed in the workforce in future. The question of the social distribution of educational opportunities is far too important both for countries as a whole and for individuals to be decided exclusively by representatives of the world of work. Hence the issue arises as to how divisions and linkages should be organized between governments, the social partners and individuals, especially with regard to finance. Another large question concerns the implementation of policies aimed at redistributing learning opportunities, not only over the entire lives of people but also between the different groups making up a modern society, where special attention needs to be given to women wishing to enter the labour market and target groups such as migrant labour, immigrants and the long-term unemployed.

Finally, there is the question of the balance between public adult education and enterprise training. The following questions are central to future policy-making: How should the goals of education and training policy in working life be defined? Who should be involved in deciding these goals? Who should control the design and implementation of training policies? Who should pay and who should be the recipient of eventual economic returns? Who should be given the opportunity to take part in adult education and training programmes? Should there be a guaranteed minimum of initial education and continuing training for all people, regardless of differences in cognitive ability and the ability to pay?

## CONCLUSION

There is a consensus in Europe that adult education and occupational training are important, for economic as well as social and cultural reasons. Recognition of the potential of adult education in upgrading the skills of the labour force and alleviating some of the negative consequences of structural adjustment in labour markets is reflected by increases in the levels of investment and participation. There is also an understanding that adult education has a role to play in helping people to cope with and take advantage of new political and economic reality. Adult education is evidently faced with challenges such as the reduction of the opportunity gap between men and women and between the initially poorly educated and well-educated segments of the workforce.

The application of 'new' economic thought to education has had far-reaching consequences, especially for the post-initial sector of education: programmes believed to improve productivity and competitiveness have expanded dramatically, and resources are increasingly being targeted on the categories of workers for whom the returns are expected to carry maximum economic advantage. On the positive side of the balance one can note overall growth in provision and participation, more individual freedom of choice, quality improvement and, possibly, an increase in the cost-effectiveness of adult education for employment. On the negative side there is the risk that the usefulness of the market approach to adult education is being overstated.

Countries such as the UK, Sweden and the USA, in which formal educational institutions traditionally provided most of the skills used in work, are moving closer to the model used in Japan and Germany in which there is more reliance on employer-sponsored industrial training. This makes good sense, as the latter approach is likely to be more cost-effective in developing skills for work and structural adjustment. But there is more to life than work, and certainly more to education than training. Adult education is obviously faced with a hard dilemma concerning its future development, as it seems doubtful whether the ideals of lifelong education can be given real meaning in the context of a training market model.

# REFERENCES

ABS (1990) *How Workers Get their Training, Australia 1989*, Canberra: Australian Bureau of Statistics, Commonwealth of Australia.

Arvidson, L. and Rubenson, K. (1991) *Education and Training of the Labour Force in the EFTA Countries*. Report prepared for the seminar New Challenges in the Education and Training of the European Workforce, Stockholm, 13–14 June 1990, Stockholm: Swedish National Board of Education.

Bengtsson, J. and Wurzburg, G. (1992) 'Effectiveness research in continuing education: merely interesting, or actually relevant?', *International Journal of Educational Research*, 17(6): 527–535.

Benton, L. and Noyelle, T. (1991) *Adult Literacy and Economic Performance in Industrialized Countries*. Report prepared for CERI/OECD, New York: Conservation of Human Resources, Columbia University.

BIAC (1991) *BIAC Position Statement to the OECD Intergovernmental Conference on Further Education and Training of the Labour Force*, Paris, 26–28 June 1991, Paris: Business and Industry Advisory Committee to the OECD.

Boot, P. A. (1990) *Further Education and Training of Adults: Provision, Participation, Economic Impact and Policy Options*, The Hague, The Netherlands Ministry of Social Affairs and Labour.

CEDEFOP (1987) *Vocational Training Systems in the Member States of the European Community*, Berlin: European Centre for the Development of Vocational Training.

CEDEFOP (1990) *Vocational Training News Flash, 1990 No. 2*, Berlin: European Centre for the Development of Vocational Training.

Charmes, J. and Salome, B. (1987) *In-service Training and the Development of Human Resources: Five Asian Experiences*, Development Centre Studies, Paris: OECD.

Clement, W., Drake, K., Fong, P. and Wurzburg, G. (1991) *A. Comparative Analysis of National Strategies for Industry Training: Australia, Sweden and the United States*. Paris: OECD, Directorate for Social Affairs, Manpower and Education.

Cramer, G. and Van der Kamp, M. (1991) *Feiten en cijfers over de volwasseneneducatie* (Facts and Figures on Adult Education). Utrecht: RVE adviescentrum volwasseneneducatie.

Dahlberg, A. and Tuijnman, A. (1991) 'Development of human resources in internal labour markets: implications for Swedish labour market policy', *Economic and Industrial Democracy* 12(2): 151–171.

EC (1989) *Joint Opinion of the Social Partners Relating to the Role of Education and Training in the Internal Market*, Luxembourg: Office of Official Publications of the European Communities.

EC (1990a) *Continuing Vocational Training Statistics in EC Member States: Comparisons*, Brussels: Commission of the European Communities, Task Force Human Resources, Education, Training and Youth (Unpublished, draft, 15 January 1990).

EC (1990b) *Social Europe. The Social Aspects of the Internal Market, Vol. III*. Brussels: EC Directorate-General for Employment, Industrial Relations and Social Affairs.

EC (1990c) *Council Decision for Establishing an Action Programme for the Development of Vocational Training in the European Community* (FORCE), Brussels: Council of the European Communities.

Finland, Ministry of Education (1990) *Developments in Education 1988–1990 in*

*Finland*, Report by the Ministry of Education to the 42nd Session of the International Conference on Education in Geneva. Reference Publications 15, Helsinki: Ministry of Education.

Houtkoop, W. and Felix, C. (1990) *Volwasseneneducatie in Europe* (Adult Education in Europe). Utrecht: RVE adviescentrum volwasseneneducatie.

Husén, T., Tuijnman, A. and Halls, W. D. (1991) *Schooling in Modern European Society: A Report of the Academia Europaea*, Oxford: Pergamon Press.

Mincer, J. (1989) 'Human capital responses to technological change in the labor market', Paper presented at the Conference on Economic Growth at SUNY, Buffalo, New York, 26–27 May 1989.

Mincer, J. (1991) 'Job training: costs, returns, and wage profiles', in D. Stern and J. M. M. Ritzen (eds), *Market Failure in Training? New Economic Analysis and Evidence on Training of Adult Employees*, Berlin: Springer Verlag.

Netherlands, Ministry of Education and Sciences (1989) *Richness of the Uncompleted Challenges Facing Dutch Education* (Reviews of National Policies for Education, The Netherlands Report to OECD), The Hague: The Netherlands Ministry of Education and Sciences.

Norway, Ministry of Education and Research (1989) *Development of Education: 1988–1990*, National Report of Norway to the 42nd Session of the International Conference on Education in Geneva, Oslo: The Norwegian Ministry of Education and Research.

OECD (1988) *Technology, Flexibility of Manufacturing, and Industrial Relations*, Paris: OECD, Directorate for Science, Technology and Industry.

OECD (1990a) *OECD Employment Outlook 1990*, Paris: OECD.

OECD (1990b) *Technological Change and Human Resources Development: The Service Sector*, Document CERI/CW/90.02, Paris: OECD/CERI.

OECD (1991a) *Report on Training Statistics*, Document SMEI/MAS/ED/WD(91)2/REVI, Paris: OECD.

OECD (1991b) *Further Education and Training of the Labour Force in OECD Countries: Evidence and Issues*, Document SME/MAS/ED/WD(91)5, Paris: OECD.

Poland, Ministry of National Education (1990) *The Development of Education within 1989–1990*. Report for the Unesco International Bureau of Education in Geneva, Warsaw: Ministry of National Education.

Ritzen, J. M. M. (1989) 'Economische aspecten van de volwasseneneducatie' (Economic Aspects of Adult Education), *Economische-sociale Berichten*, 11(1): 43–47.

SCB (1990) *Personalutbildning 1975–1989* (Industry Training 1975–1989), Örebro and Stockholm: Statistics Sweden.

Torp, H. and Skollerud, K. H. (1990) *Organisasjon, arbeidsmiljö, og mobilitet: resultater fra arbeids- og bedriftsundersökelsen* (Organization, Working Environment and Mobility: Results of Employment and Industry Research), Rapport 90:9. Oslo: Institutt for Samfunnsforskning.

Tuijnman, A. C. (1990a) 'Recurrent and alternation education', *The International Encyclopedia of Education, Supplement II* (510–513), Oxford: Pergamon Press.

Tuijnman, A. C. (1990b) 'Adult education and life career', *The International Encyclopedia of Education, Supplement II* (362–368), Oxford: Pergamon Press.

Turkey, Ministry of National Education (1990) *Development of Education 1989–1990*, National Report of Turkey to the 42nd Session of the International Conference on Education in Geneva, Ankara: Ministry of Education.

# Chapter 3

# Scrambled eggs
## Social policy and adult learning

*Alan Tuckett*

Charting the changes in public policy affecting adult learners is a complex task. Whilst adult learning in Britain is a mass activity – with some six or seven million adults engaged in formal or informal systematic programmes of study each year – it is at the same time almost invisible.

Adults are, on the whole, marginal to the institutions in which they participate. So, whereas adults aged over 21 have become an absolute majority of participants in universities, often studying part-time, public debate about higher education continues to focus on the provision of full-time undergraduate courses for school leavers. Adults now comprise a majority of the students in further education colleges – yet those institutions were built, staffed, structured and timetabled to make provision targeting the second quartile of ability of 16- to 19-year-olds.

Although adults are the clear focus of Local Education Authority (LEA), Regional Council and voluntary sector adult education programmes, and a key target group for community education services, explicit provision for adults accounts for less than 1 per cent of central government education expenditure. In this context, it has proved difficult for institutions, authorities and for central government to overcome the diversity and fragmentation of delivery systems, and to plan coherently to meet the needs of adult learners, even if such planning were to have been an agreed priority of central government.

However, there has until recently been fragmentation in central government itself in creating the policy context within which provision for adult learners might develop. The two Departments of State which until their 1995 merger had the greatest involvement with issues affecting adult learners, the Department for Education (formerly the Department of Education and Science) and the Employment Department, have had markedly different approaches to adult learning, and little effective dialogue. There has been less still with other ministries with responsibilities for adult learning, such as the Department of Health or the Home Office.

## EDUCATION POLICY

Mass provision of small-scale, largely uncertificated provision for adults, maintained with a minimum of commitment from public funds, reflected the priorities of the Department of Education and Science from at least the mid-1950s. During the immediate post-war era LEA provision for adults expanded rapidly, doubling during the period 1950–1970, with a growth in the arts, in new leisure activities, in the study of modern languages – especially when people began to take foreign holidays. A major reassessment of LEA strategy took place during the 1970s and 1980s, prompted by the Russell Report on 'non-vocational' adult education (DES 1973), and *The Disadvantaged Adult* (Clyne 1973). Both documents contested the common assumptions of the 1950s and 1960s, that the key issue was to increase the volume of provision on offer, in the belief that it was equally accessible to everyone. They pointed out that the demand-led adult education provision of these years excluded people with literacy problems; speakers of languages other than English; working class people; people with disabilities; unemployed people; and black people. Nothing was done to adopt the recommendations of the Russell Report when it was published in 1973, even following a change of government. The Secretary of State created an Advisory Council for Adult and Continuing Education rather than the National Development Council the Russell Report recommended.

Rather, it was the LEAs which responded to the challenges in the Russell Report to develop major new curriculum areas, changes in the style and structure of programme delivery, new forms of programmes operated in association with statutory and voluntary agencies, cooperative initiatives across education sectors, and a revision and revitalization of areas of traditional strength in the adult education programme. The Russell Report led to new forms of collaboration between local providers and broadcasters, in particular in the field of adult literacy, and that provided a significant additional stimulus to the process of curriculum change in adult education. Above all, the Russell Report led to an understanding that a central, critical question for providers of learning opportunities for adults is *'Who participates?'*.

After the Russell Report practical measures were taken to target under-represented groups. Whilst providers jettisoned the vocabulary of 'disadvantage' many accepted the challenge to make adult education accessible to those who had benefited least from initial education. The adult literacy campaign was backed by government funds, after a field-led campaign, given teeth by the well-publicized decision of the BBC to screen prime-time programmes for adults with literacy problems. Initiatives followed to teach English to speakers of other languages; to take adult learning opportunities out of the institutions and on to high-rise inner city housing estates; to develop programmes of work for unemployed adults; to create ladders of opportunity for people with learning difficulties to fulfil their learning potential; new courses were developed offering adults the chance to study a broad range of subjects in preparation for entry to higher education or to certificated work-related further education. These initiatives were, characteristically, begun in urban LEAs, in response to locally identified need. In Sheffield and in Derbyshire, but particularly in the Inner London Education Authority (ILEA), the cumulative effect of the changes in curriculum, outreach and targeting was a transformation of the student body (Tuckett 1988). At its best it could be shown that adult education was successful in reaching people who felt themselves failed by the initial education system.

From time to time central government did act to support the generalization of locally developed initiatives. Home Office legislation provided funds for people immigrating to the UK from the Commonwealth, recognizing that their language learning needs were a legitimate claim on the national purse. In the early 1980s there was a brief spurt of active government, with the establishment of the PICKUP programme, to stimulate colleges and higher education bodies to provide customized education for business and industry; the REPLAN programme, started to stimulate local responses to widespread unemployment; and, following the creation of the Unit for the Development of Adult Continuing Education (UDACE), encouragement was given to the establishment of educational advice and guidance services. Some encouragement was given, too, to improve training opportunities for part-time tutors through Educational Support Grants to LEAs; and in the later 1980s Government encouraged the development of Access courses to create a more secure route for mature student entry to higher education. There was, too, a continuing Government commitment to adult literacy and basic skills work. Overall, however, central government avoided large-scale initiatives in the field of adult learning. Change where it happened was initiated locally, and only later, if at all, picked up by Government.

Government has been particularly wary of addressing the weakness of some LEA provision. Since the 1944 Act LEAs have had a statutory duty to secure adequate provision for the further education of adults. However, politicians and officers continue to describe adult education as a discretionary service, and to treat it as an easy target for sudden cuts when budgets are tight; and the courts have been unwilling to challenge an authority's judgment about what constituted adequacy.

The result of this weakness in legislation, and in the enforcement of existing legislation, is an enormous variation in the range, volume and quality of offers available to adults in the different parts of the country. It has also been possible for more than half the volume of adult education provided by the ILEA in 1988 to be cut by its successor authorities with no effective review of the impact of such reductions on Londoners' learning opportunities.

## TRAINING POLICY

If government education policy for adults was to leave things substantially alone, it has been an increasing feature of training policy in the UK to intervene with nationally driven initiatives. From the creation of the Manpower Services Commission (MSC) in the early 1970s, but particularly since the publication of *A New Training Initiative* (MSC 1981) and its successor, *Towards an Adult Training Strategy* (MSC 1983), there has been a consistent recognition that the UK could not solve its needs for a skilled and flexible workforce solely by focusing on the preparation of young people newly entering the labour force. At the same time, there has been a marked shift from the priorities of the MSC at the beginning of the 1980s, to those of its successor bodies more than a decade later. At the beginning of the period there was large-scale youth unemployment and growing adult unemployment; during the 1980s there was a dramatic increase in part-time employment, large numbers of women entered the paid labour market, and as a result of demographic and industrial pressures, the UK faced labour and skills shortages, which persisted in areas of the economy through the early 1990s, whilst Britain was enduring its sharpest and longest drawn out recession for more than fifty years.

*A New Training Initiative* (MSC 1981) identified four kinds of need that would not be met by improving arrangements for the supply of young workers: the need for unskilled adults, or those with narrow manual or office skills, to have a fresh start in growth areas of the economy; the need for updating workers whose existing skills had grown rusty or outdated; the aspiration of skilled workers to seek progression to more responsible work; and the needs for new and additional skills to be grafted on to existing levels of competence in response to new opportunities in the market for individuals and for firms. *Towards an Adult Training Strategy* (MSC 1983) added the need to take account of the special needs of people with disabilities, language needs or basic skills needs, and the need for good-quality information and advice to ensure that adults made effective, informed choices about training. To back the analysis, the MSC introduced a range of short-life but large-scale programmes, including the Community Enterprise Programme, the Community Programme, RESTART and Employment Training, each of which suffered from the confusion between throughput and output. Productivity gains in manufacturing industry can be measured by increasing the number of products produced with the same or diminished investment of capital and labour. The model transfers uneasily to full-time education programmes designed to teach adults to read.

Employment Training (ET) and RESTART were introduced following the publication of a Department of Education White Paper, *Training for Employment*, which explained the case for a new programme for unemployed adults in terms with just a hint of blaming the individual:

> First, many job seekers – particularly those who have been unemployed for six months or more – lack the skills to fill jobs our economy is generating. Second, many long-term unemployed people have lost touch with the job market, and lack motivation to take up a job, training or other opportunities. Third, there is evidence, particularly in the more prosperous parts of the country, that significant numbers of benefit claimants are not genuinely available for work.

On the basis of this third observation, it became harder in many parts of the country, following the introduction of ET, for unemployed adults to study part-time in further education colleges under the '21 hour rule', a convention applied by the Department of Health and Social Security (DHSS) which enabled adults to study for up to 21 hours a week whilst registering as available to work and continuing to claim benefit. The introduction of ET was accompanied by stricter definitions of 'available for work', particularly in areas where unemployment had fallen, with the result that significant numbers of people were obliged to discontinue their studies.

Yet by November 1988, a new White Paper, *Employment for the 1990s*, recognized that the UK needed to foster a learning workforce, and that demographic and industrial change meant that a million women would be needed in increasingly skilled jobs in the workplace, that black people, older workers and people with disabilities would need to be recruited and persuaded to undertake training to become more skilled if the UK was to maintain its share as an industrial country in increasingly global markets. As with other training policy papers throughout the 1980s, *Employment for the 1990s* assumed that employers and individuals would meet the costs of this expansion of training.

To encourage this expansion Training and Enterprise Councils (TECs) and their Scottish analogues, Local Enterprise Companies, were established in the wake of the White Paper as independent training companies, with Boards dominated by local businessmen, to replace the publicly accountable Area Manpower Boards. A further incursion into the powers and responsibilities of local authorities followed, when TECs were given the power of veto over 25 per cent of LEA budgets for work-related further education. This continued a process established in the early 1980s, when the LEAs were required to submit work-related further education plans, and later Further Education Colleges were required to submit their development plans to the MSC, in order to secure a proportion of their budgets. The Government could reasonably point to the improvement in strategic planning in LEAs resulting from work-related further education planning exercises, and the closer links between education and industry that resulted from it. However, the faith placed in TECs, each of which was limited to a local geographical region, in meeting regional and national skills shortages, as well as serving their local communities, was further evidence that the Conservative Government was sceptical about too much central planning. The market, rather than society, could be relied on to meet needs. As the Trades Union Congress observed in *Skills 2000* (TUC 1989: 5), 'in no developed economy is the market vested with such power over training today' and nowhere else 'is it considered that individual investment decisions will provide the sort of trained workforce that a developed economy of the next century will need'.

Belief in the efficacy of markets was combined with a political commitment to the reduction of public expenditure. As Margaret Thatcher argued in July 1978:

> If our objective is to have a prosperous and expanding economy, we must recognise that high public spending, as a proportion of GNP, very quickly kills growth. Every penny they take is taken from the productive sector of the economy in order to transfer it to the unproductive part of it.
>
> (quoted in QueenSpark 1992)

Training, just as much as uncertificated adult education, was seen as a consumption 'good' – something you could spend your surpluses on in good times; not as an investment 'good' like capital expenditure. As a result there was a consistent tension between the analysis developed by MSC, and its successor bodies, the Training Agency and TEED, and the cash-limited actions of Government taken to stimulate adult learning in and for the workplace. The Government's hope in creating TECs was to secure new monies from the private sector to overcome this impasse. Evidence to date suggests that investment in training has held up, despite the severity of the recession; but the Boards of TECs have taken up the refrain of their public sector colleagues in arguing for an increase in public funding, as an investment in the future of the country.

## NATIONAL EDUCATION AND TRAINING TARGETS

The policy adopted in the 1988 White Paper was significantly influenced by a series of reports published in the 1980s which argued that the British workforce is less skilled, less flexible and less qualified than its international competitors (Ball 1991; Cassels 1989; CBI 1989; TUC 1989). There was a recognition that a commitment to training varied widely between different economic sectors, and that too much of the training offered was narrowly job specific. A consensus emerged that there was a need for a massive expansion of the amount of training in the economy, improvement in the level of skills in the workforce and the potential workforce, and continued learning throughout life. The consensus was given a focus in the national training targets formulated by the Confederation of British Industry (CBI), and endorsed by the TUC, which Norman Fowler, as Secretary of State for Employment, accepted in a speech in the City in 1989, and which, following some hiccups of policy, Government adopted as the centrepiece of training policy in 1991/92.

The targets identify separate goals for foundation learning for young people, and lifetime learning targets aimed at the adult workforce, and for employers (identified in terms of the national system of vocational qualifications (NVQs), created following the establishment of a National Council for Vocational Qualifications in 1986). The targets for lifetime learning were ambitious:

- by 1996, all employees should be taking part in company-driven or developmental activities;
- by 1996, 50 per cent of the workforce should be aiming for NVQs, or units towards them, and should have individual action plans to which their employers, as well as they themselves, are committed;
- by 2000, 50 per cent of the workforce should be qualified to at least NVQ Level 3, or its academic equivalent (A level);
- by 1996, 50 per cent of medium to larger organizations need to be recognized as Investors in People.

To date, whilst there has been encouraging progress towards the achievement of the Foundation Targets, as increasing the participation rate of young people has been the principal focus of training policy, the lifetime targets are a long way short of being achieved. The National Institute of Adult Continuing Education (NIACE), among others, has argued in a number of reports (McGivney 1990; NIACE 1990, 1993; Tuckett 1992; Uden 1994) that to have any hope of achieving them it will be necessary for the Departments of Education and Employment to harmonize policy, to maximize the benefits for adult learners. The 1995 merger of these Departments may help to achieve this goal.

After more than a decade of pulling in opposite directions, the National Education and Training Targets provided a focus for close collaboration between the two Departments – collaboration which was given a fillip in a 1990 ministerial reshuffle that brought Tim Eggar as Minister of State from Employment to Education, with a portfolio including further education, and saw Robert Jackson move from Education to Employment. The White Paper *Education and Training for the 21st Century* (DES and ED Group 1991) was a tangible outcome of cooperative working, when it was published under the sponsorship of both Departments.

## EDUCATION AND TRAINING FOR THE 21ST CENTURY

It is worth looking at the impact of the White Paper and subsequent legislation on provision for adult learners. The first announcement of the key policy proposal in the White Paper came at a time when the Conservative Government was under acute pressure arising from the unpopularity of the poll tax. Many felt that the decision to take £2 million of expenditure out of local control was a political expedient. However, the case for giving a higher profile to further education was a powerful one, given the commitment to the achievement of the national targets. LEAs remained schools-led and schools-dominated bodies, whereas further education seldom received the attention and support needed to transform the vocational training record of young people in the UK. Government believed that releasing polytechnics from LEA control in 1989 had been an unqualified success in releasing energies for expansion, and was keen to extend the same freedoms to the colleges, despite the fact that colleges, unlike higher education institutions, almost exclusively recruit from their local areas.

Adults were addressed almost as an afterthought in the first volume of the White Paper, despite the fact that they represented a majority of the college population. In the second volume of the paper, less than two pages was given to them. The focus of the paper was clear – that further education should be sharply focused on improving skills. To this end, funding for courses leading to academic and vocational qualifications, basic skills provision, some special needs work, English for Speakers of Other Languages, and Welsh in Wales were to be national priorities funded through a Further Education Funding Council (FEFC). On the subject of providers the wording of the White Paper on adults is elegant, but perhaps misleading:

> Further education for adults comes from a wide range of providers. The bulk of full-time work takes place in further education colleges. Much other provision is also made in colleges, but some is made in adult education centres; in schools; in adult residential colleges; and by the [Workers' Education Association] and other voluntary bodies.
>
> (DES and ED Group 1991, Vol. 2, p. 8)

No one reading this would recognize from the text that the vast bulk of adults study part-time, that colleges cater for half as many adults as free-standing adult education centres, or that the bulk of literacy and basic skills work was made through adult education centres. The White Paper did make clear that colleges were now to be the key bodies responsible for the local delivery of services, which they might, if they chose, contract out to other providers, including LEAs.

Apart from this skills-focused 'national' curriculum for adults, it was recognized that there might be a continuing demand for education designed to meet 'the leisure interests of adults', but this was to be a local concern, and any subsidy would need to be found from the resources otherwise available to local authorities:

> Public expenditure on education for adults will be concentrated on the courses that can help them in their careers and in daily life.
>
> (DES and ED Group 1991, Vol. 2,)

Publicly funded adult learning then needed to be concentrated exclusively on the skills crisis in the UK. If adults wished to learn other things, they should be expected to pay for them. No recognition here of the role adult services play in prolonging active citizenship in an ageing society; no recognition of its role in helping people resettling under the Care in the Community programme to rebuild relationships in neutral settings; no recognition either of the informal role of education, helping adults as parents, workers and citizens – and, critically, given the aspirations of the White Paper, no recognition that for many people, in particular for many women, what the White Paper disparagingly calls 'leisure' education is the critical first step on an academic or vocational education journey.

The philosophy underpinning the policy had been elaborated by Sheila Lawlor of the Centre for Policy Studies in a paper written at the time of the previous education legislation, when the ILEA was being abolished. Her argument was a sharp critique of the cross-party agreement that ILEA's adult education service was admirable, and needed to be protected:

> It is by no means self-evident that an Education Authority ought to divest resources from pupils of school age in order to subsidise an extensive variety of adult courses, many of them peripheral.
>
> (Lawlor 1988)

Education for Lawlor was redefined as schooling, and provision for adults seen as money taken away from schools where it belonged. She went on to elaborate proposals for ILEA's successor authorities, and by implication for other authorities:

> Adult education should not continue to be – or even be thought of as – a service provided by LEAs ... Adult education institutes should

offer those courses for which there is a need, and a demand; they should be financed through fees – which would have to be raised – and through business and industrial support. They might also be eligible for grants in respect of training from the DTI or MSC. Competition between different institutions for students would keep standards up and fees down. Leisure or sports classes, or those meeting a social need, might qualify for social services or other local authority grants ... Individual institutes and colleges should be encouraged to become self-governing, self-financing and competitive as quickly as possible. To promote this, the responsibility of the LEA for providing adult education should be terminated.

(Lawlor 1988)

Reading the White Paper after *Away with LEAs* (Lawlor 1988) it is difficult not to believe that the drafters of the Paper accepted Lawlor's view. However, large numbers of others did not. The House of Lords has throughout the post-war period harboured supporters of adult learning. They were early to criticize the proposals. Lord Beloff, in particular, was withering in his scorn for the failure of the policy to value learning for its own sake. Adult education organizations, coordinated by NIACE, provided a detailed critique of the policies (NIACE 1991a, 1991b, 1991c); the National Federation of Women's Institutes encouraged every one of their 9,000 local branches to write to MPs about the threat to women's opportunities for learning (Home and County 1992); and a coalition of the local authority associations, the Workers' Education Association, the Open University Students' Association and NIACE and other organizations gathered more than 500,000 signatures on a petition calling for the proposals to be dropped from any legislation. MPs received a larger postbag on the proposals affecting adult learners than on the poll tax. When adult education was caricatured as flower arranging for fun, by Government supporters, the campaign identified a merchant banker who had gone to evening classes in Brixton for industrial retraining, opened a florist's, giving jobs to some fellow students, and now sent black junior staff to the same class for in-service training; and *The Independent* (MacLeod 1991) gave prominence to the story. The press and broadcasters gave the campaign consistently sympathetic coverage, portraying Government policy as clumsy and heartless.

The White Paper was published in May 1991. By July, in a Parliamentary answer the Government signalled its intention to modify the proposals, and to limit the transfer of adult education budgets to the new proposed Further Education Funding Council (FEFC) solely to those sums already committed to the new sector's curriculum responsibilities. This was confirmed at a September press conference, called to 'clarify' the Government's policy. By the time the Bill was published in October 1991 there were other, modest, changes to the policy. The WEA, and the four London colleges, nationalized in 1988 as a result of their outstanding liberal studies programmes, were to be spared the straitjacket limiting their funding only to certificated courses covered by Schedule 2 of the Bill. LEAs were given statutory responsibility to secure adequate facilities for further education for all those areas not covered by the new FEFC; and powers to provide in FEFC areas. FEFC was given a parallel blend of duties and powers. Adequacy was defined to take account of distance, equipment and style of teaching and learning. If the colleges were to be the lead institutions, it was clearly recognized that there would be a continuing role for LEA and voluntary sector bodies across the curriculum.

During the passage of the Bill no amendments were secured on the face of the legislation, despite a sustained critique, and considerable disquiet from Government supporters in the Commons as well as the Lords. However, many of the arguments of critics of the Bill were picked up in turning the Act into practical measures to be implemented. A major concern throughout the passage of the legislation was the right of a college to overrule the bid of an external institution for FEFC funding. The offer of an appeal to the Council overcame this difficulty. Quality assurance worried NIACE and others, with responsibility for adult learning now split between the new Office for Standards in Education (OFSTED) and the FEFC's Inspectorate. Painstakingly, over two years, OFSTED and FEFC have explored how best to collaborate in this area. Far from excluding external providers in its first two years of work FEFC in England has welcomed and encouraged expansion in the sector, as adults represent a key source of the expanded student population necessary for the Council to meet its ambitious growth targets. In Wales FEFCW recognized another important concern of adult educators – that it is more expensive to reach under-represented groups – by agreeing to pay a premium for the recruitment of students from economically disadvantaged areas, identified by postcodes.

Most satisfying of all has been the acceptance by Government that for many students, general education provides a vital progression route for academic and vocational courses. As Tim Boswell argued in 1993:

> It is quite unusual for adults who have not had the best experience with the formal educational process to move straight into a qualification-bearing course. I entirely accept the argument that adults may be drawn back into learning by joining, for instance, a non-vocational course which may instil the confidence needed to try to update their skills.
>
> (Boswell 1993)

There have, however, been significant costs. A generation of experienced officers and inspectors were lost to adult learners at the time of the reorganization resulting from the Act. Responsibility for policy affecting adult learners, in colleges and in LEAs, now rests too often with staff with a range of other duties. As a result, the subtlety of provision fit for purpose has been lost. In many LEAs, and notably in inner London, the continued financial pressures on local government have led to ever greater cuts in budgets, as authorities respond to the need to delegate the maximum available sums to schools, to offset the threat of schools opting out of LEA control. Adult education organizers, responding to this, and the opportunities for growth offered by FEFC, have adapted courses to fit the new qualifications-focused FEFC curriculum. This has, of course, kept a range of provision in place, but has led to a spectacular drop in the number of older people studying (NIACE/MORI 1994). The absence of a minimum benchmark of LEA provision, backed by Government, continues to threaten the stability of offer, on which effective expansion of adult participation can be built.

For the new complex and fragmented system to work for adults a premium needs to be put on measures designed to ease movement between institutions, and to give effective advice to potential learners. Whilst moves to create modular courses, credit accumulation and transfer arrangements; to assess and accredit prior learning; and to move to competence-based education and training all continue apace, Open College Networks, which have played a key role in facilitating progression for learners from community-based learning to more formal study, continue to be vulnerable. Educational guidance services for adults have, at the same time, been closing, as the new vocational guidance services piloted by the previous Employment Department take over responsibility.

It is hard to read all this as the product of coherent planning by Government; easier rather to see policy as the often almost accidental by-product of debates between central and local government, or between Departments of State, or between different divisions in a single Department. This can be seen in the messy compromises surrounding the funding of adult learning. The decision to award tax relief to students investing in courses leading to NVQs gave an important impetus to participation – yet the Treasury has so far been unsympathetic to arguments that learning is a transferable skill, and that any investment in learning will benefit the country's drive to create a skilled and learning society. However, those arguments were persuasive when Value Added Tax (VAT) affecting education was reviewed (perhaps because the National Federation of Women's Institutes was once again forceful in lobbying). When public provision of adult education was, broadly, exempted from VAT ministers explicitly accepted that you cannot tell a student's purpose from the title of a course.

A good case can be made for arguing that the Government has done more to make policy affecting adult learners coherent in the last two years (1992–94) than in the last decades. Undoubtedly, some of this derives from the sympathetic cross-departmental work undertaken by the junior minister, Tim Boswell. More, perhaps, derives from the increased public attention adult learning commands since the 1992 Act, fostered by the success of successive Adult Learners' Weeks. However, the fragility of the situation is revealed by the 1994 Budget provision cutting the additional £1,000 in grant received by anyone over 29 studying full-time on a course attracting a mandatory grant, after being in paid work. The measure affects 130,000 people, and can scarcely be squared with the commitment to improving access, essential to the achievement of the national targets.

All in all then the policy picture remains complex – with adult learners in different parts of the country enjoying wildly different opportunities to study, as a result of a range of disconnected decisions made by bodies working to very different goals. What is astonishing is that so many adults find the loose and baggy monster of post-compulsory education and training accessible enough to take on programmes of study that transform their lives. How much more might be achieved if some basic agreements could be made, about the minimum levels of provision everyone should have within easy reach; about the financing of adult learning; about how much the individual, employers and the state should contribute to enable the rhetorical commitment to the learning society to be put into practice.

## REFERENCES

Ball, C. (1991) *Learning Pays*, Interim Report, London: RSA.

Boswell, T. (1993) 'The value and diversity of adult education' (Speech given to the NIACE Annual Study Conference, April 1993), *Adults Learning*, 4(10), June.

CBI (1989) *Towards a Skills Revolution: Report of the Vocational Education and Training Taskforce*, London: CBI.

Cassels, J. (1989) 'Demographic change and the marketplace', in D. Blandford and A. Jameson (eds), *Building Partnerships in Education*, Cambridge: CRAC.

Clyne, P. (1973) *The Disadvantaged Adult*, London: Longman.

DES (1973) *Adult Education: A Plan for Development* ('The Russell Report'), London: HMSO.

Department of Education and Science and Employment Department Group (1991) *Education and Training for the 21st Century*, Cmnd 1536, London: HMSO.

Home and County, January 1992, 'WI's White Paper Campaign'.

Lawlor, S. (1988) *Away with LEAs*, London: Centre for Policy Studies.

McGivney, V. (1990) *Education's for Other People: Access to Education for Non-Participant Groups*, Leicester: NIACE.

MacLeod, D. (1991) 'Adult education changes alarm staff and students', *The Independent*, 2 August 1991.

Manpower Services Commission (1981) *A New Training Initiative*, Sheffield: MSC.

Manpower Services Commission (1983) *Towards an Adult Training Strategy*, Sheffield: MSC.

NIACE (1990) *Learning throughout Adult Life*, Leicester: NIACE.

NIACE (1991a) *Education and Training for the 21st Century*, Vol. 1, *A NIACE Response*, Leicester: NIACE.

NIACE (1991b) *Education and Training for the 21st Century*, Vol. 2, *A NIACE Response*, Leicester: NIACE.

NIACE (1991c) *The White Paper, Key Points on Adult Education from Responses Received*, Leicester: NIACE.

NIACE/MORI (1994) *What Price the Learning Society?*, Leicester: NIACE.

NIACE (1993) *The Learning Imperative*, Leicester: NIACE.

QueenSpark Publishing Collective (1992) *Brighton on the Rocks*, Brighton: QueenSpark Books.

Trades Union Congress (1989) *Skills 2000*, London: TUC.

Tuckett, A. (1988) *The Jewel in the Crown*, London: ILEA.

Tuckett, A. (1992) *Towards a Learning Workforce*, Leicester: NIACE.

Uden, T. (1994) *The Will to Learn*, Leicester: NIACE.

# Chapter 4

# Competitiveness, technological innovation and the challenge to Europe

## *Alan Clarke*

Since its creation, the European Community[1] (EC) has been committed to improving the competitiveness of industry with a view to strengthening the economies of its member states, a policy reaffirmed in a recent Community White Paper, *Growth, Competitiveness, Employment – The Challenges and Ways Forward into the 21st Century* (Commission of the EC 1993). The shift in the balance of economic and industrial competition in the last few decades has, in part, been the result of advances made in technology and, for some time, the technological lead gained by the USA and Japan has been at the root of European anxiety. Accordingly, one of the prime objectives of European industrial policy has been to stimulate and promote technological innovation and to encourage the use of new systems and applications.

Efforts to ensure economic viability through innovation have, however, been attended by uncertainty about the impact of innovative technologies and applications on the content and organization of work, on skill needs and employment. This chapter reviews some of the findings of research into the nature and effects of technological innovation and its implications for both industry and the individual worker. It looks at the role of the EC in meeting this challenge and reflects on some of the strengths and limitations of EC initiatives in this field.

## POLES APART – THE TECHNOLOGY DEBATE

The expectation that technological innovation would open new markets for new products and services and would ensure economic growth was offset by a polarity of opinion concerning its possible impact on employment. In the early 1980s one school of thought argued that innovative technologies would provide new job opportunities, a higher level of employment and greater job security (Wakeham and Beresford-Knox 1980). Another fostered the 'job-killer' thesis (Jenkins and Sherman 1979), claiming that technological innovation constituted a threat to employment and the environment and thus to the security and well-being of the individual and society. The adherents of this school predicted a substantial drop in the demand for labour and the redundancy of existing skills – fears evoking all the features of large-scale unemployment. A third 'agnostic' school preferred to reject or ignore the importance of technology (Evans 1982) or took the view that it was impossible to predict its impact on employment (Sleigh *et al.* 1979). None, however, appeared to quarrel with the findings of the report of the Rathenau Commission (1980) on the impact of microelectronics applications on employment in The Netherlands, which concluded that more jobs would be lost by *not* introducing new technology than by introducing it.

Opinions also differed with regard to the deterministic qualities of technological innovation and its effects on skill needs. Some assumed that innovation would lead to an overall increase in the demand by industry for higher-level skills and competencies; others predicted a general drop in skill standards (Sorge 1983). Although the argument in support of 'technological determinism' has meanwhile been rejected in favour of what d'Iribarne (1983) has termed a *culture technologique*, the dynamics of technological innovation remain evident.

## The pace and scale of innovation

New technologies and their related applications have not been introduced and disseminated at the rate and on the scale predicted or feared. Rarely has technological innovation had the revolutionary impact witnessed in the printing industry – and prophesied for other sectors – where, overnight, jobs and even whole trades became redundant as a result of the introduction of microelectronics and computer technology. Where extensive changes have occurred, they have for the main part been more gradual and their effects less immediate. Nevertheless, despite their short period of evolution, the penetration of these technologies in process and product industries, clerical and service sectors has been considerable.[2]

What induces firms to innovate? In most cases, the underlying motive is that of competition. In order to remain or become more competitive, firms may choose to introduce new technologies and applications to raise the standard and quality of their products, for example by reducing manufacturing tolerances or by improving process control. They may wish to increase their output and cut production times, or they may be interested in improving product flexibility through the development of new materials or a new product line. Other firms may aim at lowering the unit cost of their products, and whilst some may opt to export work or transfer plant or manufacturing units to 'low-wage' countries, others may choose to employ new, labour-saving technologies.

Why, therefore, have innovative technologies not been introduced on the scale and at the rate expected? A study conducted in the UK (Christie *et al.* 1990) showed that the most common difficulty experienced by nearly half the users of microelectronics applications surveyed was the lack of people with specialist microelectronics expertise, in particular in microelectronics engineering. The next most common problem cited was that of finance, a problem seen to have its roots in the general economic situation of the firms and in the high cost of technological development, in particular for product applications. The shortage of workers with appropriate skills, especially maintenance workers, was named as a further factor limiting the diffusion of new technology and its economic exploitation, especially in manufacturing and construction (Bowen *et al.* 1990).

The scale on which new technologies have been introduced was found to differ according to the size of the firms and factories, with larger firms absorbing the technology at over twice the rate of smaller firms (Northcott *et al.* 1985). The study showed that in Europe, the level of absorption of new technologies by smaller firms (under 200 employees) differed considerably from country to country. This phenomenon may result from differences in the general economic system or standing of the countries in question or may be linked with differences in the structure of their industries. It may also be a consequence of different forms of work organization, levels of worker competence and the mode and standards of training in these countries – notions which would require further research.

The rate and scale of absorption is also related to the performance record of companies and plants, their ability to adapt to structural change, and their development expectations (Evers *et al.* 1990). Growth motives (positive sales expectations, improvement of the production process, competitive advantage) play a much greater role in the decision to invest in new technologies than defensive or reactive motives (shrinking sales, more innovative competitors).

The level of diffusion of innovative technologies also differs according to the sector of the economy, i.e. manufacturing – product and process innovation – and the service/clerical sectors. In 1984, the International Labour Organisation reported that 51 per cent of manufacturing firms in the then Federal Republic of Germany employing more than 20 workers used microelectronics technology, the figures for France and the UK being 38 and 47 per cent, respectively (ILO 1987). More recent estimates indicate that approximately two-thirds of manufacturing firms in these countries have adopted microelectronics. The use of microelectronics in process applications has been far higher than in products (ratio about 3:1), although there has also been a considerable growth in the latter area. A survey conducted by the Policy Studies Institute (PSI) (Northcott 1986) showed that in 1981 the firms surveyed were using microelectronics in about 20 different kinds of product, whereas the figure for 1983 was in the region of 110, and for 1986 over 160.

An indication of the scale of introduction of advanced technologies is also provided by the diffusion rate of automated equipment. It has been estimated, for example, that by 1990 more than 250,000 computer numerically controlled (CNC) machines and over 30,000 robots would be in operation in Europe (Drucker 1990). This represented a tenfold increase since the early 1980s.

In all the member states of the EC, and in particular the more industrially developed countries (France, Germany, Italy and the UK), there has been a steady trend away from manufacturing towards the service and clerical/administrative sectors. In recent years, these latter sectors have experienced a rapid growth in the use of information technology, an important factor being the development of powerful, low-cost, personal computer systems. The design of versatile, standardized, user-friendly software packages for word-processing, database, graphics and spreadsheet functions, and the development of complex remote information access and networking systems known as local and wide area networks (LANS and WANS) have provided added stimulus (Bowen *et al.* 1990: 129)

The highest adoption rate is to be found in office applications, especially in banking, insurance and carrier services, with the trend moving away from single-function to multifunctional office automation systems. However, after a slow start, the retail sector is gathering pace, linking up sales and stock control functions with purchasing and financial transactions using systems such as the Electronic Point of Sale (EPoS) system. Through this system both large stores and small shops can enter and process data which are transmitted via WANs to a central computer at head office.

Despite the various constraints, it is expected that technological innovation in the manufacturing and service/clerical sectors will continue to gain momentum. The implications are examined in the following sections.

## The impact of innovation on employment

Technology is but one of many factors affecting levels of employment, work content and skill needs. A given technology will change during the process of its diffusion, the direction of change often being steered by unpredictable socio-economic forces, themselves influenced by the emergence and diffusion of new technologies (Sorge 1987). Studies and analyses which aim to establish or verify the effects of technological innovation must therefore be carefully designed and caution exercised in the interpretation of the findings. Seldom will the causal relationship be immediately apparent, as when workers are made redundant following a conversion of plant to fully automated robot systems. More usually, innovative technologies will be phased in, the effects being less instant.

A number of the studies already cited provide information on the impact on employment of technological innovation. They indicate, for example, that those firms which are highly innovative are those in which the level of employment tends to be maintained, and that non-innovation is more likely to lead to a greater loss of jobs. Where there have been job gains attributable to technological innovation in manufacturing, these mainly relate to the group of skilled electrical workers, technicians and engineers with electronics and electromechanical skills. Redeployment often calls for reskilling and adaptive training. Where jobs have been lost as a result of the introduction of new technologies, it has been the unskilled and semi-skilled production workers who have been affected most. Job losses amongst skilled workers have been less severe, particularly amongst those acquiring new competencies in information technology applications.

Whilst microelectronics applications are to be found on a broad scale throughout the service sector, for example, in the distributive trades, in warehousing and in the medical field, information technology is used most extensively in office automation. A West German study (Höflich-Häberlein and Häbler 1988) which investigated the influence of micro-electronics applications in service industries showed that, overall, innovative technology has a neutral employment effect, with staff reductions in some firms and sectors being offset by staff increases in others.

Whether in factories, warehouses or offices, the introduction of new technologies often leads to changes in work organization and in hierarchical structures. This also has implications for management. It is expected that, in general, there will be an increase in the number of professional and senior clerical jobs and a drop in the demand for junior and intermediate managers as the new technologies reduce the need for routine supervision and coordination functions. Some junior management tasks will be taken over by senior clerical staff supported by on-line technology. Junior clerical jobs are also expected to decline in number and many of the remaining tasks (for example, fragmented data preparation and entry) may then be performed by part-time staff.

The effects of technological innovation are both cumulative and interactive, its influence on levels of employment depending considerably on the effect it has on job content and work structures, and on the type and level of skills which the new technology and systems require.

## Job content and work organization

The introduction of new, advanced technologies and applications such as computer-assisted design (CAD), computer-assisted manufacturing

(CAM), flexible manufacturing systems (FMS), sophisticated stock control and movement systems, and office automation have had a significant impact on job content and on the work environment. Many simple, repetitive, and mostly unskilled tasks have been eliminated. The introduction of encapsulated processing units has improved safety and has meant that workers are less likely to be exposed to hazardous substances and engaged in extreme physical exertion. Thus, in many cases innovation has improved the quality of work tasks and has raised the level of responsibility of the individuals required to perform them.

Changes in the content and nature of work often call for new, more appropriate forms of work organization, although research has shown that different industrial cultures respond in different ways. Both in manufacturing and in offices, technological innovation is seen to produce two principal forms of work organization (Brödner 1985). The 'Taylorist model' (TM) or 'technocentric approach' is characterized by a form of work organization and performance which calls for little flexibility and initiative on the part of the worker. The Taylorist approach tends to produce monotonous and routine jobs and to have a deskilling effect on the workforce. The second model incorporating 'new production concepts' (NPC) or 'anthropocentric production systems' (APS) provides for a more integrated approach to work processes in which the human factor plays a more significant role. The production process is more flexible, requiring a more qualified workforce, and research has revealed that with this form of work environment the economic benefits in terms of productivity tend to be higher. This is the tenor of a study concerned with the division of labour and rationalization in industrial production in the car manufacturing, machine-tool and chemical industries (Kern and Schumann 1984).

Other studies point to differences in national and company 'cultures' which may affect the choice of work organization and hence the relative distribution and general level of skills (Hartmann et al. 1983). Hartmann et al. show that there is a significant difference, for example, between British and German firms regarding such practice. Whereas German firms are seen to be convinced of the importance of employing craft skills when employing new technology, and appear to act according to the NPC model, British firms, in accordance with the traditional TM model, tend to use noticeably fewer skilled workers. The implication is that whenever new technologies are implemented according to the TM model, it is not necessary for the education and training systems to deliver highly skilled craft workers and technicians. The NPC approach, on the other hand, requires a workforce with higher-level skills, in many cases with system programming capabilities. The general trend in most industrialized countries appears to be in the direction of the latter model, and it is the one which the EU tends to favour.

The anthropocentric approach to work organization also brings into the debate the issue of worker participation. Many of the reports and studies on the management of change (Bowen *et al.* 1990)[3] indicate the expediency of involving the workforce in decision-making processes relating to innovation, and granting them greater responsibility for the introduction and management of innovative technologies. Consultation and participation of workers in decisions on organizational change also feature in the provisions of the *European Social Charter*.[4] Such participation presupposes a realignment of management philosophy concerning work organization, and the transformation of skill profiles at all levels.

From research undertaken in relation to office work, it is concluded that here, too, decisions to introduce new technologies should not be the sole preserve of management. It was found that organizational problems are minimized and new equipment and systems more effectively used when the users are involved in their selection. As in manufacturing, this presupposes that management and staff are familiar with both the potential and the possible negative implications of technological innovation. Again, it has been found that with the introduction of flexible hierarchies, office staff will generally experience an upgrading of the content and status of their respective jobs and functions.

## Skill needs in a changing environment

The changes in work content brought about by technological innovation have a decisive influence on the type and level of skills which are in demand.[5] In order to anticipate and respond to changing skill needs, policy-makers and curriculum designers rely on a variety of research methods and instruments. Some may gauge the supply of and demand for skills on the basis of econometric studies and labour market movements monitored on a regular or continuous basis. Others may draw on the findings of representative surveys of firms and interviews with employers and employees. Others base their decisions on the outcome of research and studies they have commissioned or which have been undertaken by independent researchers and institutes. Yet there is no blueprint for the finely tuned assessment and prediction of skill needs arising from the introduction of innovative technologies. Nevertheless, the results of research undertaken by national institutions and the EU since the early 1980s allow a number of general conclusions to be drawn.

First, the pattern of skill needs would not appear to depend on the state of the economy nor on the level of unemployment in the country concerned (Merle *et al.* 1990) and the trends identified display marked similarities independent of the industrial geographies and structures of the regions in which they occur.[6] The use of microelectronics applications and new materials in products, processes and service functions affects skill profiles in all sectors and at all levels, with the general trend being towards *skill enhancement* rather than *deskilling*. In manufacturing, with the increased use of automated processes, the skills emphasis is switching from production (the operator) to the preproduction stage (planning and design), and moving from *manual* to *mental* skills. As pointed out earlier, this trend is accompanied by a marked decline in the need for lower-level skills, with the consequence that many unskilled and semiskilled workers are displaced or made redundant.

Whilst there is a strong and persistent demand for more highly qualified workers, this is coupled with a call for broader and more flexible skills, or 'multi-skilling' (Bessant 1989: 41). As a result, traditional occupational boundaries are becoming blurred. In manufacturing, many operatives are required to have skills and knowledge extending beyond their traditional area of competence. For example, they may be called on to diagnose faults and carry out minor repairs themselves and to recognize when specialized maintenance staff must be called in. In recent years, there has been a growing need for operatives and maintenance staff to acquire 'interdisciplinary skills'. In some countries, this has led to the creation of new occupations, for example that of the frequently cited 'mechatronics engineer' combining mechanical and electronics skills. The demand for multi-skilling has also been stimulated by changes in the organization of production away from the assembly line to group assembly units. This combining of different skills is not, however, limited to the technical field; with the growing complexity of production systems, there is a growing demand for operators and technicians with organizational and managerial skills and management with technical skills (BIBB 1991).

The spread of complex and advanced manufacturing technology, for example, computer numerically controlled (CNC) machine tools, flexible manufacturing systems (FMS) and robot systems, has raised the demand for maintenance staff with higher-level skills in a variety of disciplines. Both in manufacturing and the service sector there is a marked need for (and a serious lack of) maintenance staff, and although the increased use of automated and self-diagnostic systems may result in a drop in the skills requirement for certain maintenance tasks, the human factor continues to be a vital resource. This staff will, however, be confronted with a growing need to acquire core skills in computer science and electronics engineering (Butcher Committee 1985).

Plant and equipment is not normally replaced in a single operation but is more likely to be phased out. Consequently, for some time 'old' and 'new' technologies will exist side by side. This requires operators and maintenance staff to have the necessary skills to deal with different generations of machinery. For example, telecommunications systems in many countries combine mechanical and electronic switching systems, and accordingly, a maintenance worker must be familiar with both electromechanical and electronic switching (Penn 1990).

Studies on office automation in France and Germany (Lane 1985) indicate that new office technologies induce a need for higher-level skills. In Germany it was found that routine, monotonous tasks were confined to unskilled or temporary staff. However, computerization appeared to reduce the proportion of poorly qualified clerks and give incentive to employers to upgrade their existing staff. French companies have in the past tended to recruit only those with a high level of qualification, adopting a long-term strategy to account for needs resulting from future technological developments. British companies, on the other hand, tend to recruit office staff with few formal qualifications and give little thought to the design of appropriate work structures and systems for new office technology (Steedman 1987).

'Multi-skilling' is also becoming a feature of the service sector, especially in firms providing 'telematics services' (network administration, messaging services, database communications, electronic data interchange). These firms show a growing need for staff with data-processing and telecommunications skills to have a knowledge of other areas or disciplines, for example, finance and retailing (Strobel 1986). Similarly, staff of customer support services are required to have additional skills in business organization and personnel management.

At a higher level of qualification, there is a great shortage of software and 'telematics' engineers, systems designers and analysts in manufacturing and the service sector. Although there has been a rise in the number of graduates from universities, business schools and polytechnics with degrees in computer studies, the demand is still much greater than the supply. In particular, there is a need for software designers and analysts with appropriate knowledge of the users' field of activity.

In manufacturing, in the service sector and in office work, the introduction of innovative technologies is tending to break down traditional hierarchical structures, resulting in more complex forms of personal interaction (Mandon 1985). More emphasis is being placed on the need for so-called 'generic' or interpersonal skills – the ability to think in terms of operational systems, to analyse and solve problems, to be adaptable and able to work in a team environment, to communicate and demonstrate reliability (Aubrun and Orafiamma 1990). Whilst these skills or competencies are not new, it is significant that they should be given such a high rating in the list of skill needs quoted, for example, by employers.[7]

The skill profiles of management are also undergoing change. As indicated in the section on the employment effects of innovation, senior management will tend to carry out functions previously fulfilled by intermediate or junior managers. Managers in industry, especially those involved in the introduction and management of IT equipment and systems, will need to become more technically competent. Similarly, in the service sector, the demand for junior managers is likely to decrease as IT reduces the need for routine supervision and control. In the retail sector, for example, local managers of chain stores have forfeited much of their responsibility following the introduction of centralized control and decision-making mechanisms incorporating automated warehousing and data-transfer system (Bowen *et al.* 1990: 130).

In concluding this section, it is noted that while job content and skills are influenced by a range of factors, these developments seldom cause an occupation or individual skills to become completely obsolete. There is also evidence that, with the exception of the core IT industries, technological innovation will not in itself create a whole range of 'new skills' but will require the modification, adaptation and, in some cases, upgrading of existing skills. Demographic trends and changes in consumer attitudes and behaviour are, however, expected to open new areas of activity and job opportunities where new and traditional skills will be in demand on a larger scale. In Europe, the general decline in the birthrate and longer life expectancy have changed the structure of the age pyramid significantly. More people are living longer, staying healthier and, with present-day ease of travel, are tending to become more mobile. The resulting consumer demand must be met by the leisure, hotel and catering industry which, in turn, is expected to experience a demand for appropriate skills. On the other side of the equation, there will be a greater need for skills in occupations concerned with the health and care of the elderly.

Another area which is expected to offer potential for the development of new skills is that of the environment and its protection. Consumers are becoming more concerned about the burden modern materials and production processes place on the environment, and industry is being required to meet increasingly stringent standards. It is therefore to be expected that here, too, more advanced technologies and applications will be required for production and quality control, and that this will raise the need for appropriate skills. These may in time become elements of traditional occupational profiles or may form part of a separate, new environmental discipline.

It is the task of the policy and decision-makers in the member states to find an appropriate training response to these new and changing demands for skills and competencies. The following sections describe the role and involvement of the EU in this changing scene.

## THE ROLE OF THE EU IN MEETING THE NEW AND CHANGING DEMANDS FOR VOCATIONAL EDUCATION AND TRAINING

Responsibility and authority for vocational training was assigned to the European Community through the *Treaty of Rome*.[8] In Article 118 of this treaty, provision was made for the *promotion of close cooperation between the member states in the social field*, specific reference being made to *basic and advanced vocational training*. Article 128 called for the *establishment of general principles for implementing a common vocational training policy*. On the basis of these and other provisions, the EC has developed and implemented numerous policies and programmes in this field, many of which relate to changing skill and training needs.

In the 1980s, the efforts of the EC, and especially the President of the Commission, Jacques Delors, became directed more strongly towards political and economic convergence and integration, and resulted in the development and propagation of concepts such as a 'European Labour Market', a 'European Area of Technological Innovation' and a 'European Social Area'. In 1986, these efforts culminated in the adoption of the *Single European Act*,[9] the prime aim of which was the realization of a 'Single European Market' as of 1 January 1993. This led to the member states giving added focus to the question of skill deficits, standards and the mutual recognition of qualifications. The issue of competitiveness became a foreground concern, not only with regard to the relationships of the Community with third countries, such as the USA and Japan, but also amongst the member states themselves.

In the mid-1970s, with the implementation of the EC *Social Action Programme*,[10] the EC had already reacted to the perceived implications of technological innovation. In its proposal to Council, the Commission pointed out that:

> technological developments . . . will continue to cause many structural changes in the employment market, bringing about the disappearance of many existing jobs and the demand for new skills [and that] better training facilities will benefit industry . . . in helping it to adapt more efficiently to a rapidly changing technological and market situation.

At that time, however, attention centred on the needs of socially disadvantaged persons, and especially the more vulnerable groups of society, such as young people with poor schooling, the children of migrants, women and workers with a low level of skills. To meet the needs of these groups, the action programme envisaged, amongst other things, the improvement of vocational guidance, preparatory training, retraining and rehabilitation.

The *Single European Act* resulted in a reorientation, with attention being placed more on the importance of developing skills to meet the needs of industry and business enterprises in the member states in order to develop and maintain European competitiveness. This motive became the cornerstone of many of the vocational training policies and programmes introduced by the EC in this period and may explain the move away from the more socially oriented concerns for the disadvantaged group. Human resource development became a central feature in the discussion of vocational training, documented in 1989 by the administrative decision of the Commission to withdraw certain areas of responsibility from Directorate-General V (then Directorate-General for Employment, Social Affairs and Education) and to create a new Task Force: Human Resources, Education, Training and Youth.[11] This transformation coincided with a substantial increase in the human and financial resources allocated to this area, and resulted in the development of a series of new and more ambitious vocational training initiatives, such as the 'action programme for the vocational training of young people and their preparation for working life' (PETRA)[12] and the 'action programme for the development of continuing vocational training in the European Community' (FORCE).[13]

Added impetus was given to EC vocational training policy with the signing of the *Treaty on European Union*[14] in Maastricht on 7 February 1992, amending the *Treaty of Rome*. Article 123 of the original treaty, laying down the terms of reference of the European Social Fund (ESF),[15] was reworded to the effect that the Fund should, amongst other things, serve 'to render the employment of workers easier and . . . to facilitate their adaptation to industrial changes and changes in production systems, in particular through vocational training and retraining'.

A new Article 126 formally established and reinforced the competence of the EC for *general education*, a provision lacking in the initial Treaty. The new Article 127 defines Community responsibility for vocational training in more explicit terms, specifying that 'the Community shall implement a vocational training policy which shall support and supplement the action of the Member States, while fully respecting the responsibility of the Member States for the content and organization of vocational training'.[16] It goes on to stipulate that EC action shall aim to 'facilitate adaptation to industrial changes, in particular through vocational training and retraining'. Finally, an important formal constraint on EC action in the field of vocational education and training was included in this Article, namely the exclusion of 'any harmonization of the laws and regulations of the Member States'. This restriction is of special significance when appraising EC vocational training initiatives.

Apart from its formal obligations under the various treaties, the EC bears a heavy responsibility for the development of vocational training as a consequence of its own strong commitment to the promotion of technological innovation through its science and technology research and development activities. Through these, in comparison, high-budget R&D programmes,[17] the EU has itself – if only indirectly – encouraged and supported changes in skills supply and demand.[18]

This involvement and the results of research on skill needs led the EC to develop a series of programmes serving the design, development and testing of new approaches to vocational training. In addition to PETRA and FORCE, these included programmes such as COMETT,[19] ERAS-MUS,[20] DELTA[21] and EUROTECNET.[22] These are too many and too varied to be adequately described here, and any attempt to assess their impact and utility must, of necessity, be fragmentary.[23]

Many of the programmes developed in response to the changes invoked by technological innovation had their roots in two EC framework programmes. These were the Resolution of the Council of 2 June 1983 concerning vocational training measures relating to new information technologies[24] and the Resolution of 11 July 1983 concerning vocational training policies in the European Communities in the 1980s.[25] These resolutions pursued two main objectives: the development and promotion of vocational training initiatives to stimulate economic activity – especially through the exploitation of innovative technologies – and initiatives serving to offset and remedy the adverse effects of innovation, with emphasis on the more vulnerable members of the workforce. The first objective concerned action to develop the skills needed by the labour market – skills which would revitalize industry and promote employment. The second objective – more strongly pronounced in the resolutions cited – was directed at achieving a socially responsible approach to innovation. The key elements of this policy line were job creation, equality of opportunity, and measures to meet the needs of workers at risk – in particular young people with poor schooling – and of the long-term unemployed. Both objectives stressed the need for provision to be made for the retraining and further training of workers *throughout their working lives*, and both called for the improvement of worker awareness concerning the implications of innovation and their involvement, for example, in workplace design.

It was also the declared EC policy to develop appropriate guidance and counselling services, to promote cooperation between industry and the public authorities and to involve the *social partners*[26] in the implementation of the various measures.

## How has the EC performed?

Most of the initiatives concerned with a training response to the challenge of technological innovation have covered a very broad spectrum, focusing on many of the features of change described earlier in this chapter. They have served to develop new training approaches to innovation, have identified and demonstrated good practice and have ensured the

exchange of knowledge, information and experience amongst practitioners, policy-makers and decision-makers in the member states. In
particular, they have stimulated and supported transnational cooperation
in this area on a wide scale. In the fulfilment of these objectives, the EC
may therefore be considered successful.

Where these EC initiatives have tended to fall short of their objectives
is in their treatment of the *social implications of innovation*, in particular the
needs and interests of those whose jobs and skills were most likely to be
affected by technological innovation – older workers whose skills have
or will become redundant, the semi-skilled, the unskilled and the
unemployed. These programmes have also given only marginal consideration to the issue of *equality of opportunity*. It may be concluded from an
analysis of the outcomes of the programmes that this is not so much a
consequence of the regulatory or institutional constraints to which EC
policy and action are subject, but is due rather to the general shift in
focus of EC training policy from the target-group approach to one
concerned more with human resource development as a means of
meeting the needs of industry and improving competitiveness – a policy
seemingly based on the assumption that the weaker members of society
will automatically benefit from economic and industrial development, an
assumption which may be questioned.

A general weakness of many EC initiatives is their tendency to focus on
the achievement of results and products within their (short) lifetime, giving
little consideration to their *evaluation* and (longer-term) *development and
exploitation*. This observation is documented, for example, in the external
evaluation report on the COMETT programme, which emphasizes the need
for priority consideration to be given to the 'diffusion and marketing of the
COMETT outputs . . . and in the more effective promotion and delivery of
the programme at Member State level' (Coopers and Lybrand 1989). These
weaknesses would appear to result, on the one hand, from inconsistency
between the demand of the member states (through the Council of
Ministers) for urgent and effective action in response to technological
innovation, and the unwieldy and time-consuming consultation, policy and
decision-making process required to develop and implement EC initiatives,
a circumstance of which the Commission itself is fully aware,[27] but may also
be a consequence of general programme planning and design.

## PERSPECTIVES FOR FUTURE VOCATIONAL
## EDUCATION AND TRAINING ACTIVITIES OF THE
## EUROPEAN UNION

From its own research activities and the experience and knowledge it has
gained from the programmes it has conducted over the last decade, the
EU is conscious of the need to develop a global training strategy which,

although respecting the differences in the structures and content of vocational education and training (VET) systems in the member states, and
observing the principle of subsidiarity, will provide an appropriate
response to the challenges of innovation. Such a strategy calls for greater
coherence in the design and implementation of EU initiatives, providing
for interaction not only amongst the VET initiatives themselves, but
between these and the technical and scientific research and development
activities of the Union. It is also essential that the maximum benefit be
drawn from these initiatives. This requires the systematic and continued
development and exploitation of the results and products of these
initiatives. For this purpose the impact of the EU activities in the
member states should be the subject of regular analysis and evaluation.

The EU would appear to have taken steps in this direction with its
new, global framework programmes SOCRATES (relating to education)
and LEONARDO DA VINCI (vocational training) adopted in 1994 and
1995. The latter programme aims to consolidate and rationalize the
activities and outcomes of the PETRA, FORCE, EUROTECNET and
COMETT programmes, establishing a common framework of objectives
and measures designed to support and supplement action by and in the
member states. LEONARDO has been provided with an estimated
budget of ECU 620 million for activities from 1995 to 1999. As its
general objectives, it will pursue the main lines of action set out in
Article 127 of the Treaty of Maastricht. In particular it aims to promote
the concept of *life-long learning*, encouraging and promoting training
activities to enable the individual to adjust better to economic and social
changes. In consolidating its activities, the programme sets out to support
the member states in their efforts to improve the quality of their training
systems and policies, above all through the promotion of transnational
cooperation, and through the exchange of trainees, specialists and
decision-makers. The programme also makes provision for studies,
surveys, analyses and data exchange to serve as a yardstick for providers
and policy/decision-makers. These activities will be directed towards
anticipating demand, achieving transparency in the field of skills and
qualifications, and obtaining and disseminating information on new
forms of training, training investment incentives and statistics on training
provision and financing.

The effectiveness of EU vocational education and training activities in
a world faced with rapidly changing skill demands will depend considerably on its ability to overcome the legal, regulatory and administrative
barriers which have hitherto hindered or impeded its activities. It will
need to review and revise its organizational and management structures
in order to move from a shorter- to a longer-term strategy and to ensure
a cohesive approach to and interaction between its various initiatives.

It is important that the VET activities of the EU are not developed and implemented 'in isolation' but are treated in the broader context of economic and labour market developments. The Commission White Paper on growth, competitiveness and employment describes at length and in detail the challenges facing the EU into the next century and stresses the need for a comprehensive and cohesive approach to the issue. The effectiveness of the EU effort in this field will, however, depend not only on the achievement of an integrated, 'interdisciplinary' response but also and especially on its ability to overcome the legal, regulatory and administrative barriers which have hitherto hindered or impeded its activities and forced it to adopt a shorter- rather than a longer-term strategy towards a changing work environment and its inherent economic and social implications.

In its efforts to promote industrial development and combat unemployment, the EU will need to search for and develop special initiatives for the more vulnerable members of society, as figures testify that economic recovery is not necessarily accompanied by a drop in unemployment. Although past initiatives of the EU for this group of people may not have been as fruitful as had been hoped, it may be claimed that, in analogy to the conclusions of the Rathenau Commission (1980) on the impact of innovation, the situation of this group would conceivably be less favourable had they not been implemented.

## NOTES

1 With the signing of the *Treaty on European Union* (the 'Maastricht Treaty') on 7 February 1992, the name 'European Union' was adopted in place of 'European Community'. As reference is frequently made to events and developments in the period before Maastricht, these terms are used inconsistently in this chapter.

2 The potential influence of microelectronics applications is summarized in a statement – still valid – by the former Advisory Council for Applied Research and Development:

> It is the most influential technology of the twentieth century because: (i) it both extends and displaces a wide range of intellectual or intuitive skills; (ii) it is all-pervasive; (iii) it is still advancing rapidly; (iv) it is very cheap and getting cheaper; (v) it will become more abundantly available from international sources and (vi) it has exceptional reliability.
>
> (Advisory Council for Applied Research and Development (1978)
> *The Applications of Semi-Conductor Technology*, London: HMSO,

3 Hugget, C. (1988) *Participation in Practice. A Case Study of the Introduction of New Technology*. EITB Report No. RC22. Watford. European Union Skills Needs Monitoring Project: a series of surveys conducted by the Commission of the EC (Task Force: Human Resources, Education, Training and Youth) in 26 regions of Europe on behalf of the European Parliament (unpublished reports – 1991). The project was subsequently extended to cover 31 regions.

4 *Community Charter of the Fundamental Social Rights of Workers* (1990), Luxembourg: Commission of the EC. In the UK it is usual to refer to the

'Social Chapter' when discussing the issue in the context of the 'Maastricht Treaty'. The Charter was adopted by 11 Heads of State or Government. (Of the 12 member states, the UK did not subscribe to the Charter.)

5 The author has intentionally avoided the debate on the concepts underlying the terms 'skills', 'competencies' and 'qualifications', which, for the lack of international norms, frequently give rise to confusion and misunderstanding in the European discussion. Therefore, wherever appropriate the shorter term should be taken to imply the broader concept.

6 EC Skills Monitoring Project.

7 For example in the series of regional surveys conducted by the EC Commission as part of the 'Skills Needs Monitoring Project', and Industrial Research and Development Advisory Committee of the Commission of the EC. IRDAC (1990) *Skill Shortages in Europe*, Brussels: EC Commission.

8 The 'Treaty Establishing the European Economic Community', signed by the six founder states in Rome on 25 March 1957.

9 Official Journal of the European Communities (OJ), No. L169, 29 June 1987.

10 Adopted by the Council of Ministers in January 1974.

11 At the time of writing this chapter, the Task Force was about to be made into a separate Directorate-General of the Commission (*DG XXII – 'Education, Training and Youth'*).

12 Council Decision of 1.12.1987, OJ No. L346 of 10.12.1987, amended by Council Decision of 22.7.1991, OJ No. L214 of 2.8.1991.

13 Council Decision of 29.5.1990, OJ No. L156 of 21.6.1990.

14 OJ No. C191, 29.7.1992.

15 Whilst the European Social Fund served to finance a host of vocational training activities, and especially initial training measures for disadvantaged persons, there was little coordination with or interaction between these initiatives and other Community vocational training initiatives – a feature raised again later in the chapter.

16 The principle of 'subsidiarity'.

17 As a measure of EU investment, more that ECU 11 billion (1 ECU equivalent to approximately £0.8) has been earmarked for this purpose under the 'fourth framework programme for research and technological development' for the period 1994–98. By comparison, the budget estimate for the Community vocational training programme LEONARDO, which is to run from 1995 to 1999, amounts to ECU 620 million.

18 A review of EU research and development programmes in science and technology is to be found in the Commission guide *EC Research Funding – A Guide for Applicants* (1990) 2nd edition, Brussels: Commission of the EC.

19 'Community action programme in education and technology' – a programme designed to promote cooperation between universities and industry.

20 'European action scheme for the mobility of university students' – a student exchange programme.

21 'Development of European learning through technological advance' – an initiative to promote the use of innovate technologies in education and training, with emphasis on distance learning.

22 A network of demonstration projects designed to promote technological innovation and good practice in the field of training.

23 The profiles of many of the EC initiatives implemented in the 1980s and early 1990s are described in the *Guide to the European Community Programmes in the Fields of Education, Training and Youth*, published by the Commission in 1993.

24  OJ No. C166 of 25.6.1983.
25  OJ No. C193 of 20.7.1983.
26  EU terminology for employers' and employees' organizations, i.e. confedera-
    tions of industry and trade unions.
27  Commission of the European Communities – DG IX/E5 (1989), *The Euro-
    pean Commission and the Administration of the Community*, European Documenta-
    tion series No. 3/1989, Luxembourg: Office for Official Publications.

## REFERENCES

Aubrun, S. and Orofiamma, R. (1990) *Les compétences de 3ème dimension:
    Ouverture professionelle?*, Paris: CNAM-C2F.
Bessant, J. (1989) *Microelectronics and Change at Work*, Geneva: ILO.
Bowen, P., Senker, J. and Senker, P. (1990) 'Skills implications of information
    technologies for the European Community', unpublished report for the
    Commission of the European Community, University of Sussex: Science
    Policy Research Unit.
Brödner, P. (1985) *Fabrik 2000: Alternative Entwicklungspfade in die Zukunft der
    Fabrik*, Berlin: Sigma.
Butcher Committee (1985) *Report of the Butcher Committee on Skills Shortages and
    Information Technology*, London: HMSO.
Bundesinstitut für Berufsbildung (BIBB) (1991) 'Qualifikationsentwicklung
    und Qualifikationsbedarf', unpublished report submitted for the 1991 CEDE-
    FOP Forum, Berlin, 25–26 September 1991.
Christie, I., Northcott, J. and Walling, A. (1990) *Employment Effects of New
    Technology in Manufacturing*, London: PSI.
Commission of the European Communities (1993) *Growth, Competitiveness, Em-
    ployment – The Challenges and Ways Forward into the 21st Century*, Luxembourg:
    White Paper Bulletin of the EC, Supplement 6/93.
Coopers and Lybrand (1989) 'Executive summary', para 16, 'Concluding observa-
    tions, in
d'Iribarne, A. (1983) 'Technologies nouvelles, qualifications et éducation –
    l'intérêt d'une approche culturelle et sociétale', in B. Lutz (ed.), *Technik und
    sozialer Wandel*, Frankfurt.
Drucker, P. (1990) 'The emerging theory of manufacturing', *Harvard Business
    Review*, (3), May–June.
Evans, J. (1982) 'The worker and the workplace', in G. Friedrichs and A.
    Schaff (eds), *Microelectronics and Society: For Better or for Worse*, report to the
    Club of Rome, Oxford: Pergamon.
Evers, H.-J., Becker, C. and Fritsch, M. (1990) 'The nature of employment
    effects of new technology', in E. Matzner and M. Wagner (eds), *The Employ-
    ment Impact of New Technology*, Aldershot: Gower.
Hartmann, G., Nicholas, I., Sorge, A. and Warner, M. (1983) 'Computerized
    machine tools, manpower consequences and skill utilization: a study of
    British and West German manufacturing firms', *British Journal of Industrial
    Relations*, 2(2): 221–231.
Höflich-Häberlein, L. and Häbler, H. (1988) 'Applications of microelectronics
    in selected West German industries', Infratest paper presented at a 'Meta-
    Conference', Berlin, December 1988.
ILO (1987) *Training and Retraining – The Implications of Technological Change*,
    Report 3, Fourth Regional Conference, Geneva, September 1987.
Jenkins, C. and Sherman, B. (1979) *The Collapse of Work*, London: Eyre Methuen.

Kern, H. and Schumann, M. (1984) *Das Ende der Arbeitsteilung? Rationalisierung in der industriellen Produktion*, Munich: Verlag C. H. Beck.

Lane, C. (1985) 'White collar workers in the labour process: the case of the Federal Republic of Germany', *Sociological Review*, 33(2), May.

Mandon, N. (1985) *Technologie et travail, l'informatisation des activités de bureau – Tome II: L'évolution des situations de travail individuelles et le Devenir des groupes professionnels – le cas du secrétariat*, Paris: Collection des Etudes.

Merle, V. *et al.* (1990) 'Difficultés de recrutement des entreprises et gestion locale de l'emploi', cited in a report on skill trends produced by CEREQ for the 1991 CEDEFOP Forum, Berlin, 25–26 September 1991.

Northcott, J. (1986) *Microelectronics in Industry – Promise and Performance*, London: PSI.

Northcott, J., Rogers, P., Knetsch, W. and de Lestapis, B. (1985) *Microelectronics in Industry: An International Comparison*, London: PSI.

Penn, R. (1990) 'Skilled maintenance work at British Telecom: findings from the social change and economic life initiative', *New Technology, Work and Employment*, 5, Autumn.

Rathenau Commission (1980) *Societal Consequences of Microelectronics*, The Hague: State Publishing House.

Sleigh, J., Boatwright, B., Irwin, P. and Stanyon, R. (1979) *The Manpower Implications of Micro-electronic Technology*, London: HMSO.

Sorge, A. (1983) 'Polarization of skills in the future?', *Vocational Training*, 11: 22, Berlin: CEDEFOP.

Sorge, A. (1987) 'Strategische Orientierungen des Einsatzes neuer Techniken und Arbeitsmarkt', in F. Buttler, K. Gerlach and R. Schmeide (eds), *Arbeitsmarkt und Beschäftigung, Neuere Beiträge zur institutionalistischen Arbeitsmarktanalyse*, Frankfurt.

Steedman, H. (1987) 'Vocational training in France and Britain: office work', *National Institute Economic Review*: (120): 58–70.

Strobel, P. (1986) 'Télématique et emploi', synthesis report *Technologie Emploi Travail*, Paris: Ministry for Research.

Wakeham, P. and Beresford-Knox, J. E. (1980) *Microelectronics and the Future*, London: IMS.

## Chapter 5

# Learners of the future
## Preparing a policy for the third age†

*Tom Schuller and Anne Marie Bostyn*

### INTRODUCTION

There are some fourteen million adults aged over 50 in the UK. Until now, there has been no initiative at national level to produce a coordinated or coherent policy to meet their educational needs. In 1991 the Carnegie Inquiry into the Third Age was set up. Its remit was to investigate the position of older men and women across a wide range of policy areas, and to make recommendations for future action. The areas selected include employment, pensions, health, volunteering and citizenship as well as education. Separate studies – nine in all – have been conducted in these areas. Their analyses and recommendations have been drawn together into a final report (Carnegie 1993). [1993 was] designated as European Year of the Elderly and Intergenerational Solidarity; the Inquiry is thus very timely, though it was originally conceived before the European decision was made. The context, in almost all industrialized countries, is one of ageing populations involving greater longevity but also healthier older people, declining economic activity rates for older men, and increasing pressure on social benefits and health care budgets. The essential issue round which the Inquiry has developed is the extent to which older people can be enabled to play an active part in society, according to their own choices. As far as educational policy is concerned, there were questions to be asked about the extent to which institutions, local authorities or national policy-makers took account of the needs of older people, directly as a group with specific needs or indirectly as members of the wider population. The study on education was carried out at the University of Edinburgh's Centre for Continuing Education and was published in autumn 1992 (Schuller and Bostyn 1992). Our task was to cover as far as possible all the learning opportunities open to third agers. The objectives were defined as follows:

† This chapter is an edited version of an article which appeared in the *Journal of Education Policy*, 8 (5), 1993.

- to give an account of current participation by third agers in formal and informal learning activities;
- to identify the key issues involved in education, training and information for older adults;
- to suggest policy options.

This chapter discusses the policy context of the study. It gives a general summary of the current situation, and provides a framework for further policy analysis. It also contains a list of the policy options which we presented to the main Inquiry; some but not all of these have been taken into the body of the final report. First, however, we discuss briefly the definitional or conceptual issues involved.

## 'THE THIRD AGE'

We have already used three terms as if they were interchangeable: older adults, those aged over 50, and third agers. Life-cycle analysis is a relatively underdeveloped field in the UK, especially in the sociological context. [. . .] Studies of the later end of the life cycle have been largely the province of those engaged in the field of social policy, whose analytical frameworks and concerns were shaped by the structure of public welfare, a notable consequence being the identification of old age with pensionable status. In short, the categories were defined by the happenstance of policy format, and rarely scrutinized within a wider social science context.

It has not been the task of the Carnegie Inquiry to redress this analytical deficit. Nevertheless a number of factors have contributed to a growing awareness of the need for a broader approach. First, demographic projections of an ageing population have generated significant policy concern over the social expenditure and health care implications. Ageing is seen exclusively as a problem to be coped with, and solutions sought to the projected costs of caring for old people. [Second], stemming mainly from a politically charged debate whose epicentre is in the USA, has come a growing awareness of the ethical, conceptual and political problems surrounding the notion of intergenerational justice – and, indeed, the deceptively simple notion of 'generation' itself (Laslett and Fishkin 1992).

Third, labour market trends have meant that large numbers of older men have left the labour force. In the UK, economic activity rates for men aged 60 to 64 have decreased from over 80% in 1971 to barely over 50% two decades later. It should be stressed that this is largely a male phenomenon. As DeViney and O'Rand (1988) have pointed out for the USA, separate age–gender categories need to be distinguished. Older women have maintained their economic activity rates, and if one looks at the age-groups younger than that immediately preceding retirement age, their rates have even increased. We therefore have an interesting example of a policy issue which is now achieving prominence because it affects men, but which has been of relevance to women for a long time without gaining such recognition. [. . .]

Increased longevity and earlier retirement (*de facto* rather than formal) have opened up what could loosely be called a new phase in life, where significant numbers are expected to spend a considerable amount of time in reasonable health after they have ceased formal employment. Peter Laslett (1989) has provided a structure for defining whether or not a society can be said to include a third age, basing this on life expectancy at 25, survival rates at 70, and wealth levels needed to sustain active citizenship in old age. It is important to underline the way our conceptions of age and ageing are socially constructed, and can be expected to change over time.

The Carnegie Inquiry opted for a compromise. Operationally most of the studies were encouraged to use a broadly chronological definition, setting the starting point for the third age at 50. There was considerable discussion within the Inquiry about whether there should in any sense be an upper limit to the field. On the one hand it was clear that any chronological age would be arbitrary, and that one of the main thrusts would be the need to avoid discriminatory age segregation; on the other hand it was important that the Inquiry should not be dominated by the needs of the dependent elderly, important though these are, since the whole point was to broaden the political understanding of age. In the event it was agreed that there should be no defined upper limit, but that the focus should be on how to cater to the needs of the active older population. In the end, therefore, the Inquiry's definition emerged as functional rather than chronological:

> We have defined the third age as the period of life when people emerge from the imperatives of earning a living and/or bringing up children and, without precedent in our society, are able to look forward to perhaps twenty of more years of healthy life.
>
> (Carnegie Inquiry 1993: iii)

## DEFINITION OF THE FIELD: EDUCATION, TRAINING AND INFORMATION

It followed from the definition of the third age as starting at 50 that not only should employment be a major field of study, but learning should be construed as more than simply education unrelated to work. The division between education and training has long been the subject of policy debate within the UK (Finegold *et al.* 1990). Here, perhaps surprisingly, was a chance to bring the two together in a single set of policy recommendations – 'surprisingly' because it is precisely for this age-group that training is often considered irrelevant. The conjoining of education and training itself represented an attack on the conceptualization of age and the stereotyping of older people which regarded them as by definition excluded from economic activity. We shall return to this later in the chapter when examining the notion of the social economy of the third age. The decision naturally added greatly to the complexity of the task, since it extended the range of statistical sources and experiences on which we had to draw in order to formulate key issues.

On top of this came the decision to include informal learning opportunities. For those involved in analysing or even describing the field of adult education this has always been a problem. Tough (1976), for example, made a considerable impact with his investigation of adult learning projects which showed that although relatively few adults recorded themselves as participating in adult education in the formal sense, many more were actively engaged in organized learning projects. Furthermore, the major study carried out by Sargant on behalf of the National Institute for Adult and Continuing Education (NIACE) in 1990 (Sargant 1991) showed that the number of people who attended classes was only a small proportion of those who could be described as involved in education. The difficulty, of course, is where to draw the line, since anyone who is not wholly routinized could in one sense be described as learning on a day-to-day basis. The most obvious area in which this applies is that of the mass media. Many TV and radio programmes are highly informational and may also develop skills of various kinds but to include all viewing and listening would swamp the analysis of formal provision and offend against our commonplace understanding of education; more immediately, it would displace the policy focus to a level where the formulation of policy options would become a matter of broadcasting policy or of cultural policy generally.

Nevertheless our remit was extended to include informal learning opportunities. With an overall time span for the study of 18 months, we drew on three main sources:

- A variety of *statistical* sources. These included national published statistics; figures produced specially for us from data banks such as the Labour Force Survey; and published and unpublished data from other studies. We discuss below some of the methodological difficulties involved in synthesizing these sources.
- *Existing literature*. A number of competent surveys exist, covering both provision and the learning abilities and processes of older adults (e.g. Withnall *et al*. 1983; Glendinning and Percy 1990; McGivney 1990).

- A number of *small-scale surveys*. These included structured question-naires to all members of the Association for Educational Gerontology, and to all Universities of the Third Age in the UK (over 100 at the time of the study, and increasing rapidly); surveys of educational providers based on a common framework of questions to be used in group discussion; case studies of a small number of employers and TECs/LECs; a survey of voluntary organizations on the training of older volunteers; group discussion with members of ethnic minority groups; and a survey of student motivations and benefits in Norfolk LEA and Wandsworth College. Many of these had low response rates, but they were not designed as representative investigations in the strict sense; they were intended to cover a range of interested parties, eliciting views on a common set of issues. These focused on obstacles to participation and learning; notions of good practice; and proposals for steps forward.

## THE 'STOCK' POSITION: SNAPSHOTS OF EDUCATIONAL GENERATIONS

This section summarizes where we are now as a result of educational policies since the First World War. The key points are:

- *The great majority of older people had little initial schooling.* Roughly two in three people over 50 and under the state pension age (60/65) left school at 15 or earlier, compared with one in four of those under 50 (Table 5.1).
- *This initial disadvantage has not been corrected by subsequent education.* Table 5.2 shows the levels of qualification reached by respondents in the 1987 British Social Attitudes survey. These may have been gained in initial education or later on through continuing education. The figures confirm the age differences in educational attainment, most obviously for those with no formal qualifications: the proportion declines stead-ily, from 73% of those aged 70 + , to 46% of those aged 50–54 and 42% of the population as a whole.
- *The two great social divides of sex and class have had a major and sustained impact on the distribution of educational opportunity.* Although women's initial schooling was not much shorter, their level of qualification is significantly lower. Only 2% of women over 50 have a degree and 67% have no qualifications at all. The respective figures for men are 7% and 53%. As for social class, nearly nine out of ten unskilled or semiskilled workers have no qualifications at all. That some relationship between education and occupational level exists is predictable; its sheer strength is striking.
- *Each succeeding generation is better educated than its predecessor, as measured by length of initial schooling and possession of formal qualifications.* Table 5.3

Table 5.1 Age finished full-time education (%)

| Age finished F/T education | All ages M | F | First age M | F | Second age M | F | 50–54 M | F | 55–59 M | F | 60–64 M | F | All under 3A M | F | All 50–60/64 M | F |
|---|---|---|---|---|---|---|---|---|---|---|---|---|---|---|---|---|
| 15 or under | 36.0 | 33.0 | 7.0 | 7.2 | 31.1 | 31.5 | 62.1 | 59.5 | 67.3 | 66.7 | 75.0 | | 25.4 | 25.9 | 67.9 | 63.0 |
| 16–18 | 50.0 | 54.3 | 83.3 | 83.4 | 51.3 | 53.3 | 27.4 | 32.1 | 24.1 | 26.3 | 18.1 | | 58.8 | 60.2 | 23.4 | 29.3 |
| 19–24 | 12.6 | 12.2 | 9.8 | 9.4 | 15.8 | 14.5 | 8.7 | 8.0 | 7.1 | 6.7 | 5.5 | | 14.3 | 13.3 | 7.2 | 7.4 |
| 25+ | 1.4 | 0.5 | – | – | 1.9 | 0.7 | 1.8 | 0.4 | 1.5 | 0.3 | 1.4 | | 1.4 | 0.5 | 1.5 | 0.3 |

Source: Dept. of Employment: Labour Force Survey (1990)

Table 5.2 Respondents' highest educational qualification (%)

| | A. All ages | | B. 50+ (1) Sex | | (2) Occupational Class* | | | | | (3) Age | | | | |
|---|---|---|---|---|---|---|---|---|---|---|---|---|---|---|
| Qualification | M | F | M | F | (1) | 2 | 3 | 4 | 5 | 50–54 | 55–59 | 60–64 | 65–69 | 70+ |
| Degree | 8 | 2 | 7 | 2 | (41) | 12 | 1 | – | – | 5 | 4 | 4 | 4 | 3 |
| Professional qualification | 13 | 20 | 13 | 20 | (36) | 33 | 8 | 2 | – | 16 | 13 | 12 | 10 | 9 |
| A level | 9 | 4 | 6 | 4 | (6) | 7 | 6 | 2 | – | 5 | 5 | 4 | 7 | 4 |
| O level | 19 | 11 | 10 | 11 | (9) | 16 | 12 | 4 | 6 | 18 | 16 | 12 | 5 | 6 |
| CSE | 8 | 4 | 10 | 4 | (–) | 3 | 12 | 4 | 1 | 8 | 8 | 6 | 8 | 5 |
| None | 42 | 67 | 53 | 67 | (8) | 28 | 61 | 86 | 87 | 46 | 54 | 62 | 64 | 73 |

Source: SPCR; British Social Attitudes (1987)
Note: * 1 = professional, 2 = intermediate, 3 = skilled, 4 = semi-skilled, 5 = unskilled. (Numbers in Category 1 are too low to have significance)

shows how this pattern has changed over time. The key feature is the steady increase in the level of qualifications. The proportion of those with degrees rises from around 5% for those aged over 50 to over double (11%) for people in their thirties, whereas the proportion of those with no qualifications declines from two in three for those over 60 to fewer than one in five for those aged 20. Within the third age, the pattern is repeated; three out of four men aged 60–64 left school at 15, compared with three out of five of those born ten years later.

*Table 5.3* Highest qualification by age-group (%)

| Qualification | 20–29 | 30–39 | 40–49 | 50–59 | 60–69 | Difference (old–young) |
|---|---|---|---|---|---|---|
| Degree or equivalent | 8 | 11 | 8 | 5 | 5 | –3 |
| Higher education below degree level | 9 | 13 | 11 | 9 | 6 | –3 |
| GCE A level or equivalent | 15 | 11 | 7 | 4 | 2 | |
| GCE O level or equivalent/CSE Grade 1 | 34 | 23 | 16 | 10 | 6 | –28 |
| CSE other grades/ commercial qualifications/ apprenticeship | 15 | 9 | 11 | 11 | 12 | –3 |
| Foreign or other qualifications | 2 | 3 | 4 | 4 | 3 | 1 |
| No qualifications | 18 | 30 | 44 | 57 | 65 | 47 |

*Source*: OPCS *General Household Survey 1988* (HMSO 1990) Table 7.5

The figures discussed so far show how low the initial education base is for third agers. This has changed over time, although the UK remains well down the league in the average level of initial schooling with more young people leaving with no qualifications than in most countries. The lowness of the base is accentuated by the levels of participation in the intervening period, i.e. by current third agers during their second age. The 1990 NIACE survey (Sargant 1991) shows that 81% of those aged 65 or over and 77% of those aged 55–64 have not studied since completing their full-time education. Thus four out of five in the older age-group have not participated in any kind of formal education in the fifty or so years since they left school. This compares with a figure for the total population of 63% – itself hardly something for national self-congratulation, when set alongside countries such as Sweden, where every year some 1.5 million out of six million adults attend study circle courses (see

Rubenson 1988). Most third agers have therefore gone a very long time without participating in formal learning; and distance in this context is to be measured not only in calendar years, but also in terms of the distance they perceive to exist between their current position and the probability of education – they consider that they are very unlikely to participate or to want to participate. This becomes particularly important when we consider the probable impact of the cohort effect on future demand.

## PARTICIPATION RATES IN EDUCATION AND TRAINING

### Education

Table 5.4 summarizes our estimates of overall enrolments in formal education. It shows that roughly three-quarters of a million adults aged over 50 enrol annually in some form of adult education. The figures require some explication.

Local authorities are the major providers of adult education. Total enrolments in local government provision were calculated at some 1.6 million in a 1991 HMI report (HMI 1991). Woodley and his colleagues, in what is still the most comprehensive survey of educational participation by adults, showed that 19% of the participants in local classes in 1981 were aged 60 or over (Woodley et al. 1987: Table 3.1). Extending this to take account of the 50–60 age group gives an enrolment total of some 400,000.

For further education (FE) the best figures available were for England alone. These show that in 1989 just under 127,000 people aged 50–74 enrolled in FE courses where age is recorded. Other enrolments where no age is reliably recorded totalled 115,000, and applying the same age ratio yields a further 13,200 third age enrolments, making a total for England of 140,100. Applying the same ratio to the rest of the UK gives us an estimate of some 150,000 as the grand total.

The WEA figure of 60,000 is based on an estimate that around one-third of the Association's total of 180,000 are third agers. For university extra-mural departments we have set the proportion slightly lower, at 25% of the 1988–89 total of 271,000. Pre-retirement estimates are based on calculations made by the Pre-Retirement Association; they should be set against a total of nearly 600,000 people who are within five years of the state retirement age.

The other figures are drawn from statistics gathered by the relevant institutions or sectors on an age basis, and involve a lower degree of estimation. But to balance these crude enrolment figures we have attempted in Table 5.4 to provide a weighting by length of course, for

*Table 5.4* Third age enrolments in education (estimate for 1989/90)

| Type | (a) Enrolments (000) | % of total | (b) Average hours per enrolment | Total hours (000s) | % of total |
|---|---|---|---|---|---|
| Adult education (local authority) | 400 | 54 | 30 | 12,000 | 36 |
| Further education | 150 | 20 | 30 | 4,500 | 14 |
| Workers/ Educational Association | 60 | 8 | 20 | 1,200 | 4 |
| Pre-retirement education | 30 | 4 | 10 | 300 | 1 |
| University of the Third Age | 20 | 3 | 100 | 2,000 | 6 |
| National Extension College | 4 | 1 | 150 | 600 | 2 |
| Open College of the Arts | 2 | | 150 | 300 | 1 |
| Open University (ug) | 10 | 1 | 400 | 4,000 | 12 |
| (Assoc) | 1 | | 200 | 200 | 1 |
| Higher education: | | | | | |
| non-univ. | 7 | 1 | 800 | 5,600 | 17 |
| univ. degree | 1.2 | | 800 | 960 | 3 |
| univ. extra-mural | 70 | 8 | 20 | 1,400 | 4 |
| Totals | 755 | 100 | | 33,060 | 101 |

clearly enrolments vary greatly in the extent to which they involve a time commitment.

The roughest average, in the sense of the one which probably has the widest variation around the mean, is that for further education. The average of 30 hours underwent several revisions as we consulted various parties.

## Training

Statistics on overall participation in organized training were if anything harder to come by. It is surprising, since at least one regular and major survey – the Labour Force Survey (LFS) – includes relevant questions. The problem is that the LFS asks about training received in the last four weeks. Responses to this showed that some 7% of older men (50–64) and 8% of older women (50–59) had received training in that time, giving a total of just under 400,000. It would only be reasonable to multiply that figure by 12 to give an annual rate if all training lasted for a short time. In fact, about one-quarter received training that lasted for anything from a week to a year, and another quarter's training was 'ongoing'. It therefore seemed reasonable to multiply the LFS figure by a factor of two to three, yielding an estimated total of just under a million.

However, another survey (Training Agency 1989) reported that 14% of those aged 55–59 and 23% of those aged 45–54 had received vocational training in the last three years. It would be unreasonable simply to divide by three to give an annual rate since a proportion will receive training every year. Instead, we divided by two, and this gave a figure of rather less than half that of the LFS survey. We conclude that an estimate of 650,000–700,000 might be in order – some 13% of the relevant age-group. This means that only just over one in ten of employed third agers receive any training at all in a given year.

Two points should be noted. The first is that older women show higher participation rates in training than older men. The second is that the proportion of older people receiving training has increased quite significantly in recent years. In 1984, for example, 4.1% of men and 4.2% of women aged 50–54 had received training in the last four weeks according to the LFS; the figures for 1990 were 9.4% and 9.8% respectively. This rate of increase is faster than for younger age-groups, but it was from a far lower base. The 1990 figures for men and women aged 25–49 were 15.0% and 15.6%.

## ASSESSING PROVISION: A FRAMEWORK FOR EVALUATION

We have presented above a statistical account of current provision. [. . .] But figures alone offer little guide as to the adequacy of the provision. As Percy observed, concluding his analysis of three different data sets from the 1970s and 1980s:

> These surveys just about enable us to subscribe to a generalised statement such as this: 'we know that for those of pensionable age (and thereabouts) current (i.e. at the time of asking) participation in classes (i.e. all classes: work-related education may make little difference to the figures) is in the range of 2–7%. About two-thirds of this age-group have never participated in classes. The remaining (25–30%) have done so in the past, but are not at present doing so.
>
> (Percy 1990: 31)

To go further, we need some kind of framework which will allow current provision to be evaluated against a number of different criteria.

*International comparison*

Potentially a useful way of gauging how the UK stands. There is, however, no uniform approach to gathering information, though the advent of 1993 as the Year of the Elderly and Intergenerational Solidarity provides an opportunity for this (cf. the establishment of the European Observatory on older people). An overview from the Unesco Institute of Education draws on a variety of sources from different years and shows estimates of participation rates ranging from 2.3% (1975) to 15% (1990) amongst the 65 + age-group in the USA, 2% and 6% for those just over and under 65 respectively in Finland (1979/80), 3.7% and 10% for similar age-groups in Canada (1984) and 5–10% for those aged 50 + in The Netherlands (1990) (Belanger 1992). No country appears outstanding in its educational provision specifically for older people, although the USA can claim to have pioneered interesting initiatives and to have witnessed the strongest antidiscrimination statements. There are certain areas in which the UK can claim to be reasonably advanced, for example with the Open University and community education. Against this must be set the great overall deficit in the initial and continuing education and training of the population as a whole, now documented in numerous analyses. The contrast is sharpest with the Scandinavian countries, where participation in adult education is so much more firmly part of the culture, with participation rates of 23% and 16% recorded for the 60–64 and 65–74 age groups respectively in 1982–83 (Rubenson 1988).

*Progress over time*

One of the key features of the debate on third age policies is its long-term character. The UK has already passed through one phase of population ageing, and has several years to build up full momentum before entering the next. There are areas where rapid action is needed; but at another level longer-term objectives need to be set, and mechanisms for monitoring progress towards these objectives need to be installed.

*Rising expectations*

Whatever judgement is reached on the current position, we cannot as a nation pronounce ourselves satisfied. Targets will continually recede. This is in part a prediction, on the basis of confident projections of increasing demand, but also a prescription: it is a sign of a civilized country that policy is geared to raising as well as meeting aspirations. However difficult it is to define 'needs', there is a ratchet effect which should be anticipated and welcomed: aspirations generate 'needs' which, when met, prompt fresh aspirations.

*Social distribution*

Gross numbers give some guide to performance. The distribution of opportunity and achievement is a different matter. How far do certain groups appear to be systematically under-represented? What has been done to correct this, or at least to ensure that realistic opportunities have been available to these groups even if they have not taken them up? These are questions which should be present in an overall review.

*Quality*

As important as quantity. We have established benchmarks relating to the numbers participating in education and training, and indicated the amount of other learning taking place. Performance cannot be measured only by head-counts or budgets. The final dimension, therefore, has two aspects: the quality of learning as experienced by the learner (in essence, the quality of consumption) and the effectiveness of the learning. In other words, measurement of progress has to cover not only the numbers learning and the distribution of learning opportunities, but also what the outcomes are. This applies equally to education and training, though obviously in very different ways.

This final point requires some elaboration. For much of adult education, especially where this is distinguished from vocational training, objectives are hard to define in advance and with clarity. Personal development can be achieved in a number of ways. Arguably, research into adult education has concentrated too much on participation rates and too little on what effect participation has had on individual lives, and on social and community life more generally. [ ... ] The focus has been on inputs rather than outcomes. In the Carnegie report we identified a number of aspects of good practice, based on returns from practitioners and students. Here we present some empirical evidence derived from one of the component studies, and one associated issue of considerable significance to anyone concerned with evaluation, at whatever level.

We carried out a survey of students in two different locations: Wandsworth College, a large adult education institute in Inner London; and Norfolk LEA, where questionnaires were circulated through a number of outlets. The response rate was low, especially in Norfolk, but the results (see Table 5.5) are based on several hundred returns. The survey revealed a consistent pattern of students reporting benefits which exceeded their original expectations and motives, especially in areas of increased confidence and social interaction.

The overall results are encouraging to the institutions concerned, and raise some interesting issues – note, for example, the very sizeable

*Table 5.5* Survey results from Wandsworth College and Norfolk LEA

| Reported aim | % stating aim | % reporting benefit |
| --- | --- | --- |
| To keep my mind active | 72 | 72 |
| To develop knowledge of a subject | 64 | 68 |
| To make new friends | 45 | 57 |
| To develop a practical skill | 40 | 42 |
| To gain more confidence | 35 | 40 |
| To have some time away from home | 33 | 40 |
| To make up for opportunities lost when younger | 32 | 36 |
| To develop skills for further study | 23 | 27 |
| To develop my qualifications | 11 | 25 |
| To develop better health | 22 | 23 |
| To be more involved in the community | 21 | 22 |
| To develop a sporting skill | 6 | 9 |
| To help me get a new job | 5 | 9 |
| To help me in running a business | 6 | 7 |
| To help me in my volunteer work | 15 | 15 |
| To help me with my current job | 9 | 9 |
| To do something creative | 48 | 40 |
| To improve my career opportunities | 8 | 7 |

increase in the number who improved their qualifications even though this had not been a significant original motivation. The point, however, is that there is a very wide range of expectations and that the outcomes are not satisfactorily captured by any competence-based approach. Not only is more research needed particularly in the area of effectiveness, but this should include a range of methodologies such as classroom observation, group discussion and longitudinal study. [. . .]

The associated issue is that of unintended outcomes. Only a proportion of the adults who enrol in classes have a precisely defined outcome in mind. Even for these, there will often be outcomes which they have not expected, which may be favourable or unfavourable and which may be revealed only some time after the activity has ended (Pilley 1993). Quality is therefore a particularly problematic notion in this field given the specific and personal nature of much third age learning.

## THE SOCIAL ECONOMY OF THE THIRD AGE

The framework provided above needs to be set in a wider context. Policy discussion of learning opportunities for older people requires an appreciation of the broad costs and benefits involved. Here we argue for a new social economy of the third age, which takes into account both the actual and potential contributions made by older people, and conversely the costs of failure to make adequate provision.

- The loss of *economic output* caused by the expulsion of older people from the workforce in the 1980s has been estimated at some £7 billion (Bosanquet 1986). Pifer (1991: pers. comm.) has argued that in very general terms we lack the methodology for estimating the benefits of investing in basic skills training. The notion that the payback period for training is coming down sharply is obviously favourable to the case for investing in the training of older workers, but has yet to be proven empirically. Nevertheless, it is highly plausible [. . .] that the arguments for investing in a skilled workforce [. . .] apply with similar strength to older workers. There is an added dimension. Not only is the future potential of an older worker lost if he or she is not given training; the existing body of skills is dissipated, probably for ever, if the worker is removed from the workforce or is not allowed to pass on these skills to succeeding generations.
- We cannot find 'hard' studies which demonstrate a link between learning and *health*. Once again this is more likely to be due to the absence of serious applied research than to the absence of any such relationship. Given the costs of dependency, investment in measures which directly or indirectly sustain independence as long as possible stands a high chance of paying itself back quickly. Can education help to achieve the 'rectangularization of morbidity', so that as people live longer, the extra years are taken up with active healthy living and a swift death, rather than with a long, slow decline? Again this has both an individual and a wider application. Not only is it desirable that individuals should keep themselves healthy; it is also important, at a crudely instrumental level, that third agers, many of whom are involved in caring for others, should retain that capacity. The value of the services delivered by all carers has been estimated at between £15 and £24 billion annually (FPSC 1989). What are the costs of allowing a 60-year-old woman who is caring for an elderly relative to lose her motivation and energy, becoming dependent herself and forcing others to take on the responsibility she has so far shouldered, compared with the costs of basic educational provision? Access to adult education may not of itself be sufficient, but it may play an extraordinarily cost-effective part in preventing or postponing dependency in various forms.
- Linking the issues of national economics and individual well-being is that of *personal finance*. We have not said much in this chapter about this as an increasingly important area of control, as pensions and other arrangements become more complex and responsibility for them devolves more upon the individual. A recent Gallup survey showed that a third of the respondents did not understand their pension benefits.

Less than half of these were worried by their ignorance, but the consequences of such a lack of knowledge are potentially catastrophic. [. . .]

- Less quantifiable of all – indeed in one sense positively incompatible with quantification – is the loss of *cultural* contribution if third agers are deprived of learning opportunities. Laslett has made the case for third agers as 'cultural trustees', with an obligation to maintain, explain and practise all forms of cultural activity, covering craft production, creative arts, popular culture and intellectual activity.

> Time, or leisure rather – and a means to use it – has ceased to be the monopoly of an élite made up of hundreds, thousands, or at most in tens of thousands of persons. It is becoming a commodity of millions of our citizens, our elderly citizens, those in the third age. Some way, therefore, must be discovered to entrust them with our cultural future, and by the same means to relieve them of the burden of their present indolence.
>
> (Laslett 1989: 202)

Alongside this quite traditional notion of culture Laslett argues for enhanced political activity on the part of older people, referring to the as yet unrealized potential of the third age in the political sphere. To this list of cultural activities can be added volunteering and citizenship (Midwinter 1992).

## CONCLUSION: EDUCATION POLICY RECOMMENDATIONS

Our study contains forty-three policy options for consideration by the Inquiry. These cover the three major elements – education, training and information – and are directed at a number of different levels: national and local government, employers and educational institutions. Some of them have been incorporated directly into the final report of the Inquiry (Carnegie 1993). Here we reproduce those relating to education.

### Government (national)

- *A clear policy statement on the rights of older people to a broad range of educational opportunity.* This would be an important assertion of the status of third agers as full participants in society.
- *All relevant educational bodies* – most particularly, local education authorities, the Higher and Further Education Funding Councils and their constituent members – *to have a clear obligation towards adult learners, including older adults.* This obligation will take different forms at different levels. For the Funding Councils, for example, it would be a matter of setting priorities through financial incentives to support

suitable institutional policies and practices, notably in earmarked support for continuing education with a specific outreach character.

- *The duty on local education authorities to secure sufficient provision of adult education to be confirmed, accompanied by adequate resources.* If capping is to continue, central government should admit a level of local financing which allows LEAs and others not only to make statutory provision for schools but also to be able to have a reasonable budget for adult education. Formulae such as the Standard Spending Assessment should acknowledge the particular needs of older learners.
- *Financial support to be significantly reweighted in favour of part-time provision.* This applies both to the financing of *institutions* and to that of *individuals*. In higher education the fee-grant system to be reviewed in this light. More generally, discretionary awards for part-time study to be increased.
- *Co-ordination of and support for distance learning providers* (pre-eminently the Open University, but also the Open College of the Arts, National Extension College, etc.) with particular reference to older learners with problems of mobility. This would include incentives for education institutions which are not themselves providers of distance learning to collaborate in this, for example in the provision of tutorial support groups or of access to physical resources such as libraries, and to IT.

## Government (local/regional)

- *Local authorities to prepare an explicit policy statement on older learners,* interpreting and complementing statements at national level.
- *Local authorities to set and monitor targets for participation,* to be expressed in terms of numbers or proportions of local population groups, together with more qualitative goals.
- *Local authorities to ensure that as broad a range as possible of learning opportunities is offered to older adults,* recognizing that genuine breadth can only be achieved by major efforts to enable potential students to articulate their needs and participate in curriculum development. Full use should be made of school buildings, in the evening and during school holidays.
- *Local authorities to promote collaboration between education and other local/ regional services, notably health, social services and voluntary organizations.* Such collaboration might take place at policy/management levels, with joint planning groups; but it might also take such forms as cross-placements of staff and joint professional training, both initial and in-service.
- *Financial support and fee policies to be designed to help those with least initial schooling and those who cannot afford full (or even reduced) fees.* A review is

needed of the effective targeting of financial support, recognizing the tension between universal and selective support.

- *Local authorities to support local education guidance networks and services, combining comprehensive information with advice and access to taster courses.* This should be acknowledged as especially important for certain groups, notably ethnic minorities, where mother-tongue guidance is often needed.

## Educational institutions

- *Institutions to issue a policy statement which defines their general attitude to older learners, but which also sets a framework for admissions, curriculum development and evaluation.*
- Where institutions commit themselves seriously to meeting the needs of *older learners* they will need to consider: (i) *outreach initiatives* to reach groups who are not in the learning habit; (ii) *scheduling and location* of provision; (iii) *appropriate learning environments*; (iv) *curriculum development*; (v) *guidance and information.*
- *Staff development will almost always be needed*, at several different levels: from senior management to receptionist.
- *Institutions will need to consider how far they make separate provision for third agers.* Different institutions will follow different policies in this respect, and rightly so, but the outcomes of these different policies should be properly monitored.

Education policy for the third age encapsulates a number of issues of general salience. First, there is the need for immediate action to counteract the inequalities of history, as generations of older people enter and live through retirement with little in the way of educational support and no embedded learning habits. Second, there is a need for a longer-term perspective which recognizes that policies appropriate for the next century cannot be introduced in a single parliamentary session but which establishes firmly the basis for continuing development. Third, policy analysis in relation to this age-group brings forward once more the issue of coordination between different policy areas; in particular between education and training, but also between formal and informal learning. We pointed earlier to the paradox that the notion of the third age is largely associated with life after work and yet policies which did not address learning at work would miss the mark. Similarly the new technologies, which are so conspicuously associated with the young, have major implications for the extent to which older people are able to realize their learning potential. Libraries, cable learning channels and computer networks offer enormous scope for people whose mobility may be relatively limited. Yet the challenge is to link these to the social contexts of learning which older people value so highly.

# REFERENCES

Belanger, P. (1992) 'L'éducation des adultes et le vieillissement des populations: tendances et enjeux', *International Review of Education*, 38(4): 343–362.

Bosanquet, N. (1986) *A Generation in Limbo*, London: Public Policy Centre.

Carnegie Inquiry (1993) *Life, Work and Livelihood in the Third Age*, Carnegie Inquiry into the Third Age Final Report, Dunfermline: Carnegie UK Trust.

DeViney, S. and O'Rand, A. (1988) 'Gender – cohort succession and retirement among older men and women, 1951 to 1984', *Sociological Quarterly*, 29(4): 520–550.

Finegold, D. *et al.* (1990) *A British Baccalaureat: Ending the Division Between Education and Training*, London: Institute for Public Policy Research.

FPSC (1989) 'Family care in focus', *Family Policy* 6, London: Family Policy Studies Centre.

Glendinning, F. and Percy, K. (eds) (1990) *Ageing, Education and Society: Readings in Educational Gerontology*, Keele: Association for Educational Gerontology.

HMI (1991) *Education for Adults*, London: Her Majesty's Inspectorate, Department of Education and Science.

Laslett, P. (1989) *A Fresh Map of Life*, London: Weidenfeld and Nicolson.

Laslett, P. and Fishkin, J. (1992) *Justice between Age Groups and Generations*, New Haven: Yale University Press.

McGivney, V. (1990) *Education's for Other People: Access to Education for Non-Participant Adults*, Leicester: NIACE.

Midwinter, E. (1992) *Citizenship*, Research Paper 8, Carnegie Inquiry into the Third Age, Dunfermline: Carnegie UK Trust.

Percy, K. (1990) 'Opinions, facts and hypotheses – older adults and participation in learning activities in the UK', in F. Glendinning and K. Percy (eds), *Ageing, Education and Society: Readings in Educational Gerontology*, Keele: Association for Educational Gerontology.

Pilley, C. (1993) *Adequacy and Effectiveness in the Education of Adults*, Edinburgh; Centre for Continuing Education, University of Edinburgh.

Rubenson, K. (1988) 'Swedish adult education policy in the 1970s and 1980s', in S. J. Ball and S. L. Larsson (eds), *The Struggle for Democratic Education. Equality and Participation in Sweden*, New York: Falmer Press, 117–136.

Sargant, N. (1991) *Learning and 'Leisure': A Study of Adult Participation in Learning and its Policy Implications*, Leicester: NIACE.

Schuller, T. and Bostyn, A. M. (1992) *Learning: Education, Training and Information in the Third Age*, Research Paper 3, Carnegie Inquiry into the Third Age, Dunfermline: Carnegie UK Trust.

Tough, A. (1976) 'Self planned learning and major personal change', in R. M. Smith (ed.), *Adult Learning: Issues and Innovations*, Illinois: ERIC Clearing House, 58–73.

Training Agency (1989) *Training in Britain*, Sheffield: Training Agency.

Withnall, A., Charnley, A. and Osborne, M. (1983) *The Elderly*, Vol. II of *Review of Existing Research in Adult and Continuing Education*, Leicester: NIACE.

Woodley, A., Wagner, L., Slowey, M., Hamilton, M. and Fulton, O. (1987) *Choosing to Learn*, Milton Keynes: SRHE Open University Press.

# Chapter 6

# Educating cheap labour†

## *Mechthild Hart*

## THREATS, CRISES, AND OTHER LOOMING DISASTERS

[. . .] In his essay 'Education and the Sony War', Joel Spring (1985) summarizes the economic developments which have taken place since 1960. The fact that American companies were losing ground in international competition owing to delayed capital investments and declining productivity led to a twofold appeal to education: better basic skills training or 'career preparation' in order to expand the pool of workers qualifying for low-level jobs thereby keeping wages from climbing, and 'increased graduation requirements in mathematics, science, and other academic fields', producing new graduates who 'will lead US industry to victory in the worldwide technological competition' (Spring 1985: 124). [. . .]

Shor (1986) makes a similar point in his discussion of the 'real needs' of business:

> One is a limited supply of highly-trained personnel. A second is an oversupply of middle- and lower-range labor. A third is high-level research and development in a handful of major universities. A fourth is a curriculum which adjusts students to the labor market, as well as to the domestic and foreign priorities of the corporations. A fifth outcome is education as a business activity itself, an open market for business goods and services.
>
> (Shor 1986: 128)

It is against this background that I want to examine the proposals and arguments presented for training and educating the future labour force. By keeping in mind the overall concern of business for a large pool of workers with good work habits and basic skills, a critical look at the

---

† This chapter is an edited version of a chapter which appeared in *Working and Educating for Life*, London, Routledge, 1992.

arguments put forth reveals a number of glaring inadequacies, and above all a lack of analyses which would do justice to the complex interplay of the multiple factors and relationships contributing to the current situation, a complexity which is not explained by simply painting the picture of a 'looming human capital crisis' (Perelman 1984). One of the consequences of describing and explaining work-related developments within these narrow parameters is an overall structure of argument that is ridden with contradictions, and marked by unwarranted assertions, stated but unproven relationships between isolated facts, an absence of concrete and specific evidence, and a reliance on emotionally charged language. [. . .]

It is worth looking at the argument in some detail. In *A Nation at Risk*, for instance, the decline of the American educational system is deplored, thereby holding it fully responsible for current economic problems. Consequently, so the authors of the report argue, the only road to economic recovery is improved schooling, education, and training. In short, the educational system is both 'the problem and the solution to the economic crisis' (Shor 1986: 108). No proof is offered for this causal connection. Rather, it relies on its considerable emotional appeal which is drawn from many sources of actual and potential fears and worries of a population confronted with the dismal state of public education, the diminishing power of unions to protect pay cheques or jobs, with worker displacement, unemployment, and a fast rate of obsolescence of work-related experience and skills. This report, like others, seems to draw its persuasive power primarily from the presumed direct connection between the 'economic crisis' and a deficient human capital. Once that connection is made, the primary task is to present information on demographic trends (who *are* these deficient workers?) as well as changing and increasing skills requirements for the jobs of the future (what *are* the skills needed by the future workforce?). However, precisely because the relationship between education/training and jobs (in the form of performance, work-related tasks and skills, employment opportunities, etc.) is far from unidirectional and clear-cut, concrete, detailed, and convincing evidence cannot be brought forth in favour of this connection.

This is one of the reasons that facts and myths are so enormously entangled in these accounts. The overall message is all too clear, however: the problem of threatened economic competitiveness or economic decline resides with the individual. In other words, the entire weight of the current 'productivity decline' is placed on the shoulders of 'an unproductive population' (Shor 1986: 110). Questions of international economic competition that have led to a new international division of labour, plant closures and relocations due to high capital mobility forever in search of 'cheap labour', urban decline leading to geographical and social isolation of large inner city populations, sexual and racial discrimination (to name only a few factors which directly contribute to the current reality of work) – all these questions are ultimately reduced to the simple explanation that people lack certain skills. While the concerns with illiteracy, lack of so-called basic skills, and with uncertainty about skill requirements of future jobs are all highly legitimate, the mystification of the true causes of these and other problems makes training proposals which idealize the complex and ambiguous link between work and education highly dubious (Gleeson 1986: 56). Without a clear understanding of these causes, however, proposals for various training schemes and programmes will contribute mainly to 'reducing expectations, limiting aspirations, and increasing commitments to the existing social structure' (Shor 1986: 38–39) by feeding on justified fear and anxiety about future survival possibilities.

## THE WHITE MALE WORKER – A VANISHING SPECIES?

In a special report titled 'Human capital: the decline of the American workforce', *Business Week* (19 September 1988) depicts the problem as one that arises because 'employers must now dig deeper into the barrel of the poorly educated' because labour markets have tightened (Bernstein 1988: 104). The 'decline' is brought on by the fact that the future workforce will consist of a higher percentage of women, minorities, and immigrants and a correspondingly lower percentage of white men. As described by Dole (1989), these are the 'populations where the human resource investment has been historically inadequate – women, minorities and immigrants'. [. . .]

A relationship is established mainly by the quasi-automatic association of women, minorities, and immigrants with low-grade human capital. Additionally enveloped by a language of threat, gloom and doom, existing prejudices against women, minorities, and 'aliens' are easily mobilized. I believe that these are, above all, the fears of white men who, in the future, will no longer be the majority of workers (although still favoured by employers, see below). Such fear is expressed, for instance, in the language used in the following quote, where the authors warn of the 'increasing percentage of *non-White, non-male* workers and illiterate workers' (Spikes 1989: 10, my emphasis), creating an immediate and unquestioned association of non-white and non-male with less valuable than male and white, particularly by placing these terms in juxtaposition with 'illiterate workers'. [. . .]

Although without a solid empirical base, the structure of the argument is revealing. It appears to serve primarily an ideological function as it directly feeds into a notion of skill which is 'saturated with sexual bias'

(Phillips and Taylor 1980: 55). Not only are skills in general sex-stereotyped as typical women's and typical men's skills, but the unilateral equation of women's work with low-skilled labour weaves in and out of skills' definitions and corresponding wage differentials. Ironically, the same skills that were previously expected from women as practically natural givens, above all manual dexterity, patience, and attention to detail, now reappear as 'higher skills' for which the (male) workers have to be retrained. The switch from handling '100-pound wire that was 0.6 inches in diameter' to the use of fibre optics 'which means splicing very delicate fibres – like a brain surgeon, almost' is interpreted as a 'skills gap'. The hundreds of thousands of South East Asian women doing the intricate wire bonding work in the microchip industries of multinational corporations were certainly never compared with brain surgeons, and their skills were likewise not considered 'high'.

The picture painted of minorities is equally one-sided, over-generalized, and therefore highly misleading. The existence and growth of the Black 'underclass' cannot be denied. However, the over-emphasis on Black teenage pregnancy, high-school drop-out rates, the references to crime, drug use, and single-parent families paint an overall picture of total 'disorganization' and 'disintegration', directly feeding off White racist fears. [. . .] 'Explanations' of this problem consist of vague references to 'racism'; mainly, however, the reasons are found to lie in 'cultural factors, and in the frustration and apathy' on the side of the members of the underclass itself (Garland 1988: 123). Why the cities are in decline, why large numbers of minorities are geographically isolated, without access to decent schooling, job opportunities, or to information about the latter – these questions are not addressed. Neither is the part 'the economy' itself may have played in this demise.

There is another hidden dimension which needs to be addressed. In discussions emphasizing the high illiteracy rate and general cultural disorganization of 'the disadvantaged' it remains entirely unclear to what extent these people are not part of a general labour surplus that will most likely never be absorbed or even tapped into. We need to look at this situation not only within the context of the world market and the global economy which is characterized by an overall trend towards a growing labour surplus. Johnston and Packer's comment (1987), that the 'unprecedented opportunity' for minorities to enter the labour force 'over the next 13 years' is a 'sanguine outlook' which is 'far from assured', is one of the more realistic statements found in the literature[1] [. . .]:

> given the historic patterns of behavior by employers, it is more reasonable to expect that they will bid up the wages of the relatively smaller numbers of white labor force entrants, seek to substitute

capital for labor in many service occupations, and/or move job sites to the faster growing, more youthful parts of the country, or perhaps of the world.[2]

(Johnston and Packer 1987: 91)

The history of discrimination against minorities regardless of educational background or preparation is similar to that of women. [. . .]

Perelman (1984) indirectly supports the view that not much is to be gained by concentrating on 'the disadvantaged', although he approaches the issue from another angle. His main concern is to provide an argument for building a large, comprehensive adult education 'learning enterprise', modelled after the (idealized) 'free enterprise system', and built on the principles of privatization, decentralization, and open competition. His concern with an undue emphasis on youth and the disadvantaged, and a corresponding neglect of the 'masses of workers in the middle' (Perelman 1984: 22) by adult educators, can be interpreted as a practical business decision since the 'mainstream of work-force adults' (ibid. xvi) is certainly a more likely and reliable clientele than the 'disadvantaged' who are generally 'hard to reach'. [. . .]

## A WIDENING SKILLS GAP?

If we look at the statistics and numbers presented, there is no doubt that the skills of the future will look different, and in many cases require higher levels of literacy. It is not clear, however, precisely how large the increased demand will be, and, more importantly, how many workers will be needed to fill these jobs requiring higher literacy levels. As stated in Chynoweth (1989: 13), 'depending on the definition, estimates of national illiteracy range from as low as 0.5 percent to as high as 50 percent of adult Americans'. Apart from different kinds of definitions that may exist concurrently, any one definition is prone to change as well. [. . .]

Lee (1988: 28), for instance, who talks about a 'quiet crisis in basic skills', does not state what percentage of the actual workforce is and will be affected by illiteracy or what the ratio of available jobs and illiterate workers will be. Very similar to the alarmist report in *Business Week* (19 September 1988), an impression is created of an overall workforce plagued by illiteracy, and of a school system that churns out more illiterate than literate students. Lee cites an example, however, which throws some light not only on the magnitude of the problem but also on the *real* crisis: a New York telephone company tested 21,000 applicants to fill 780 vacancies. He reports (Lee 1988: 29) that 'only' 16 per cent, i.e. 3,360 of those applicants, or more than four times as many as were needed to fill the jobs, passed the test. Can this really be interpreted as a 'widening skills gap', or do we have to focus our attention on the 'widening jobs gap' instead, where 21,000 applicants are competing for 780 positions? This does not take away any importance from the fact that a high number of people are lacking basic literacy skills – but this is a problem that needs to be discussed and addressed in its own right rather than misinterpreted as a danger to productivity and economic growth.

In general, numbers of workers involved, as well as the actual skills requirements, are entirely blown out of proportion. It also remains unclear (and undiscussed) from which groups of people the new job entrants will be recruited. 'The workforce' is a mythical construction, as we need to talk about a labour market which is highly segregated, divided, and stratified. Thus, to say that 'of all the new jobs that will be created over the 1984–2000 period, more than half will require some education beyond high school' (Johnston and Packer 1987: 97) does not state whether this trend is new or one that affects the groups of people deplored as unskilled. It plays, however, into the 'higher skills' argument. As the statistics presented by Johnston and Packer (ibid) show, if ranked by percentage of growth, the top 50 per cent of all jobs that are growing include lawyers and judges, scientists, technical and health professionals, managers, writers and artists, etc. but do not even include the fastest-growing occupation, i.e. services. Obviously, these occupations have traditionally not been drawing from 'women, minorities, and immigrants'.

The overall picture regarding past, current and future levels of educational attainment of the workforce as a whole, or of certain special groups like women or minorities, is far from equivocal. First of all, since the 1950s there has been a steady and continuous rise of educational attainment. As reported by Cyert and Mowery (1987: 66), the share of the labour force without a high school diploma declined from 50.3 per cent in 1959 to 18.5 per cent in 1986. In addition, the share of those with at least a college degree doubled over the same time span. Likewise, Perelman (1984: 15), after deploring the 'looming human capital crisis', complains of an overabundance of 'college-educated members of the workforce' and warns of 'a rising tide of overeducated and underemployed graduates'. In her discussion on the reasons for growing workers' alienation, Munelly (1987: 80) summarily states that 'workers are now more highly educated than at any other time in our history'. The evidence presented by Cyert and Mowery (1987) fully supports this view. This evidence also contradicts the portrayal of the workforce of the future as deteriorating because of the higher percentage of women and minorities. In fact, as they write (Cyert and Mowery 1987: 67), 'changes in the racial and gender composition of the future US work force will have a minimal impact on aggregate levels of secondary or post-secondary attainment'. Not only will the increase of minorities be relatively small (a rise from 13 per cent in 1984 to 15 per cent in 1995), but the educational gaps between Whites and minorities have been narrowing (Cyert and Mowery 1987: 66, 70).

Above all, no solid evidence exists for the claims about an overall decline or deterioration of the workforce, and discussions on the growing illiteracy of large numbers of Americans, or on the 'widening skills gap', need considerable qualification. The same is true for the claim that the jobs of the future will require higher skills. Johnston and Packer (1987), for instance, make the following statement:

> Although the overall pattern of job growth is weighted towards higher-skill occupations, *very large numbers of jobs will be created in some medium to low-skilled fields.* In absolute numbers, the biggest job creation categories will be service occupations, administrative support, and marketing and sales, which together account for half of the net new jobs that will be created. In the service category, the largest groups are cooks, nursing aides, waiters, and janitors. Among administrative support jobs, secretaries, clerks, and computer operators predominate. In marketing and sales, most of the new slots will be for cashiers. With the exception of computer operators, *most of these large categories require only modest levels of skill.*
>
> (Johnston and Packer 1987: 100)

The authors continue by stating that even for those moderately skilled jobs 'workers will be expected to read and understand directions, add and subtract, and be able to speak and think clearly'. In other words, the overall expectations may be higher with respect to previous skill levels, although the skills themselves are fairly 'basic'.

The discussions on lack of basic skills among workers already employed and among new applicants fairly consistently point to large numbers of both these groups to show some deficiencies in written communication and computational skills. As reported by Cyert and Mowery (1987: 25), the Office of Technology Assessment estimated that roughly 20 per cent of those displaced from employment from 1979–84 'could be characterized as deficient in basic communication and computational skills'. Undoubtedly, lack of basic literacy skills constitutes a problem for the workers involved, as they may not find new employment, or lose their jobs because of the difficulty in retraining them.

Again, these figures do not in and of themselves testify to the 'decline of human capital'. They testify, above all, to large numbers of jobs which did not draw on the human capacity to think. We do not find even a hint of criticism of design and organization of work as contributing to the 'decline' of basic skills in mainstream literature. On the contrary, past efforts to adapt a workforce to the highly fragmented, Taylorized and regimented conditions of factory life are now considered simply 'inopportune'. [. . .]

Within the context of the present discussion it is important to emphasize that the millions of workers who lost their jobs over the last fifteen years were not displaced because of their lack of basic skills (apart from the fact that only 20 per cent were shown to be deficient) but because of various structural changes like plant closures, relocations, and workplace automation. Second, it is not clear how many of these displaced workers can or could be reabsorbed into the active labour force, anyhow, regardless of their levels of skill, especially considering their age. Third, the obstacles many of these workers face are frequently caused by new jobs being geared towards quite different populations than those who have been displaced. This is true particularly with respect to the fastest-growing sector, i.e the service sector, which favours the employment of women.

Nevertheless, a concern with lack of basic skills is highly legitimate. In a society that is becoming increasingly more complex, everybody should be equipped with more than 'basic' literacy skills, and the fact that so many Americans lack even these is an indictment of the society as a whole rather than of the illiterate people themselves. Furthermore, to have minimal basic skills at least gives people a chance to find employment, although this is no guarantee since the relationship between skills and jobs is far from being unidirectional.

## RE-SKILLING, DE-SKILLING, AND THE KNOWLEDGE WORKER

Arguments concerning a 'widening skills gap' not only rely on the above-cited figures concerning deficiencies in basic skills, but also explicitly or implicitly evoke the need for 'higher skills'. Through a variety of rhetorical means the overall picture that is painted for the jobs of the future is one of generally higher-level skills, i.e. abilities that go beyond reading, writing, and computing, primarily in connection with high technology and 'knowledge work'. The definitions of what constitutes 'higher skills' are as volatile as those describing basic literacy. While these definitions are highly context-specific, they are often presented as objectively given, generally valid requirements for jobs of the future. Perelman (1984: 10) is particularly optimistic about large numbers of people in the future being employed in 'knowledge-related work'. This fits well with his interest in building a huge adult 'learning enterprise' but contradicts the usual predictions of where most jobs of the future will lie.

Perelman's optimism is unfounded for another reason as well. To be

employed in knowledge-related work by no means automatically translates into 'performing functions that require uniquely human intelligence,
imagination, and creativity' (Perelman 1984: 10). This may be true most
likely for a small élite of workers, especially when one considers the
continuing trend of new information processing technology to become
'people-literate', i.e. to take over more and more of the functions of
human intelligence. This may leave only rather passive and assisting
or 'processing' functions to the 'knowledge worker'. [. . .]

The calls for higher skills are part of the larger argument concerning
the 'de-skilling' or 're-skilling' of work, particularly in connection with
the introduction of new technology into more and more workplaces.
The arguments and counter-arguments for and against re- or deskilling
are manifold, contradictory and highly confusing. The de-skilling argument was first presented by Harry Braverman (1974), and has been taken
up and criticized by researchers investigating the effect of new technology on women's office and clerical work (see, for example, Machung
1984). The re-skilling argument has so far mainly been presented in
literature identifying with the business perspective and emphasizing the
positive aspects of new technology on work.

The effect of the introduction of high technology into various workplaces is therefore highly varied, depending on a large number of
factors, including the particular category of workers affected by these
changes. In general, available evidence seems to suggest that the various
re-skilling and de-skilling processes set in motion by the introduction of
new technology not only occur along the lines of pre-established divisions but also contribute in their own particular way to the overall trend
towards a polarization of the workforce. A study conducted by Appelbaum (1987) on the introduction of new technology into the insurance
industry, for instance, shows that this change displaced a significant
number of minority women who had only recently entered clerical
positions and performed the more routine jobs which could be automated
most easily. Simultaneously, new, highly skilled clerical work, the result
of automating the more routine aspects of professional work and making
them part of clerical work, was available primarily to white women with
the necessary class background and credentials.

However, while the skills requirements rose, making work available
for certain groups of women (while diminishing employment opportunities for others, or pushing them into newly available low-skilled and
poorly paid jobs), clerical work as a whole remained sex-segregated and
essentially dead-end. We can here speak of a trend towards polarization
characterized by an elimination of middle-level (professional) positions
and thus of the career path from clerical to professional work
(Appelbaum 1987: 196). Polarization therefore occurs not only in terms
of wages, work relations, and skills or expertise, but also in terms of

dead-end and upwardly mobile positions, all of them occurring along old class, racial, and sexual lines.

There is ample evidence to show that the processes described above are characterized by considerable internal struggles where skills are often redefined by the more powerful groups to exclude the weaker ones from moving out of dead-end jobs, or from entering more prestigious positions (Cockburn 1983; Bergmann 1986). In other words, the distribution of kinds of work, and of access to work or employment is strongly related to the fact that the labour market is divided by class, race, and sex. This means that access to jobs requiring higher skills is unequally distributed along the lines of class, race, and sex, that 'higher skills' are not necessarily equivalent to higher-level or more prestigious jobs (including higher levels of autonomy or authority), or that they constitute more opportunity for advancement.

In fact, evidence exists for de- as well as re-skilling of work, depending greatly on the particular area or occupation under scrutiny (e.g. banking versus industry), as well as on the size and structure of an office or firm where new office technology is introduced (see, for instance, Zuboff 1988). The picture is further complicated by the fact that not all researchers base their discussion on the same definition, emphasizing different factors or aspects, depending on their particular interpretation, interests, as well as tacit cultural assumptions. Thus, while some researchers discuss the increase or decrease in the *technical* aspect of skills, others emphasize the aspect of *autonomy and control* as important indicators for de- or re-skilling (see, for instance, Carter 1987). [. . .]

## THE FLEXILIFE OF THE GENERIC WORKER

The universal portrayal of the workers of the future as dismally unprepared for the new demanding jobs can be seen as a way to enlarge the pool of minimally skilled entry-level workers without the intention of absorbing them into the labour market. In fact, even the most conservative reports do not envisage a full employment scenario and hope for an unemployment rate around 5 per cent. Thus, all indicators point in the direction of generally stagnant high unemployment with only slight fluctuations, and increasing forms and numbers of underemployment. Confronted with the considerable uncertainty and instability as regards employment projects, the current strong emphasis on training for jobs tends to translate into the reality of training instead of jobs, of 'learning now, jobs later' (Shor 1986: 131). This policy is officially legitimized by referring to 'constant change' where no one can predict with certainty what kind of jobs, requiring what kind of skills, will be available in the future. Shor (1986: 114) astutely observed that these training schemes are attempts to 'blur the troubling link between education and employment'. He continues:

> A weak job market amounted to a moving target which the pistol of education kept missing. Less direct aiming and less shooting meant more credibility to school and society both.
>
> (Shor 1986: 114)

This is the place for 'generic skills' to enter the picture. Generic skills are, above all, meant to contribute to intellectual ('learning how to learn'), psychological ('ready for change') as well as geographical *mobility* and *flexibility*. In other words, generic skills training is proposed as a means to adjust labour 'to long-term uncertainty in the job-market' (Shor 1986: 119).

This is precisely the ideological core of the general or generic skills argument. Those who try to hold on to the continuity of their life history and experience are now met with the indictment of being 'habit-bound', or of 'fearing change' (Johnston and Packer 1987: 68). Again, this rhetoric is reminiscent of the imperialist or patriarchal language that speaks of tradition- or custom-bound peasants, natives, or housewives unwilling to be 'integrated' into the process of modernization. The rhetoric of constant change, flexibility and mobility today has replaced the older one of responsibility and commitment, and a corresponding indictment of irresponsibility and lack of commitment levelled against those who changed jobs frequently on their own account. Furthermore, the call for flexibility is reserved exclusively for the workers themselves, a perfect illustration of the 'view from above'. In light of such an entrenched idea, to require business or 'the economy' to adjust to the needs of its workers appears scandalous.

Dewey's concern for truly educational principles in the context of a vocational education which adapted workers to the existing industrial regime today attains a new urgency, as well as an additional twist. It is no longer sufficient to educate a workforce which can adapt and live with the regimentations of factory life. This would directly contradict the need for flexibility and versatility. What is called for is a psychological, mental and behavioural preparation for living with instability, and for being able to think of oneself in terms of a renewable, exchangeable and updatable resource rather than in terms of a human being with unique experiences, hopes, wishes, and dreams.

The psychologically (as well as socially) highly problematic aspect behind the euphemisms of 'constant career change' and 'multiple-option flexilives' (Handy 1984) is rarely addressed. For instance, the built-in obsolescence and proposed throw-away nature of one's work-related experiences and competencies may seriously conflict with a psychological and social need for constancy, or for continuity in one's personal history in order to be able to develop and sustain a sense of self, and a supportive community. Handy (1984: 163), who sees the 'flexilife' as not only inevitable, but also an ultimately desirable form of future existence, asserts this necessity for 'a sense of person', but nowhere addresses the question of how this sense is to be achieved. It seems that it is to remain a privilege of the 'professional' to develop a sense of self through her or his work, and to cultivate an identity that is tied to her or his work experience, to a sense of creativity and purpose, including the experience of accumulating, developing and deepening her or his competence – some of the prime characteristics of 'good work'. To be sure, under conditions of corporate industrialism and of generally alienated labour, these aspects of good work have long since been eroded for the majority of the working population. The new and universal emphasis on flexibility and mobility seems to add, however, the finishing touch, extinguishing the last traces of the 'traditional work ethic [which] stressed the integration of work and personal development' (Carlson 1982: 135).

Personal development is part and parcel of the communicative collaborative aspect of human work (Wirth 1983), which in most workplaces is expressed in informal work relations rather than in the formal organization of work itself. Under conditions of the generic 'flexilife', inherently social, interactive relations are restructured into individual attributes like 'accurate empathy' (Klemp 1982) which can be packed up and carried into a number of interchangeable workplaces or environments. Equipped with her/his generic skills, which are 'durable, versatile, transferable, open-ended, and elastic', the worker becomes the ideal human capital 'virtually immune to obsolescence' (Klemp 1982: 53). This represents a dramatic intensification of the trend found in many adult education programmes towards packaging the curriculum, and towards fragmenting the educational content into individual, disconnected competencies which confront the learner as externally given, objectified behaviour, dissociated from subjectivity or unique experiential background. In many ways, the generic worker of the future, this 'human capital virtually immune to obsolescence', is strangely disembodied, with the possibility of interference by subjective, history-bound experience to a large extent eliminated.

Furthermore, the ideal worker becomes a self-sufficient nomad, migrating with moving job possibilities, keeping specific ties to neighbourhoods, friends and family suspended enough not to interfere with the need for mobility. Stable, long-lasting social networks may, however, become more important for people as the uncertainty of employment opportunities increases. They may be absolutely necessary for spiritual as well as material survival. People who are unwilling to move because they rely on established social networks rather than risking both unemployment and absence of such support do not display rigidity, inflexibility or 'fear of change' (a reproach which is levelled especially against middle-aged and old workers – see Johnston and Packer 1987: 82–3), as much as a realistic assessement of actual chances for survival.

In sum, the new *generic worker* must be able to adjust to indeterminate change, and is characterized by low expectations regarding pay, work conditions, and above all job security. Ideally, a workforce of generic workers must be either suspicious or directly afraid of any unionization attempts. Finally, such a workforce must be able and willing to shoulder an unusual amount of work, since in all likelihood the new jobs will not be enough for the workers to get by, but will have to be combined with other employment (occasional, seasonal, temporary, etc.) as well as work associated with providing unpaid social and personal services. In short, the new workers will be 'working like women' whose 'flexible working patterns' (Rothwell 1986) have already made them into the preferred labour force in many instances.

This parallel has not passed unnoticed. As Handy, the proponent of 'multiple-option flexilives' and 'portfolio-lives', writes:

> [a flexilife] is, in fact, the kind of existence that the last few generations of women have been well used to, moving between work and family, mixing part-time work with home responsibilities, balancing career priorities with a concern for relationships in the home and, in many cases, having to abandon one for the other.
>
> (Handy 1984: 162)

And, he continues:

> It is ironic that just as women have begun to win their fight to lead the kinds of lives that men lead, those lives are beginning to shift towards the pattern from which women are escaping.

Women's 'flexilives', i.e. the unspecificity of their skills, and, consequently, their universal availability for any kind of task, are part and parcel of the sexist division of labour, and of women's subordinate position in society in general. In fact, women's flexibility and versatility constituted a major component of the overall devaluation or 'cheapening' of female labour. This pattern is repeated in the calls for the new generic worker. Here, too, flexibility and mobility, coupled with low expectations and a high degree of adaptability to existing social structures, have to be seen as part of the general trend towards devaluing all human labour, turning 'human resources' more and more into quasi-natural resources. [. . .]

## CONCLUSIONS

The preceding discussion revealed that currently predominating responses to changes in the global market system move mostly within a production-oriented paradigm of economic development, with an over-whelming emphasis on skills and techniques, preparing students for work in hierarchical organizations. Such a paradigm generates an interpretation of the current crisis which screens out the most important and most troubling aspects of this crisis: the increase in precarious, unstable work relations, the growing North/South division, the feminization of poverty in conjunction with a new sexist division of labour, and the continued destruction of the environment.

Furthermore, a strictly technological–industrial model of work is reflected in a model of education that derives its prime legitimation from its direct individual or economic pay-off appeal. Today, the bond between education, training and work, always troublesome, complex and contradictory, is mystified into a simple, direct, cause–effect relationship, drawing education increasingly into the narrow sphere of bottom-line thinking. Because of the overarching importance of the issue of work for adult experience, a narrow, instrumental view of work translates into a view of education which places 'immediate relevance' and efficiency above concerns for overall human development and well-being.

Despite the rhetoric of sweeping change, major themes and questions that testify to the true nature of contemporary social and economic developments escape a thinking whose vision is blurred by its obsession with 'productivity' and 'economic growth'. These are questions concerning the human and social consequences of economic decisions, the equitable distribution of resources, and long-term ecological sustainability. Adult education proposals that would seriously address these issues would not only be very different from those which emphasize skills, techniques, and an overall adjustment to a technologically defined change, but would also fill the meaning of practicality and relevance with new content. Preparation for work would have to include the development of critical knowledge of the larger social and political context of work, production, and work relations. Models of work would have to be discussed that are outside the orbit of technological–industrial work and production and that are not tied to the orthodoxy of abstract economic growth. If we interpret the crisis as one of increasing poverty, diminishing natural resources, and continued ecological disaster, we have to look at the issue of work and of production quite differently. Ultimately, we need to arrive at a new understanding of growth and productivity which entails different ways of dealing with nature and with human beings, that preserves rather than destroys, and that produces human well-being rather than consuming natural and human resources.

## NOTES

1 By living in a highly segregated city like Chicago, one easily gets the impression that the inner city Black population has been entirely given up by society (including business). Deploring these people's skill levels nevertheless serves an important political purpose: to justify the dismissal or social neglect of these populations.
2 As reported by CBS '60 Minutes' (18 February 1990), employment agencies blatantly and systematically discriminate against minorities, especially those who apply for jobs which bring them in contact with the public.

## REFERENCES

Appelbaum, E. (1987) 'Technology and the redesign of work in the insurance industry', in B. D. Wright (ed.), *Women, Work and Technology*, Ann Arbor: The University of Michigan Press.

Bergmann, B. (1986) *The Economic Emergence of Women*, New York: Basic Books.

Bernstein, A. (1988) 'Where the jobs are is where the skills aren't', *Business Week*, 19 September 1988.

Braverman, H. (1974) *Labor and Monopoly Capital*, New York: Monthly Review Press.

Carlson, D. (1982) 'Updating individualism and the work ethic: corporate logic in the classroom', *Curriculum Inquiry*, 12 (2).

Carter, V. (1987) 'Office technology and relations of control in clerical work organization', in B. D. Wright (ed.), *Women, Work, and Technology*, Ann Arbor: The University of Michigan Press.

Chynoweth, J. K. (1989) *Enhancing Literacy for Jobs and Productivity*, Washington, DC: The Council of State Policy and Planning Agencies.

Cockburn, C. (1983) 'The material of male power', *Feminist Review*, 9, in (1983) *Brothers: Male Dominance and Technological Change*, London: Pluto Press.

Cyert, R. M. and Mowery, D. C. (eds) (1987) *Technology and Employment*, Washington, DC: National Academy Press.

Dole, E. (1989) 'America's competitive advantage: a skilled workforce', *Adult Learning*, 1(1).

Garland, S. R. (1988) 'Why the underclass can't get out from under', *Business Week*, 19 September.

Gleeson, D. (1986) 'Further education, free enterprise and the curriculum', in S. Walker and L. Barton, *Youth, Unemployment and Schooling*, Milton Keynes: The Open University Press.

Handy, C. (1984) *The Future of Work*, Oxford: Basil Blackwell.

Johnston, W. B. and Packer, A. H. (1987) *Workforce 2000*, Indianapolis: Hudson Institute.

Klemp, G. O. (1982) 'Three factors of success', in T. B. Jones (ed.), *Liberal Learning and Business Careers*, St Paul, Minnesota: Metropolitan State University.

Lee, C. (1988) 'Basic training in the corporate schoolhouse', *Training*, 25(4).

Machung, A. (1984) 'Word processing: forward for business, backward for women', in K. B. Sacks and D. Remy (eds), *My Troubles Are Going to Have Trouble with Me*, New Brunswick: Rutgers University Press.

Munelly, C. (1987) 'Learning participation: the worker's viewpoint', in V. J. Marsick (ed.), *Learning in the Workplace*, London: Croom Helm.

Perelman, L. J. (1984) *The Learning Enterprise: Adult Learning, Human Capital and Economic Development*, Washington, DC: The Council of State Planning Agencies.

Phillips, A. and Taylor, B. (1980) 'Sex and skill: notes towards a feminist economics', *Feminist Review*, No. 6.

Rothwell, S. (1986) 'Working like women', in P. Ekins (ed.), *The Living Economy*, London: Routledge and Kegan Paul.

Shor, I. (1986) *Culture Wars*, New York: Methuen.

Spikes, F. (1989) 'Educating the workforce', *Adult Learning*, 1(1).

Spring, J. (1985) 'Education and the Sony war', in J. W. Noll (ed.), *Taking Sides*, Guilford, Connecticut: The Dushkin Publishing Group.

Wirth, A. G. (1983) *Productive Work – In Industry and Schools*, Lanham, Maryland: University Press of America.

Zuboff, S. (1988) *In the Age of the Smart Machine*, New York: Basic Books.

# Chapter 7

# The age of leisure†

*Ken Worpole*

That 'ace caff with quite a nice museum attached', formerly known as the Victoria and Albert Museum, in the course of making redundant some ten senior academic staff at the end of 1988, issued in one of its many press statements a sentence describing the changes as being the result of having 'to apply the best practices of the leisure industry' to the future running of the museum. In Bath in 1988, crane manufacturer Stothert & Pitt, one of the West Country's oldest firms, learnt that it was to be broken up and sold by its new owners to release its 15-acre site for redevelopment; high land values had made the site much more valuable for shops, offices and leisure facilities than for traditional manufacturing. Former steel town Corby is soon to become the home of Wonderworld, the 'complete leisure city', which will feature a 4,200-seat concert hall, hotels, luxury villas, sports stadium and golf course, and endless other attractions and spending opportunities. The economic and social restructuring currently being undertaken in the name of 'leisure' in Britain seems to be happening faster than the political process can cope with.

Spending on leisure in Britain is now worth over £70 billion a year. Unevenly spread, subject to all the continuing inequalities of class, race, gender and geography, nevertheless in total there is more free time and more money to spend on enjoying it than ever before. Much critical thinking in the past has concentrated on inequalities at work, in housing, in education, in life chances; it is now time to think about how we address the problem of inequalities in a world of seeming abundance and free choice. What is the leisure boom really all about?

To start with, it is now almost exclusively defined in terms not of activity, of doing things, but of spending. A survey from the Henley Centre claimed that consumer spending in 1987 on leisure was divided between spending on 'Creative Leisure' (3.8 per cent) and 'Non-Creative

† This chapter is an edited version of a chapter in Corner, J. and Harvey, S. (eds) (1991) *Enterprise and Heritage: Crosscurrents of National Culture*, London: Routledge.

Leisure' (96.2 per cent). Their definition as to what distinguishes the two kinds of leisure may be contested in many ways; nevertheless, the absolute disparity between spending on participatory and non-participatory forms is fairly stark and certainly disturbing.

Leisure then is defined as spending: on alcohol, on eating out, on books and magazines, on buying radios, television sets and video equipment, on holidays, on admission prices for the cinema, theme parks, spectator sports and so on. Leisure has become yet another economic sector, and therefore much more amenable to the rhetoric of enterprise and business than to the age-old dream of free association, rest from work, play, a feeling of community and the creation of art and culture. In fact for many people in the past leisure actually took the form of active resistance to the disciplines of work. Today one person's leisure is for many others low-paid, part-time and casual work. [. . .]

## SHOPPING AS LEISURE

One of the most important issues which arises from the new leisure boom is the fairly recent but already commonplace assumption that a major form of leisure in the modern world is shopping. This has been argued by both Right and Left, and not unconvincingly. Shopping for clothes, records, books and furniture is seen as an important part of people's wish to establish their own personal style and cultural identity. But the rapidity with which High Street rental values and capital expenditure costs have now to be recouped through customer flow and turnover means that cultural styles have to change faster at the point of sale than they do at the point of cultural production. Hence pastiche. A clothes designer I talked to in the course of some research on craft industries in the Southern region in 1988 complained that whereas there used to be only two seasons a year in the shops, they now wanted to change stock six times a year in order to create a faster turnover. To be out of fashion today is not to be wearing last season's outfit but last month's.

Along with the economic imperative of high turnover has come the continuing process of monopolization within the retailing sector, with the same twenty multiples to be found on every High Street and in every shopping mall: Benetton, Boots, Marks & Spencer, Littlewoods, BHS, Mothercare, Habitat, Burton, Dixons, Next, W. H. Smith, and more recently Body Shop, Tie Rack and a few other nationally known names. Britain now has the highest concentration of multiple dominance in Europe; in the UK 83 per cent of the retail grocery trade is controlled by multiples, compared to 26 per cent in Italy, 27 per cent in Sweden and 64 per cent in France. Of the 240,000 retailers in the UK today, the

top 500 firms take 75 per cent of all shopping trade, and of that the top
ten retailers take a massive 30 per cent. Cinema distribution and exhibition has for a number of years been in the hands of just two companies,
Rank and Cannon, and bookselling, though economically buoyant, is
now largely in the hands of three giant firms. [. . .] The 'repertoire' of
goods on offer in the multiple stores is highly standardized, the staff
often part-time and untrained, and there is almost no connection any
more at a local level between production and consumption. Interestingly
the only local input into retailing is through the Oxfam shop and other
charity shops, which not only perform a valuable recycling function in
the local economy, but also offer the only possibility of finding non-
standardized goods.

Yet we are assured that this highly centralized and endlessly replicated
array of shops and financial services is a key ingredient of the 'new
leisure society'. Something, surely, is wrong. For in Bracknell there are
no specialist record shops, no antique shops, no picture framers, no
angling specialists, no delicatessens, no independent bookshops or health
food shops, no crafts or arts materials suppliers, no brasseries or
wine bars, no music venues, no radio or electrical goods repairs, no
designer boutiques, no second-hand bookshops, no wine-making or
home-brewing shops, no cycle shop, no hand-made pottery suppliers,
no hobbies shops, no women's centre or bookshop, no vegetarian
restaurant. So what kind of definition of leisure is being used? [. . .]

Already criticisms that every town now looks the same are echoed
widely, and the thesis that municipal leisure provision equals uniformity
now looks less convincing than it did before. The malls and shopping
centres are often designed and built by the same construction firm, fitted
out to the same specifications by the same design company, and policed
by the same firm of security guards. And the private policing of
shopping malls may well presage the shape of policing of the wider
society to come, with the rapid growth of private firms in the past
decade now accounting for there being one private police officer for
every one public officer in Britain (in 1991). For what is most astonishing
about this new age of leisure is how much policing and surveillance it
seems to need.

## THE PRIVATIZATION OF PUBLIC SPACE

The above would certainly be the view of John Hall, the entrepreneur
behind the Metro Centre in Gateshead, the largest shopping centre in
Europe and, according to contemporary Conservative rhetoric, first
stage of the economic revival of the North-East. Every inch of the
Centre and the surrounding car-park is monitored by cameras feeding a
bank of video screens in a central security control room; in addition men

with binoculars patrol the roof looking out over the surrounding landscape for any sign of trouble or 'undesirables' as they term them. A group of young people jostling each other or playing tag are moved on within seconds of a radio message being sent from the control room to the army of private security staff on patrol on the ground.

The design of the Metro Centre is such that there are no windows looking out on the surrounding Tyneside landscape; this is an architecturally structured private world. And this, quite consciously, is what Hall and his business colleagues see as a model for a future 'orderly society': the poor, the infirm, the unemployed without money, are to be excluded from this consumer paradise. [. . .]

There is little or no trade union organization amongst the people who work at the Metro Centre, and of course trade unions are not allowed either to recruit or picket in the complex because it is all private property.

And so is Basingstoke town centre, the site of a large shopping complex built on land recently sold by the Town Council to the Prudential Assurance Company. Basingstoke's most recent claim to public attention came in 1987 when the Women's Institute was refused permission to set up a charity stall in the town centre because it might be seen as undermining the business of local stores. Entering Basingstoke from the station, the only pedestrian footway into the town (a subway under the inner ring road) now belongs to the Prudential company which could, theoretically, refuse people access to the town centre if it so wished, a medieval situation if ever there was one. But in many ways much modern urban development is characterized by a conscious evocation of medieval forms: the private estates and shopping centres are designed as closed 'defensible spaces', and often have names embodying Anglo-Saxon references such as Keep, Moot, Point, Gate.

The selling of town-centre sites to private companies is a phenomenon that is rapidly gaining popularity in the energetically privatizing South: Aldershot and Dorchester are among other towns that have taken this decision – presupposing that the era of civic culture has come to an end and that the only important function left for town centres is shopping. [. . .]

Many of the newer malls are designed without seats in order to deter the non-spending citizen from overstaying his or her welcome. Daytime clashes or altercations between young people and private security guards are not an infrequent occurrence in many centres, which was not the case when shopping was a function of the public High Street. More ominously, as was reported in January 1989, in Southend the council has backed a local traders' plan to employ a private security company to monitor its still public High Street, complete with ten video cameras and

24-hour monitoring, the interests of retailers presumably coming above the interests of citizens.

## THEME PARKS AND PLAYGROUNDS

Elsewhere the private sector seems to be calling all the shots. As has already been noted, an ex-steel town, Corby, is to be the site of Wonderworld, a 90-acre £500 million theme park with a £10-per-head entry charge; Battersea Power Station (until the development company refurbishing it ran out of money in mid-1989) was to have catered for 6 million visitors a year paying £3 a head to visit the new leisure park being built there – and spending £25 on themed retailing during the 5–6 hours it was anticipated they would spend there. In presentations to potential investors the developers openly admitted that a key feature of the Battersea project was to 'break up' the family unit into serialized individuals, thus extending their length of stay and increasing their individual 'spend'. Psychologically, group identity is regarded as a negative factor in encouraging greater spending, and therefore it must be designed away. [. . .]

Trail-blazing Torbay Council has brought off a deal which will create 'Quay West', Britain's first privately controlled beach resort. The site of Crystal Palace, the great public exhibition centre of the nineteenth century, is being restored with taxpayers' money to provide a site for a Holiday Inn hotel and leisure centre, requiring Bromley Council to promote a parliamentary Bill to amend the original Crystal Palace Act to take out all the public access clauses. London's County Hall, the home of London government for nearly a hundred years, is to be sold for development as a hotel with shops and leisure provision as part of the same package. [. . .]

Is it just metropolitan snobbery to criticize all these new developments, another example of the traditional intellectual contempt for the popular pleasures of the people? Perhaps. But rapid developments such as the current leisure boom do not happen in a political or economic vacuum. In order for the private sector to flourish, the public sector rival (and former innovator) must be constrained, downgraded or made to adopt new principles. It has to be demonstrated 'that there is no alternative'. And this is exactly the pattern of recent years. An alternative tradition of catering for popular leisure has been systematically undermined!

Take for example current changes at the Natural History Museum. Following a visit by seventeen senior managers to Disneyworld in Florida in 1989, major changes have been instigated within the museum to restore attendance figures following a 40 per cent drop in visitors after admission charges were imposed in 1987. The new-look museum (£120,000 was spent on a new logo) will have new staff uniforms, three new restaurants, a new shop and new signposting. Visitors are now called customers in museum press releases, and a representative of the 500 employees at the museum has accused the administration of conscious economic élitism: 'We continually hear of ABC1s [Registrar General's social categories]. It is becoming a high-profile trendy museum . . . The thing that is insulting to staff is that we are being told that the things we did before were not very good. The Disney approach is good. Fantasy is good.'

Museum charges, savage cuts in adult education spending, residential college closures, cuts in extra-mural classes, local government cuts in public leisure provision, reduced opening hours (and in some cases, closure) for libraries, reduced spending on parks and gardens, no new capital investment in public facilities, cuts in grants to voluntary arts organizations, legislation to make parents pay for educational visits and trips; all these – direct results of government policy – have been to ensure that the private sector leisure industry will prosper and older traditions associated with the public realm will disappear and die. This is precisely what is happening in broadcasting too: the public service tradition is being undermined in order to allow a deregulated and more profitable market to take over.

## LOCAL GOVERNMENT AND LEISURE

Yet leisure takes other forms as well, and here again privatization is encroaching with confidence and speed. Competitive tendering in local government services means that some of the very best of public provision – sports centres, swimming pools, parks and gardens, municipally owned galleries, museums and theatres – could within the next decade be in private hands, and subject to pricing policies that make a clean break with the traditional principle of universal provision and access which, though flawed and often too passively interpreted, meant that there at least was a starting point for a public culture.

As with the defence of the National Health Service, defence of public sector leisure provision has to be one of critical defence. For it is clear that the traditional notion of 'universal provision', which after the settlement of 1945 became the watchword of public provision, had been allowed to atrophy from meaning 'something for everyone' to meaning 'we just open the doors and serve whoever comes in'. As a result, in education, in welfare, in health provision, and in public leisure, the most educated, the most mobile and the most tenacious have been the prime users of services, often far ahead of those most in need of them. Policy has failed to adapt to these changing circumstances and unexpected results of 'universality'; seeing the 'public' as an undifferentiated mass of people – particularly in an era of changing lifestyles and identities – has meant failing to see who precisely missed out. The 'Black Report' on the uneven benefits distributed by the National Health Service, and the educational research of Halsey, Jackson and Marsden and many others, which has pointed to the continuing over-representation of the middle classes in higher education, have both shown that failure to differentiate, failure to compensate, failure to identify unrepresentative take-up of services, have all contributed to an even greater inequality in the usage of public services than had ever been possibly imagined. [. . .]

When I and some colleagues produced a report on leisure provision in six towns in the South (Landry *et al.* 1989) we were dismayed to discover that most forms of leisure provision we visited and assessed – sports centres, swimming pools, theatres, youth venues – did no monitoring of their visitors and users and therefore were unable to identify in any way whatsoever who their customers were and, more importantly, who their users weren't! Failure to identify users by age, geographical location, gender, employed status, single-parent, pensioner, etc. meant that there was no basis for promoting the services to potential new users.

In the one case where statistics were kept – the monitoring of unemployed users of a particular swimming pool – then this group were under-represented at the pool by a factor of twenty. A lot of rhetoric about free swimming for the unemployed had failed to have any effect at all; if anything it may well have deterred people. Something was clearly wrong. The service had not genuinely been promoted or tailored to meet specific needs. This was also the case with 'women-only' swimming sessions, which have proved immensely popular in a number of places and capable of attracting a whole new range of women to swimming, yet which in some places had been programmed at inconvenient times, without a crèche and with male attendants. Public leisure provision has not yet developed a notion of differentiated audiences, requiring differentiated marketing, pricing and servicing strategies. Yet this will have to come if the public sector is to meet the challenge of privatization in the 1990s. [. . .]

The government has made some concessions to the demand by local authorities that they be allowed to stipulate some conditions of sale or award of management contract, in particular with regard to concessionary pricing schemes for disadvantaged groups, as well as responding to other social needs. But will Mecca Leisure, Brent Walker, Crossland Leisure, Trusthouse Forte or any of the other large commercial leisure operators ever have the social vision of Oxford City Council's Recreation Services department, with its 'Health for All' programme involving a widespread campaign of voluntary health and fitness testing, a policy of agreeing target groups for recreation and health promotion services, 'Look after your Heart' initiatives in workplaces and on housing estates,

AIDS awareness campaigns in every sports and recreation centre, the promotion of an Oxford 'good eating' guide (a regulatory monitoring scheme on hygiene and food quality in the city's cafés and restaurants), and the involvement of local doctors in promoting the local recreation services? [. . .]

The Sports Council sees a widening divide between provision for the generally wealthy working population and that for the poorer sections of the community, often unemployed, in urban and rural areas with a declining economic base; arguing that the latter's needs may well be adversely affected by privatization. Some Labour councils have, through inadequately conceived concessionary schemes, given the impression that they are only interested in providing for the disadvantaged, and by default have encouraged the better off to look to the private sector. The key principle surely of any notion of a civic culture is that provision must be for all, even though differentially provided?

Certainly a policy for leisure that only regards leisure as a mode of consumption will simply mirror the inequalities of wealth and power that already exist: if you cannot afford it, you cannot have it. Yet ironically it is the unemployed, the prematurely retired and the elderly, among others, who have additional time available for recreation and leisure, yet who precisely don't have the disposable income to buy it in the marketplace.

## LEISURE THROUGH SELF-ORGANIZATION AND CREATIVITY

Yet, as has been demonstrated, state or public provision has not been an unqualified success story. There is a need to develop a new approach to the public and civic realm in education and leisure. And here we come again to those pre-statist socialist ideals of [self-organization and creativity . . .]. For Britain is honeycombed with voluntary organizations devoted to an enormous range of popular and specialist arts, sports and leisure activities. They survive against the odds, and often against the indifference of local authorities and government agencies.

Still the most detailed attempt to quantify this world came in *Organising around Enthusiams: Mutual Aid in Leisure* (Bishop and Hoggett 1986). Their study of voluntary leisure organizations in two districts, one in Bristol and one in Leicester, uncovered an enormous range of activity in both. In the former area, a district with a population of 85,000, they were able to count some 300 voluntary clubs and societies, and in the latter district with a population of 68,000 they counted 228 organizations. From aero-modelling to aerobics, morris dancing to mouse-fancying, painting classes to pigeon-racing, yoga to yachting, they found a diversity of hobbies, interests and skills which could never be accommodated by the multinational leisure companies. Nationally one might well expect similar levels of participation and self-management [. . .].

Surely here is the key to a major historical tradition of leisure that we should aspire to: the question is, then, how to support and resource such a tradition without killing it dead? For ironically one of the quickest ways of destroying the 'voluntary sector' is to flood it with money and consequently professionalize it. This is likely to become a crucial issue for local authorities, as their powers of direct provision are further constrained, and yet as many of them still, rightly, aspire to protect some form of civic culture. In the intensifying ideological struggle over the meaning of 'leisure' in our society, there is some serious new thinking to do, and a lot of paternalistic baggage to throw overboard. For which political parties are yet ready to people to do things for themselves? Or, as a leisure boom based on consumption continues, likely to be found arguing for leisure as a voluntary activity?

So if one decides to move away from the notion of leisure as consumption, what might be (and often have been) the characteristics of leisure as a form of creativity and self-expression? I would suggest these themes:

- the acquisition of skills, and the pursuit of interests in depth (this surely is the tradition of most amateur hobbies and interests, whether bird-watching, pigeon-fancying, knitting and embroidery, gardening, competitive individual and team sports);
- a close link with both formal and informal modes of education and self-education – evening classes, weekend schools, Open University, specialist magazines, rallies, conferences and annual meetings;
- organization through self-management, through participation in voluntary organizations, local, regional, national and international networking;
- participation and expertise moderated by the judgement and approval of peers, rather than external or arbitrary bodies;
- sharing of resources and major capital items of expenditure, meeting in other people's houses, in church halls, in library rooms and rooms above pubs, making own equipment, swapping equipment or buying second-hand through specialist magazines;
- creating new forms of social and public space where people can meet across class lines (train-spotting, dressmaking), or specifically just among women, or through an ethnic identity, or across a wide age range (chess clubs, photographic societies, yoga classes);
- leisure as both home-based and providing networks outside the home for further development and association with peers;
- leisure as a major form of self-expression and personal identity –

people are more likely to describe themselves as a keen swimmer, photographer or stamp-collector than they are a keen shopper or theme park visitor. In the former the identity is retained by the individual, whereas in the latter the identity of the activity is always retained by the providing organization.

Yet a world of 'amateurs' poses problems. The distinction between 'amateur' and 'professional' cultural activity has bedevilled cultural theory in this century (where it has actually been registered), and certainly cultural policy too. [ . . . ]

Yet times are changing. The growth of community arts in the 1970s began to enable links to be made with forms of popular leisure and self-representation, particularly in photography, writing, and the development of neighbourhood festivals. The decision at the end of 1989 to merge the Crafts Council with the Arts Council also offers hope to those who may now feel that production for use (woodworking, pottery, knitting and embroidery, weaving, for example) can also be among the validated arts.

I am convinced that it will be much easier to elucidate leisure theory once we have overcome the historic divide between amateur and professional arts and leisure activities, and that specific project should be one of the most important priorities for cultural theory in the next few years. The pleasures of consumption are many, but so bound up are the limits of those pleasures with the economic system they reflect that they are given to us – and taken away – in the most arbitrary of ways. We are always beholden to others for these things, particularly when they come to us simply as commodities produced by an economic system that allows for very little local accountability or control. But if we regard leisure as a form of self-organization, mutual association and popular production, then we are beholden only to ourselves and our peers, and what we can learn to do with our leisure we may one day learn to do with the world beyond.

## REFERENCES

Bishop, J. and Hoggett, P. (1986) *Organising around Enthusiasms: Mutual Aid in Leisure*, London: Comedia.

Landry, C., Montgomery, J. and Worpole, K. (1989) *The Last Resort: Tourism and 'Post-tourism' in the South-East*, Stevenage: SEEDS.

# Chapter 8

# Adult education in the light of the risk society†

*Theo Jansen and Ruud van der Veen*

The concept of modernity nowadays has become a controversial one, not least by the debates that were started by the protagonists of post-modernism, according to whom the 'historical project of modernity' has failed and is (or should be) left behind in the world of today.

The aim of this chapter is to present a different view on modern developments, as articulated by the German sociologist Ulrich Beck (1986) in his concept of 'risk society' (*Risikogesellschaft*). In his view there is no such thing as a post-modern society; on the contrary, processes of modernization continue, but in a different way. We are entering rapidly into a new episode of history, where 'simple modernization' transforms itself into 'reflexive modernization'. Simple modernization was characterized by the processes which transformed the 19th-century agrarian societies into the industrial societies of the 20th century. Now we witness processes in which the conditions of these 'classical industrial societies' (class, family, neighbourhood, science, democracy) are modernized themselves. These processes Beck calls reflexive modernization and they result in what he considers a risk society. At the same time important shifts take place in the central problems of modern societies. In the industrial society the great social issue was the (unequal) production and distribution of social wealth. The risk society is characterized by the administration and distribution of different kinds of risks that are produced in and by the ongoing processes of modernization.

The relevance of the concepts of reflexive modernization and risk society for adult education is that they ask for changes in the agenda of adult educators for the years to come, at least in the western world. The eroding and fragmentation of the classical industrial society brings new frameworks for old themes, e.g. adult education and its contribution to redistribution of wealth. But, above all, these developments confront society with new themes, such as ecological safety, the danger of losing

† This chapter is an edited version of an article which appeared in the *International Journal of Lifelong Education*, 11 (4), 1992.

control over technological and scientific innovations, the internationalization of political structures, the growth of a much more flexible labour force, etc. The study and practice of adult education cannot afford to ignore these themes, if adult education pretends to contribute to solutions for actual social problems. The most fascinating question for adult education is how these new themes will be translated into new methods. Will these methods shed new light, for example, on the integration of instrumental, expressive and sociological learning, on experiential learning and on mutual directivity between facilitator and participant? These methodological themes especially are the subject of the last part of our chapter. But first we must explore further the meaning of the concept of risk society, the contours of the (forthcoming) social and personal life it contains and the themes for adult education it entails.

## RISK SOCIETY

Central to Beck's (1986) analysis of the risk society is his thesis that the main contradictions and dominant values of the industrial society are more and more overlapped and partly changed in character by the processes of reflexive modernization (Table 8.1). [. . .]

This comparison does not mean to say that problems of unequal production and distribution of social wealth are resolved in the risk society, nor that the value of economic growth would not flourish any longer. What it does mean is that the conditions under which these problems and values are shaped are changing drastically and so also are their forms and consequences. To illustrate, we will give some examples that are also highly relevant for adult educators.

Of course, there still exists a firm contradiction between capital and labour, for western societies are as capitalist as they were before. But the focus of political and economic problems is less determined by the opposition of traditional class divisions. Society is more and more shaped by the uncontrolled and unpredictable influences of scientific and technological innovations. Ecological disturbances and pollution, nuclear disasters and biogenetic developments threaten the quality of life in general and even sheer existence. New technologies for the organization of labour and communication between people (computerization, mass media) reform the organization of social life in a way that was neither foreseen nor planned by any political decision or controlling agency. The consequence of all this is the origin of new risks for social and biological life which are of an irreversible and global nature, crossing traditional class divisions and concerning the whole population, irrespective of class, sex or age. This is why Beck rather cynically formulates: poverty divides, smog unites. This holds true not only on a national but also on a world-wide scale, as Chernobyl or the greenhouse effect prove.

*Table 8.1* Comparison of characteristics of the classical industrial and risk societies

| Characteristics | Classical industrial society | Risk society |
|---|---|---|
| Central risk | Unequal distribution of life chances and goods | Global insecurity of life |
| Main causes | Unequal control over means of production | Technological/scientific innovations become uncontrollable |
| Power struggles over | Possession of means of production and distribution | Control over information and definitions |
| Main contradiction | Labour–Capital | Universal (ir)responsibility |
| Dominant value | Economic growth | Safety/ecological rationality |
| Political solution | Welfare state | New political culture |
| Social agents | Collective identities/ interests/experiences | Individualization of identities/interests/ experiences |
| Manifestations | Poverty/oppression/class-struggle/labour unions/centralization/social class/family/neighbourhood | Pollution/destruction/ expertocracy/social movements' fragmentation/autonomy/ anonymous dependency |

This development also influences the kind of political and economic struggles in the risk society and the agents who wage them. The traditional central political institutions are losing their steering capabilities *vis-à-vis* the all-embracing and pervasive effects of scientific and technological innovations. They try to react, but lack the power to plan or control effectively the deeply reforming consequences of techno-scientific developments for social life and their accompanying risks. This is one main reason why people lose their confidence in political institutions and try instead to organize themselves directly around the anxieties and interests they experience, e.g. in local action groups and new social movements. Participation in these groups, however, does not follow the traditional left–right differentiation or class boundaries, because the new risks people are resisting do not pertain to the classic issues of the (re)distribution of social wealth. Parts of the working class and the unions share common interests with parts of the management and the owners of the means of production, as they belong to 'risk-winning' branches (petrochemical industry, electronics), whereas others belong to 'risk-losing' branches (fishermen, farmers, tourist industry) and are (potential) allies for protest movements.

This state of affairs means that social inequality and the marginalization of social groups – which do not disappear in the risk society, but are even sharpened – no longer coincide with traditional class boundaries. Age, sex, race, i.e. pseudo-biological hallmarks, in combination with the level of qualifications and occupational branches, now determine social chances, so these too are the foci of resistance.

The risk society poses new questions and themes for adult education. During the 1970s, when in the western world the welfare state reached its peak, there grew a dominant ideology that saw adult education as 'emancipatory', aiming at the 'empowerment' of people, which we could describe as liberation of people from conditions that limit their thinking and acting. In the 1980s we saw a tendency to reduce the impact of these concepts, on the one hand by stressing instrumental goals ('back to basics') and, on the other hand more hidden, by reducing the concept of emancipation to the empowerment of deprived groups. Language is politics: progressive adult education became more and more reduced to work with deprived groups, developing methods that became closer to social work. In our view the aim of emancipation, empowerment, to which we still subscribe, requires a role for adult education as an initiator and agent for a broad *cultural debate* and not just a form of social policy and social work.

Adult education as an instrument for social policy, directing itself predominantly to the redistribution of societal goods and wealth (cf. Griffin 1987), still connects adult education to the paradigm of the classical industrial society. The problem is not at all that there is something wrong with striving for a more equal distribution of societal goods, but the very limited scope in defining societal problems. Reflexive modernization produces risks that not only threaten the life chances of socio-economic deprivileged groups, but the quality of life of society and even the survival of mankind. Ecological disturbances and the lack of control over techno-scientific innovations mask deeply hidden socio-cultural contradictions, which cannot be resolved within the existing political and economic institutions and dominant values. Who should rule us, who should manage us, how should we control them, are questions that have to be posed again and now on a much broader, global scale. What is needed and what will develop in the decades to come is a new political *culture*, where it becomes clearer who is responsible and in which there is much more public control over information. It is within such a broad cultural debate about responsibility and definition of the situation with respect to ecological problems and the role of science and technology that adult education will and should have its own role. If the existing institutions of adult education do not take this role, there will be new institutions. The growth of new structures and agencies of control will only be possible on the basis of a broad awareness, a reflective political culture, in which there will be more consensus about the definition of the situation and responsibility for prevention and solution. [ . . . ]

Fortunately there is among adult educators already growing attention to ecological problems, and, just as in working-class education, the ecological education takes several forms. Sometimes ecological problems are found explicitly as the theme for a course; more often a course is for an individual a vehicle, e.g. to enjoy nature more or to live more healthily, and very often ecological themes just arise in general discussions about the future of society, politics, etc. But if education is more, and it should be more, than giving a time and place to discuss these things, then adult educators should have enough expertise to facilitate these discussions in a way that helps people to understand better that what is going on is not just a problem with nature, but has to do with the heart of our culture and the way in which we organize social life.

## INDIVIDUALIZATION

A specific feature of the risk society that Beck (1986, 1988) draws attention to is processes of individualization, as in both freeing people from traditional social bonds and subjecting them to anonymous, standardizing rationalities of the state and the market. On the one hand, the traditional social and ideological ties of family, class, neighbourhood, church, etc. are weakened, which gives more freedom of choice and decision to the individual. This means that individuals become more 'self-responsible' for the planning and organizing of their lives. Using a phrase of Beck, biographies become more 'self-reflexive', i.e. formerly socially conditioned biography transforms gradually into a more self-decided and self-organized biography. Biographies are in a sense de-standardized. This is a typical phenomenon that appears along with industrialization and urbanization. One of the reasons for this is that urban culture is a more permissive culture, e.g. lifestyles and 'patterns of living together' become rather diverse and changeable during a lifetime. An additional reason for destandardizing biographies is the more dynamic situations in which people now often live, e.g. a more frequent change of job and residence, different kinds of sexual relations and households.

On the other hand, should this development be equated, not unproblematically, with a growing autonomy and emancipation of the individual subject? With the diminishing bonds with traditional social and ideological groups of reference, the individual becomes more dependent on the disciplining and uniforming institutions and procedures that dominate the political and economic system as the essential conditions for its existence. So individuals are expected to take responsibility for their own lives and to make the right decisions to further their own career chances while being dependent on conditions that they can hardly see through, and certainly not determine.

This ambiguous character of processes of individualization in the risk society constitutes a tremendous challenge to the themes of adult education and its applications of traditional life course theories (Knox 1978). Under conditions of reflexive modernization, the process of individualization entails quite a lot of pitfalls for educational adaptations because of the new circumstances individuals are confronted with. We will identify four possible pitfalls that bear direct relevance to the themes of adult education.

The first pitfall is that the liberation of traditional social and ideological ties does not 'automatically' lead to a rationalization of personal choices, but may instead lead the individual to 'discard conventions' both in social relations and in material products. For instance, the diminishing influence of traditional philosophies of life and ideologies makes people look for identity in much looser *lifestyles*, which express themselves in a person's preferences for leisure activities, home furnishing, dressing, and opinions about work and career, type of social network, linguistic usage, etc. Lifestyles are often no more than patterns of conspicuous consumption, sensitive to fashions and trends and exploited by commercial interests. So, there is a real danger that traditional religious and political values are simply exchanged for materialistic values and that this pattern of conspicuous consumption degenerates into a new superstition, a new totem (Rhode 1988). The challenge for adult education is to offer provisions, e.g. in art education and spiritual education, that help people to strengthen lifestyles to a personal art of living, a 'savoir vivre', that diminishes dependency on trends and fashions.

A second pitfall in the process of individualization is that it makes individual people responsible for situations for which they are sometimes not well prepared, or that are beyond their ability to influence. Individualization then does not mean liberation and empowerment but coercion and humiliation. A significant concept here is *important life events*; adults do not develop gradually as children do, but by fits and starts depending on challenges that life happens to present, such as a new job, a travel opportunity, the loss of a partner, etc. Important life events can be seen as *learning projects* (Tough 1979); most are self-education projects, but there is a growing dependency on experts, ranging from officials to salesmen to adult educators. Individualization means that people are confronted more often with important life events and that they have greater responsibility for organizing their own learning projects. The most important things to learn are not certain facts and practical skills, but basic attitudes such as taking responsibility and adapting to uncertainty and fear of failing, in combination with growing insights into the obstacles to self-responsibility that are erected by political and economic structures. This is the essence of what could be called the lifelong learning project of individualization and it underlies much of adult education.

A third pitfall of individualization is that *giving meaning to life* becomes more and more a private matter. For a child, it can be maintained that developing is 'becoming an adult' but, at least when you reach adulthood, development means unfolding your own identity by organizing your life according to your own purposes, yearnings, values. Where traditional ideological institutions, such as the church and the community, become weakened, these purposes, yearnings, values become privatized. In particular, going from one *stage of life* to another confronts an individual with doubts about the right direction. This is true for the still more or less standard transitions in life connected with age such as puberty, mid-life and retirement, but it is also true for other less standard transitions that are becoming more frequent, such as divorce and becoming unemployed. Because of the privatization of giving meaning to life there are fewer prescribed solutions, and so these transition periods, sometimes called *moratoria*, become longer and more troublesome and more often even an open crisis. Against this background it is easy to understand why adult education started to offer forms of counselling with respect to life transitions, of which pre-retirement courses may be the best-known and widespread example.

The last pitfall of individualization processes we will mention here is the gradual evolution of *new forms of social inequality* which mean, under the present political conditions, also a *growing* social inequality. In earlier stages of the industrial society the dependency of the labour market was seen as a collective, joint fate of certain classes in society. Now unemployment and poverty are experienced much more as an individual fate and there is even a tendency to blame individuals for their unemployment and poverty. This tendency is worsened by what can rather cynically be called a 'democratization of social insecurity'; also, people in the middle classes run a higher risk now of unemployment and poverty. This pitfall for adult education is the tendency to consolidate implicitly these new forms of social inequality by concentrating on education for isolated types of deprived groups such as unemployed older people, divorced women, young drop-outs, handicapped people, immigrants, etc. There is a double danger in doing so: not stressing solidarity between the employed and the unemployed and not stressing solidarity between subgroups of the unemployed.

## ADULT EDUCATION BEYOND INSTRUMENTALISM

Having sketched the outlines of the risk society and its relevance for crucial themes in adult education, [we will now] explore what methodological consequences this might have for the practice of adult educators. In the last few decades there has been a trend in adult education to stress instrumental learning, i.e. the transfer of knowledge and skills, giving less attention to fundamental reflection on what is taught. In the light of the developments outlined above it seems necessary for adult education to reflect once more on its critical and creative functions for individual and social life. Fulfilling functions that are merely instrumental to the dominant institutions and values of industrial society makes adult education rather a part of the problems that are characteristic for the risk society than a contribution to their solutions. Therefore adult education should leave behind its instrumental phase and (re)integrate the teaching and learning of practical skills and knowledge that people need for daily living with the stimulation of questions and public debate about the future of society and the possible designs of individual and social life.

Insofar as adult education goes beyond mere instrumental learning it is double-faced and sometimes it is really a Janus face that looks in two opposite directions. [. . .] Where adult education tries to make people more conscious and critical, it sometimes stresses the analysis of social problems and at other times focuses more on the analysis and expressions of the self. In the translation of prominent themes that the risk society poses into methodological challenges for adult education, the balanced mingling of these two orientations is an important issue.

In the following paragraphs we will make some suggestions for new ways in which adult education might give shape to these methodological questions. Our suggestions do not appear out of the blue; in fact we have labelled some developments that are already visible in society and adult education, and that makes it possible to sketch some of the methodological issues that are connected with these. Our description below is partly based on 20 in-depth interviews with practitioners in The Netherlands.

## Problem-solving networks and not just deprived groups

Many adult educators in the 1960s and 1970s, becoming aware that adult education cannot be neutral, did take sides for all types of deprived groups. In doing so adult education often drifted away in the direction of social work or political advocacy. The underlying problem is polarized thinking, as if there were nothing between neutral adult education and taking sides for a specific group. The concept of adult education as a form of cultural policy can clarify another more moderate and more effective strategy. The problems deprived groups or (political) grassroots movements are confronted with are most of the time neither caused by nor solvable by such groups alone. Their origins lie in the processes of modernization and individualization of society. So many different groups of actors are involved in the (re)production of these problems and in the possibilities to transcend them. Adult education can play a role in stimulating contacts and communication between such groups: by acting as a 'broker' it may bring together a network of actors involved in specific problems. [. . .]

A network approach seems a fertile [one for] problems like unemployment and environmental pollution, i.e. not just working with victims and advocacy groups but also with employers, officials, community agencies, wherever education can contribute to a solution.

So there is a 'third road' in between a 'neutral and values-less' adult education and an uncritical engagement and identification with specific groups or organizations. Based on thorough analyses of modernization problems and a balanced, professional attitude of both distantiation and involvement, adult education has a function as a broker in problem-solving networks. Such a function, however, also raises new questions, e.g. on which values should this be based? What types of contracts between educators and their clients are feasible? Do we need a code that describes the professional autonomy, which doctors and advocates have, when adult educators work with social movements as well as with employers?

### Reframing experiential learning

During the last decades in adult education a lot of attention has been given to the axiom that education is more than the transfer of theoretical knowledge. Countless methods and techniques of experiential learning were developed in adult education. In our interviews with practitioners we found, however, that this 'rebellious' movement, stressing experiential learning so much and so one-sidedly, is over the hill. Adult educators are now developing more balanced practices that combine theoretical learning and experiential learning, because in limiting oneself to experiential learning there is a danger of 'getting stuck' in recognizing and affirmation of what participants already know without enriching it with new knowledge coming from outside. Besides, with respect to the ecological and techno-scientific dangers, so typical of the risk society, it can be said that most of these are outside daily experience. Pollution of the earth, water and sky are in many cases as invisible or unsmellable as nuclear radiation or the biogenetic manipulations and petrochemical 'breakthroughs' in the laboratories. Their existence and the possible effects on the quality of life and health can only be shown by theoretical concepts and constructs that are always prone to controversies and disputes. And at the same time the outstanding position of high-tech information technology makes experiences of the world and communication between people predominantly 'second-hand': determined by the selections and limitations of the media that are used.

Thus experiential learning as such is deficient in supporting learners to understand and interpret the world they inhabit. There is a need for new methods that are able to supplement and critically correct the daily experience of people. Such a method is, for instance, the 'Zukunftwerk-statt' (future workshop), as developed originally by the philosopher Jung, in which, through a variety of techniques, expert knowledge is confronted by the views and experiences of a heterogeneous group of participants. [. . .]

Insofar as adult education took 'survival risks' as a subject it has often been an 'education of disasters' (Gronemeijer 1987), i.e. an education that implicitly or explicitly explained to people in how many ways the world could be ruined. The ultimate effect of such an education is a culture of pessimism, a defeatism that offers no alternatives to act for a better world. Instead of giving in to such an education of disasters, adult education should associate itself with social analyses and social movements that offer a concrete alternative for a better future. [. . .]

A representative of a centre for environmental education explained in an interview how they try to avoid doom-mongering, by taking the behaviour of people as the starting point for education. So, they do not talk much about themes like pollution and animals threatened by extinction but have developed very practical courses about 'transport', 'food', etc., trying to answer the questions of participants about what they can do in their private and local situation. The real challenge, however, is how to connect such limited and 'private' actions with the necessary changes in the political culture and structures for public control. In this respect adult education should have a function as a go-between for social movements and political and economic institutions, e.g. in stimulating communication between the ecological movement, unions of factory labourers, farmers and organizations of consumers. In this way public debates about the risks of modern life can be related to the (effects of) activities in daily routines and to the structural conditions for changing them.

## New forms of community (education)

Traditional forms of community, such as the church, class, neighbour-hood and family, are deteriorating. There is a danger and a widespread fear that, as a result of individualization, new forms of community will not emerge easily. This could become a threat for democracy because community organizations function as intermediary structures between, on the one side, the big powers of state and money and, on the other, the rather powerless mass of individuals. As such, community organizations, forming the so-called 'civic society', are important agents for critical cultural debate and social action, giving a voice and structure to opposition to the power of the political and economic systems.

Where traditional forms of community are deteriorating, new forms of community develop, and should be supported, which are more adapted to the process of individualization by being less 'totalitarian', i.e. they do not embrace so many aspects of life, have less impact on their members, are less hierarchical and more dynamic. But these new forms have their flaws:

- inter-organizational networking on broader issues becomes more and more important because the community as a whole is now falling apart in limited-purpose community organizations that fit the more specific interests of individuals;
- training of potential active members and also outreach work to attract new members becomes more important for organizations because of the higher turnover of members than in earlier years, as a consequence of more frequent changes in individual preferences;
- because individualized organizations have a more expressive character, i.e. are less hierarchical and formal and give more room to the expression of the personal views of participants, these organizations are more dynamic, there is more conflict, negotiation and reorganization.

These flaws of modern individualized forms of community point to a larger role for professional community education, supporting networking on broader issues, training new leadership, facilitating conflict-solving, outreaching for new members, etc. It indicates also another role for community education. Community education is at the same time helping people to understand the importance of organizing and helping individuals to develop their own identity and competencies through organizational activities. This becomes more true when organizing is less a traditional condition of life and more the expression of choices of conscious individuals. Because of individualization no collective, uniform identities can be presupposed as a starting point for (community) educational processes. Identities and experiences in the risk society are fragmented, volatile and provisional. So it is only in *intersubjective* communication that individuals in organizations can develop common denominators for collective goals, activities, needs, values and so on. Community education cannot in advance establish which denominators are relevant for specific organizations; it can only create as favourable conditions as possible for intersubjective communication about what should and could be shared by those involved.

## A reappraisal of liberal education

In the period of the welfare state a mainstream of liberal education in all types of local educational provision went on, although new theoretical developments of adult education did not pay very much attention to the mass of classes in foreign languages, the humanities, physical health, etc. Sometimes it was even seen negatively as contributing to making the working class a class of 'petits bourgeois'. Liberal education has, in fact, still an important function, because it has not so much to do with becoming bourgeois, but much more with becoming an individual. In a society where the amount of 'free' time has grown, free time means more than just time to relax; it becomes an opportunity to develop a personal lifestyle. Liberal education essentially supports people to overcome dependence on traditional values or materialistic values in developing a personal 'savoir vivre'. So it is time for a reappraisal of liberal education and at the same time for a greater awareness of what its modern function is and how it can be improved along those lines.

## Thematic reflection on important life events

The deeply historical and social roots of the need for self-reflective biographies that dominate in the individualized risk society give a specific function to adult education in balancing reflection on the social conditions of existence, on the one hand, and the planning and organization of personal life, on the other. In fact, adult education has a task in counter-balancing the *dominant therapeutic approach* in supporting people to take responsibility for their own lives, to accommodate the fear of freedom, to be more creative and flexible. This therapeutic approach tends to stigmatize the individual who is struggling to adapt to important life events and to apportion blame for not having proper solutions. What is needed is *a more thematic approach* to important life events, where the discussion is framed in, for example, knowledge about the sociological context of personal problems and/or in knowledge about relevant normative dilemmas. [. . .]

## CONCLUSIONS

In this chapter we have argued that new forms of adult education, both in content and in methodology, are needed to adapt the theory and practice of the field to the processes of reflexive modernization and the growing importance of self-reflective biographies that are characteristic of the risk society. But these new forms, although essentially standing in a long tradition of reflective adult education, will not be just a continuation of the traditional type. The coming to the foreground of ecological problems, increasing individualization, etc. marks a clear break, in particular with the type of progressive adult education prevalent in the welfare state of the 1960s and 1970s. We expect that adult education in the future will be more an instrument of a broad cultural policy than an instrument of social policy. [. . .] It will deal with survival problems (environment, techno-scientifics) and existential problems (personal growth, giving meaning to life) as well as (new forms of) social inequality.

It will probably differ from adult education in the period of the welfare state, in the sense that adult education will be both more modest about the autonomous contribution it can make to social problems and less convinced of a role as the messenger for all-embracing liberating ideologies. As a reaction to the former over-estimation of its role and the fading away of the 'great illusions', at least in the western world, adult educators developed in the 1980s a more professional attitude, which means in political education, e.g., allowing for pluriformity of ideas and trying to raise rational argumentation with respect to social change. We expect that this process of professionalization will not be stopped or reversed in the years to come, when political and cultural debates will become more important again. Adult educators will probably be more cautious in offering alternatives for 'the existing society'. The result will be an adult education that sticks closer to the daily hopes and worries of the learners, and is more prepared to further a dialogue between conflicting experiences, interests and ideological images and to stimulate reflection in a Socratic way, i.e., raising awareness of the crucial questions to ask instead of pretending to know the answers. Of course this will not mean a complete indifference to the content of ideas discussed; it means that adult education is not propaganda for certain ideals and solutions, but a place for critical discussion of social developments and their impact for personal and social life. Its intellectual and spiritual inspiration could be better derived from general values, such as 'the defence of human rights' and 'democratic control of society', and from an 'ecological rationality' than from partisanship with specific groups or ideologies. But such adherence does not less necessitate both sociological imagination and the capability for sociological analyses and methodological inventiveness for professional workers in adult education.

## REFERENCES

Beck, U. (1986) *Risikogesellschaft: auf dem Weg in eine andere Moderne*, Frankfurt am Main: Suhrkamp Verlag.

Beck, U. (1988), *Gegengifte: die organisierte Unverantwortlichkeit*, Frankfurt am Main: Suhrkamp Verlag.

Griffin, C. (1987) *Adult Education as Social Policy*, London: Croom Helm.

Gronemeijer, M. (1987) Milieu-educatie: een falende praxis? Of: is de milieu-beweging een educatieve beweging?, in W. Leirman (ed.), *Volwasseneneducatie en de uitdagingen van de jaren '90*, Leuven: Acco.

Knox, A. B. (1978) *Adult Development and Learning*, San Francisco: Jossey-Bass.

Rhode, C. (1988) 'Totems en trends, een cultuursociologische vergelijking', in A. de Ruyter *et al. Totems en trends, over de zin van identificatiesymbolen*, Hilversum: Gooi en Sticht.

Tough, A. M. (1979) *The Adults Learning Projects, a Fresh Approach to Theory and Practice in Adult Learning*, Toronto: Ontario Institute for Studies in Education.

# Chapter 9

# Open learning and consumer culture†

## John Field

Economic factors are central to an understanding of contemporary education. In a number of recent analyses, particular importance has been given to the influence upon education and training of those new ways of organizing work and production which have been described by terms such as 'post-Fordism' (Edwards 1993; Evans and Nation 1992; Westwood 1991). Most of these authors have chosen to focus upon education's connections with the production side of economic activity, in particular with its role in supplying the labour market with the kinds of skills and knowledge allegedly required for the 'new production concepts' (Kern and Schumann 1991). What has yet to be addressed is the consequences for education and training of the growth in consumer spending power across the western world – a growth that has been remarkably sustained over the long run ever since the Industrial Revolution, and has only come to be seriously questioned in the light of growing environmental awareness since the early 1970s.

This chapter takes issue with the view that contemporary adult education and training are a simple reflection of 'post-Fordism' in either production or employment. There are several distinct problems with such approaches. Serious flaws can be identified in the view that changes in the contemporary economy since 1945 amount to a qualitative break in capitalist organization of a kind which requires explanation through macro-theories of 'flexible specialization' and 'post-Fordism' (Pollert 1991; Thompson 1989: 224–229). Neither Westwood (1991) nor Edwards (1993) acknowledges such criticisms, empirical or conceptual, explaining developments in adult education and training with reference to the supposed characteristics of 'post-Fordism'. Further, by focusing primarily upon production, and to a lesser extent upon work (though what is meant by 'work' or 'employment' often remains unclear), they neglect the role of consumption in contemporary education.

† This chapter is an edited version of an article which appeared in *Open Learning*, 9(2), 1994.

These comments can be illustrated with reference to the recent work of Richard Edwards (1993). Edwards argued that the 'dominant organizing principle in the economy in the advanced nations had shifted by the end of the 1980s from 'Fordism to post-Fordism'. This led to the widespread use of 'flexible systems of manufacturing, customised design for specific segments of the market, and an emphasis on quality control', entailing a major restructuring of work with the replacement of 'job demarcations and pyramidal bureaucracies' by multi-skilled and flexible forms of employment, with a massive rise in the associated demand for lifelong learning. These developments in the economy, Edwards argues, have fostered a range of 'post-Fordist' reflexes in education and training, legitimated by a discourse of student-centredness, yet in fact open learning is simply an educational adjunct to the post-Fordist concern for flexibility and capitalist restructuring (Edwards 1993: 176–181). Whilst Westwood's view of post-Fordism and adult education and training differs importantly from Edwards' in emphasis, she is similarly concerned with links between post-Fordism in production and the vocationalization of adult education (Westwood 1991: 47).

This chapter has a different focus, being concerned with the education of adults in relation to consumption. I start with recent theories of consumer culture. Second, I explore implications of consumer culture theories for the education and training of adults, and particularly for open and distance learning, where Edwards (1993) rightly points to the pervasive discourse of customer-centredness. Third, I sketch a research agenda for the future, drawing upon theories of consumer culture and consumer behaviour while recognizing that neither can provide more than partial accounts of adult education and training. In general terms, adult education and training can be regarded as a form of consumption in at least four important dimensions.

- First, there have been long-term changes in the ability of adults in western societies to exercise choice in the purchase of goods and services. Of course, important pockets of poverty remain, but over the long run as all western societies – even Britain – have as a whole become more affluent, so greater numbers of individuals have been able to exercise greater amounts of choice over how they spend their money, and how they use their time (cf. Gershuny 1987). This also holds true for the demand side for educational activities.

- Second, the idea of the citizen as consumer stands at the heart of recent policy developments. This is no simple *imposition* by a heartless government: current policy reflects a fundamental ideological shift which can be discerned in many western societies (and, more recently, in the ex-communist states), and which is also expressed partly in a growing private sector of education providers. Thus the supply side is in practice increasingly dominated by a consumer orientation, however much it is articulated within a public service ideology.

- Third, education activities can be understood as consumer goods in themselves. They are optional services which are purchased as a result of *choice*; unlike schooling, much adult education is undertaken by individuals acting as free agents within a marketplace which offers differences of product and price. Choices are made at least in part because would-be students anticipate that particular educational events will be enjoyable experiences.
- Fourth, much educational thinking is dominated by human capital theories which assume that learning should foster economic growth and increased consumption. In exploiting human and natural resources ever more intensively, western societies have repeatedly and consistently opted for increased consumption rather than reduced working time (Cross 1993). It is almost unthinkable to suggest, for instance, that more education might benefit a society by leading to *less* rather than more productivity; indeed, distance and open learning is actively marketed as a means of combining learning with earning. Contemporary education and consumer culture are deeply intertwined.

It therefore follows that adult education can be understood, at least in part, as an aspect of consumer culture. Where open learning is concerned, the practices and meanings of consumption are of even greater significance than they are for more conventional educational forms.

## CONCEPTUALIZING CONSUMER CULTURE

Concepts of consumer culture have been around in different forms since at least the 1920s (Cross 1993: 156–163). Since the Second World War, however, a range of scholars and market researchers have investigated and debated the relations between consumption, economic performance and individual identity. Two issues have been repeatedly raised in these discussions which have particular significance for the analysis of education and training: first, the cultural meanings of consumer behaviour; second, the economics of consumption.

The term 'consumer culture' implies some kind of structured set of values and behaviour. Its use suggests that consumer behaviour constitutes a coherent means of communication; thus concepts of consumer culture are closely bound up with theories of communication and differentiation, with goods and services acting as 'markers'. The anthropologists Mary Douglas and Baron Isherwood have described the way that

consumption uses goods to make formal and visible a particular set of judgements in the fluid processes of classifying persons and events.
(Douglas and Isherwood 1979: 67).

Bourdieu's (1984) sociological discussion of 'taste' rests on the view that consumers actively use services or goods to establish and demarcate a distinctive social space, thus creating segmentation by economically significant markets for cultural goods and services. Consumer culture is understood as an economy of signs, used by individuals and groups to communicate messages about social position and worth.

In what might be characterized as a post-Marxist variant, this coupling of symbolic and economic has been summarized by Featherstone:

> To use the term consumer culture is to emphasise that the world of goods and their principles of structuration are central to the understanding of contemporary society. This involves a dual focus: firstly, on the cultural dimension of the economy, the symbolisation and use of material goods as 'communicators' not just utilities; and secondly, on the economy of cultural goods, the market principles of supply, demand, capital accumulation, competition, and monopolisation which operate *within* the sphere of lifestyles, cultural goods and commodities.
> (Featherstone 1987: 57)

His emphasis is upon post-war markets for commodities, where possibilities exist for consumers to express a degree of choice. However constrained, and however influenced by advertisers, spending patterns over the past 50 years have reflected consumers' growing discretion over how they spend their income; that part spent on basic physiological necessities (food, shelter and elementary clothing) has correspondingly fallen.

As a minimum, theories of consumer culture ask us to address the role of markets in the education and training of adults. This is relatively straightforward. In so far as participation in adult education and training is voluntary, it involves acts of choice, normally including a simple act of purchasing in markets where competing services exist. Such theories also ask us to consider the education of adults as an economy of signs, where learners' choices can be seen as social or private acts of communicative transaction. There are, though, difficulties with consumer culture theories in relation to adult education and training. Some are criticisms which can be made of any attempt to apply consumer culture theory: for example, it overstates the qualitative break between contemporary consumer culture (usually identified as post-1945) and previous eras, whereas it is possible to discern consumerist trends and tendencies in earlier periods (Cross 1993; Campbell 1987). Others are more specific to the nature and functioning of adult education and training in contemporary societies.

## CONSUMER CULTURE AND ADULT LEARNERS

Globally, markets for personal services of all kinds have exploded in recent years. Many personal services are widely purchased by individuals in replacement of, or in addition to, similar services which in principle are readily available through the state (e.g. personal pensions, private schooling, or health insurance). It is, then, hardly surprising if the presence of an increasingly affluent and educated consumer market should affect such a weakly developed element of the welfare state as the education and training of adults.

Culturally, too, the education and training of adults display many of the classic characteristics of consumerism. Two may serve as examples. The first is the growth of provision which is oriented towards demand for individual self-development: this can be seen in growing markets for access to improve qualifications, as well as in the thriving market for activities which offer individuals the opportunity to acquire a new understanding of and control over themselves, their body and/or their mind. The second is the growing tendency for consumers to insist upon attention to physical comfort and mental well-being in the service which they have paid for. Providers' own market research regularly points up the salience of chairs or parking space in consumer choices, as does a concern with making the consumer feel good by the use of appropriate pedagogic strategies. Equally, one could point to the commercial success of management training videos featuring comedy actors. The boundaries between education and entertainment are increasingly blurred; but what Schäfer (1991) describes as 'edutainment' is not confined to distance and open learning through new communications technologies. We can see the same processes at work both in the burgeoning of education associated with leisure or personal development interests, and in the wider consumption uses made by individuals of all kinds of adult education and training.

Though some consumer culture theorists have referred to the education and training of adults in support of their broader thesis, they have been less than forthcoming with concrete evidence, and have not identified any aspect which is distinctive to the field of adult education and training. Sociologists of consumer culture tend to regard consumption as an active process, in which identities are manipulated and then communicated to others. In practice, analyses of adult education in relation to consumer culture have tended to revert to social class analysis. For Featherstone (1991), for example, participation in adult education is typical of the 'new petit bourgeoisie' of providers of symbolic goods and services. Lacking the assurance and confidence of inherited cultural capital:

The new petit bourgeois therefore adopts a learning mode to life; he is consciously educating himself in the field of taste, style, lifestyle.

(Featherstone 1991: 91)

Featherstone is here following the general approach of Pierre Bourdieu (1984), for whom both

art and cultural consumption are predisposed, consciously and deliberately or not, to fulfil a social function of legitimating social differences.

(Bourdieu 1984: 67–68)

Here educational consumption is situated as legitimating and supporting the social distance between and within different groups.

However, problems exist with this analysis too. It is not clear that it is from the 'new petit bourgeoisie' that open and distance learning draws its students. Featherstone's 'new petit bourgeoisie' of 'cultural specialists and intermediaries' (1991: 21) may or may not constitute a primary market for open learning, or indeed for any kind of lifelong learning; if it does so, it can probably be found more in self-directed learning (as purchasers of mass-produced guides to self-improvement, perhaps) than in the more traditional settings, such as extra-mural classes. It may be that the 'learning mode' which Featherstone sees as typifying this group only has meaning insofar as it sets up a certain distance from more established and traditional forms of education and training. This is consistent with Lichterman's analyses of the largely middle-class readers for self-understanding texts such as *Women Who Love Too Much*, who apparently adopt a somewhat ambivalent attitude towards the books they read and discuss (Lichterman 1992: 427). However, this is an area where speculation is stronger than evidence.

Second, Featherstone (1991) and Bourdieu (1984) have relatively little to say about lifelong learning and individuals. Although they have a great deal to say about social groups and strata, and their strategies of social differentiation and closure, they tend to neglect the place of the individual. Yet, if education is used by adults from particular social strata as a marker *and* an expressive means of self-development, it is also centrally part of the process whereby *individuals* differentiate themselves from one another. While supply remains relatively undifferentiated taken in the round, at the level of specific events it is possible to see the adult education offer as an example of 'mass customization', with a panoply of para-educational services (guidance, information and assessment services) being used to match individual and product.

Until relatively recently, individuation was conventionally held to end with the achievement of adulthood. Indeed, the two were seen as closely interrelated. However, the discovery of adult learning in the 20th century was associated with a recognition that adult individuals can continue to change throughout their lives. Bourdieu (1984) argues that participation in lifelong learning may be related to a belief in the plasticity of identity, seeing this as specific to certain social groups. In particular, he suggest that what he calls 'relegated agents' who portray themselves in such roles as the artist *manqué* will be

> drawn to schemes of 'continuing education', a perpetual studenthood which offers an open, unlimited future, and contrasts diametrically with the system of national competitions designed to demonstrate, once and for all, that what is done cannot be undone.
>
> (Bourdieu 1984: 155)

It is not clear from this account, though, whether others than 'relegated agents' may consider themselves to be capable of greater creativity and expressivity than is demonstrated by their formal status and qualifications; nor whether they are rational in doing so.

The analyses of Bourdieu (1984) and Featherstone (1991) imply that, to explore relations between consumerism, individuation and adult education, we should look to areas such as personal development and cultural creativity. Certainly, the curriculum changes of the last fifteen years have included dramatic growth in courses offering the possibility of a new identity: assertion training, slimming, D-i-Y, bodily well-being, creative writing, interpersonal skills, counselling programmes and, above all, 'rebirthing' are all typical, and at a guess their expansion is likely to continue. However, they are still dwarfed in scale by courses on sailing, typing, languages, art history or other subjects which by all means involve the reconstruction of the self, but in a far milder form than the almost limitless playing with identity envisaged by theorists of post-modernity. Rather than innovation, they represent continuity with well-established concepts of adult development (Carroll 1991). As adult participation in education is largely voluntary, the onus typically lies on providers to take positive measures to attract and retain their clientele. Further, in most cases these voluntary learners are expected to pay a fee in return for the service which is to be provided [. . .]. Whereas in economic terms alone it seems entirely reasonable to regard voluntary adult learners as consumers, it is more problematic to regard the cultural processes of communication which surround adult education as simple examples of 'consumer culture'.

## IMPLICATIONS FOR OPEN LEARNING

Open learning is used to denote both an educational philosophy *and* a set of techniques for delivering knowledge and skills. As philosophy, open learning implies greater accessibility, flexibility and student-centredness:

it implies placing the learner rather than provider at the core of educational practice. As a set of techniques, it is characterized by the use of resource-based teaching and training, often associated with the use of new communications media. According to Edwards (1993), both senses of open learning have 'been appropriated and narrowed by government and employers for the new vocationalism' (p. 180). For Edwards, the techniques are adopted largely for cost reasons, the philosophy to legitimate the growth of post-Fordism in the production of educational materials. This may be true so far as it goes; what is even more striking, however, and what Edwards ignores, is the rapid absorption of open learning into consumption.

Economically, it is relatively simple to establish connections between open learning and consumption. On the supply side, open learning is sold in a largely unregulated and, even at degree level, at least in the UK, a highly competitive commercial market (Rumble 1992). This situation is relatively recent, of course; as little as twenty years ago, the costs of entry to the open learning market were high, demand was uncertain (higher education and foreign languages aside), the number of suppliers relatively small.

Economies of scale for some new communications technologies (e.g. satellite or cable TV, where multinationals are particularly strong) mean that a small number of producers dominate in one or two sectors of the market; but taken as a whole the market has seen a rapid growth in the numbers of suppliers – many of them relatively small-scale – offering video, cassette tapes, interactive CDs, and computer-aided and multi-media packages. This type of market is normally held to favour the consumer, by bringing a greater range of products within reach. We can see evidence in any high street: bookshops full of self-teach manuals, record shops of instructional videos, computer shops of multimedia packages, and so forth.

What of the demand side of the market, which has also mushroomed over the past two decades? Demand for open learning is as diverse as its supply. Two major kinds of purchaser are particularly influential: larger employers, who believe that open learning offers a cost-effective and targeted way of training their workforce; and public agencies from libraries to health authorities, who believe that open learning offers a cost-effective, focused way of providing services to their clients. In both cases, purchasing may be from either the external market or an internal producer–supplier. Yet the past two decades have also witnessed a sharp growth in the market of individual consumers. With growing levels of individual spending power, more people will be in a position to choose to purchase open learning resources; all other things being equal, it is likely that more will exercise that choice. In fact, the market of individual consumers has risen faster than might have been anticipated, and it has led in unexpected directions. However, other than studies of participation (Woodley *et al.* 1987), little research into the market for open learning has so far appeared. The economics of distance open learning has focused largely upon the supply side (Rumble 1992: 32). It is therefore difficult at this stage to engage in much more than informed speculation about the behaviour of consumers in the market for open learning, and on the meanings their participation may have for them. Hints may be gleaned, though, from reflection upon the material and cultural conditions which characterize the open learning market.

First, much consumption of open learning is based in the home. Home-based leisure activities are typically 'self-governed', involving those who have passed through early adulthood (Tomlinson 1986: 47). Distance open learning fits both criteria (on age, see Woodley *et al.* 1987: 23). Evidence from the supply side suggests that patterns of consumption may be very similar to those shown for similar home-based leisure activities: thus, instructional videos are probably often watched by couples or other family-based groups. Videos offering improved sexual techniques or guides to holiday resorts are examples of open learning resources which span the boundary between learning and domestic lifeworlds. New communications technologies have been applied in a dramatic colonization of home-based leisure by commercial activities, in turn allowing a rapid growth in the availability of self-directed learning from video or computers. One consequence is the spanning of conventional boundaries between learning (part of the public domain) and family (part of the private sphere).

Second, much consumption of open learning is engaged in by individuals or self-selected groups. Individualization and even privatization of learning may be one of its main attractions. Typically, I chose to learn a new foreign language through commercially sold packaged learning rather than an evening class after trying the latter, which merely brought embarrassment at what I found a slow and difficult learning process in the company of strangers. Learning with a close friend, on the other hand, was fine. As a relatively affluent and discriminating consumer, I was able to select relatively high-cost materials, and to work at them steadily over time. In this respect, distance open learning is closely connected to wider processes of individuation – that is, the social construction of subjectivity and individual uniqueness. Consumers may purchase open learning resources largely for purposes of self-gratification and/or personal autonomy on the one hand while their participation in open learning fosters the differentiation of individual identities. On the supply side, some new communications technologies, such as CDi and/or digital networking, allow for far greater differences between the services received by individuals than more established forms of distance teaching, such as correspondence or television.

Third, much individual consumption of open learning is related to attempts at personal change. Even the acquisition of a foreign language involves some risk to the individual's identity; however, more intimate 'technologies of the self' invite the learner to identify and explore an identity with which they may already be dissatisfied, and try out a new identity with which they may not yet feel comfortable and secure. This is a substantive contribution to the process of individuation – of the social construction of individual uniqueness – while the learning process may be more attractive to learners if some protection is offered from the outside world. Hence the relationship with consumption as cultural communication may be a slightly unusual one, in that it is not the process of using open learning which functions as a marker, but the *concealed* acquisition and competent display of the new skills or knowledge on offer. As Bourdieu (1984) argues, cultural capital should appear 'disinterested' (p. 23). Hence the central feature of highly valued knowledge is that it should appear to others to have come easily, almost naturally, not as the result of painful effort; distance open learning offers an opportunity for furtive learning.

Fourth, many of the new communications media used in open learning are already familiar to consumers. Younger consumers, whose operational skills with video and information technology are especially developed, are also highly attuned to using these technologies in particular ways. Essentially, these technologies are familiar from the home entertainment context. Distance open learning thus fits into existing cultural expectations and appropriations. Technologies may be appropriated in a more active way than is implied in the term 'edutainment'. Thus in the case of televisual communications, the home is often the site of a multitude of activities; the screen in the corner is a secondary activity, watched intermittently. Although you may decide to employ John Cleese if you are to sell managers the idea of watching videos about meetings, no audience will watch with attention throughout, nor will they always share the framework of meanings intended by the trainers showing the video. Whereas it is over-simple to suggest that the medium is the whole message, a simple transmission model is also wholly unreliable. Yet much open distance learning relies on precisely such a model of communication.

Fifth, open learning consumers may respond in ambiguous ways to the resources they have purchased. Lichterman describes readers of self-help psychology books as engaging in a 'thin culture', a term he uses to denote

readers' shared understanding that the worlds and concepts put forth in these books can be read and adapted loosely, tentatively, sometimes interchangeably, without enduring conviction. Readers draw on the books in ongoing relation to portions of more formally elaborated cultural frameworks and in relation to mass-mediated images of personal life.

(Lichterman 1992: 426–7)

Similarly, most open learning students are already relatively well educated (Woodley *et al.* 1987), suggesting at least one reason why open learning may also function as a 'thin culture': it attracts an unusually critical, not to say sceptical, audience, who recognize learning resources as commodities and can place a price upon their value.

Six, recent information technologies are capable of enormous variety and rapid change. When applied to distance open learning, they are thus easily absorbed into the kinds of market which thrive on fashion and obsolescence. More established formats, such as texts or broadcast programmes, tend to be marketed over a period of some years; the Open University's broadcast programmes are a case in point. More recent developments, particularly in the combining of digital networking with CDi, allow for much more rapid adaptation, including the daily (if need be, hourly) incorporation of highly volatile information. Some open distance learning materials are thus typical of so-called 'designer products', which are probably best seen as examples of 'mass customization' where typically Fordist techniques are used to produce a range of seemingly highly differentiated products.

Of course, similar forces affect the education of adults more widely, and not only open and distance learning (Field 1991). Equally, attention to consumer behaviour makes explicit the attraction for many adults of educational forms which blend learning with entertainment. Sociologists have noted that the teaching strategies typically adopted by adult tutors and trainers are often intended to please the customers, and thereby maintain attendance (Salisbury and Murcott 1992). What is significant about distance open learning is that commercial, technological and cultural trends combine with one another to reinforce the appeal of distance open learning to a consumer market which currently shows every sign of growth without limit.

## CONCLUSIONS

Consumption is, I believe, to some extent a useful perspective from which we can examine aspects of the education of adults. It is only one among a number of perspectives, and its value is bound to vary between different sectors, levels and styles of provision. Yet compared with production, reproduction and citizenship, consumption's place in the study of adult education is consistently downplayed by both scholars and practitioners.

In so far as it has been explored, consumption is associated with the concepts and practice of 'marketing'. In much continuing education, as in any public service, the concept of a 'market' remains ambiguous. Government – national and local – remains the most important single source of funding. In competition between continuing education organizations, therefore, the major threats usually concern competition for access to government funding. Ironically, then, the more market-led the organization, the more it comes to depend upon the favour of the government. Where this takes place, the marketing orientation is largely dysfunctional. Providers very sensibly put the paymaster first; this is rarely the individual learner. In public service sector organizations, the concept of consumers' charters is now commonplace. However, this represents a somewhat passive view of the consumer. What is less clear is the relationship that adult education providers might have to the development of vigorous consumers' movements, whose access to expert knowledge is likely to be stronger rather than weaker than that of many established educational organizations.

Conceptually, it is difficult to see how the analysis of adult education as consumption might develop without greater attention to the economics of continuing education generally. Currently, the economics of education generally is at a low ebb; so far as the education of adults is concerned, there is little beyond a few rudimentary cost–benefit analyses of vocational training. From the available literature, it appears that concepts of marketing are impoverished intellectually, and practically limited to advice on how to present information more attractively. Firmer empirical and conceptual grounding would be provided by a series of studies of issues such as the financing of participation and provision of different kinds of levels; of control over purchasing decisions (who decides on family spending, both of money and time?); and of the economies of scale versus the benefits of smallness in provision.

For its part, the field of adult education and training provides something of a test case for the consumer culture hypothesis. Although the field of organized adult learning might be expected to confirm the hypothesis, in practice it throws up a number of empirical and conceptual difficulties. Thus in certain areas of adult education – university extension or some kinds of industrial training, for instance – the market is dominated by learners with what might be called a 'traditional' orientation towards learning: they actively pursue the goal of access to traditionally defined knowledge, usually in the humanities, and usually presented in a teacher/trainer-centred fashion. However, the language and values of learner-centredness are more common in more 'modern' areas, such as distance open learning, at least at the level of public self-image; it may be that it is in such areas that learners tend to correspond to the personal growth/individual advancement models which are emphasized in theories of consumer culture. Certainly this possibility seems to deserve further investigation, by practitioners as well as scholars. Though the language of consumerism may jar among practitioners, patterns of participation in adult education cannot be understood even in part without reference to purchasing decisions, styles of life and levels of disposable income. This is not to say that the consumer culture hypothesis fits the fields unproblematically; rather, the fit is generally a loose one, and it is probable that the meta-theory of consumer culture will be found wanting in any serious, empirically grounded study of adult learning as a whole. Consumption is not a simple given; it may be an active, generative process as well as a passive, reproductive one. Its influence upon the development of adult education and training, and distance open learning in particular, should not be understated.

## REFERENCES

Bourdieu, P. (1984) *Distinction: A Social Critique of the Judgement of Taste*, London: Routledge.

Campbell, C. (1987) *The Romantic Ethic and the Spirit of Modern Consumerism*, Oxford: Blackwell.

Carroll, N. (1991) 'Lifestyle change marketing: a strategic approach for providers of continuing and professional higher education', *International Journal of University Adult Education*, 30(3): 31–43.

Cross, G. (1993) *Time and Money: The Making of Consumer Culture*, London: Routledge.

Douglas, M. and Isherwood, B. (1979) *The World of Goods: Towards an Anthropology of Consumption*, London: Allen Lane.

Edwards, R. (1993) 'The inevitable future? Post-Fordism in work and learning', in R. Edwards, S. Sieminski and D. Zeldin (eds), *Adult Learners, Education and Training*, London: Routledge.

Evans, T. and Nation, D. (1992) 'Theorising open and distance education', *Open Learning*, 7(2): 3–13.

Featherstone, M. (1987) 'Lifestyle and consumer culture', *Theory, Culture and Society*, 4(1): 55–70.

Featherstone, M. (1991) *Consumer Culture and Postmodernism*, London: Sage.

Field, J. (1991) 'Out of the adult hut', in P. Raggatt and L. Unwin (eds), *Transition and Change*, London: Falmer.

Gershuny, J. I. (1987) 'Lifestyle, innovation and the future of work', *Journal of the Royal Society of Arts*, June, 492–502.

Kern, H. and Schumann, M. (1991) *Das Ende der Arbeitsteilung*, Munich: Beck.

Lichterman, P. (1992) 'Self-help reading as a thin culture', *Media, Culture and Society*, **14**(3): 421–447.

Pollert, A. (ed.) (1991) *Farewell to Flexibility?*, Oxford: Blackwell.

Rumble, G. (1992) 'The competitive vulnerability of distance teaching universities', *Open Learning*, 7(2): 31–45.

Salisbury, J. and Murcott, A. (1992) 'Pleasing the students: teachers' orientation to classroom life in adult education', *Sociological Review*, 40(3): 561–575.

Schäfer, E. (1991) 'Medienverbund im Wandel. Auf dem Weg zum Edutainment?', *Grundlagen der Weiterbildung Zeitschrift*, 2(2): 65–69.

Thompson, P. (1989) *The Nature of Work*, London: Macmillan.

Tomlinson, A. (1986) 'Playing away from home: leisure, disadvantage and issues of income and access', in P. Golding (ed.), *Excluding the Poor*, London: Child Poverty Action Group.

Westwood, S. (1991) 'Constructing the future: a postmodern agenda for adult education', in S. Westwood and J. Thomas (eds) *Radical Agendas? The Politics of Adult Education*, Leicester: National Institute of Adult Continuing Education.

Woodley, A., Wagner, L., Slowey, M., Hamilton, M. and Fulton, O. (1987) *Choosing to Learn: Adults in Education*, Milton Keynes: Open University Press.

# Chapter 10

# Education and the marketplace†

## Lyn Tett

## INTRODUCTION

This chapter will argue that the marketplace model of education disadvantages both participants in, and providers of, education. [The focus will be on] post-compulsory education. The data come from a study of adult participation, progression and guidance commissioned by the Scottish Office Education Department and, in particular, from a study of progression opportunities for adult learners (Munn *et al.* 1993). This study defines progression as focusing on three broad kinds of opportunities:

- Those which targeted traditionally under-represented groups and encouraged initial return. In this sense progression was from non-participation to participation.
- Those which facilitated sideways moves within the system. Here progression might be from one subject to another, or one institution to another at the same course level.
- Those which explicitly encourage movement upwards and onwards within the system. Examples here would be clearly articulated routes from further to higher education, or from uncertificated to certificated courses.

The focus in particular will be on the first type because, I will be arguing, participation by such groups is especially problematic once a marketplace model is adopted.

## NEW RIGHT IDEOLOGY

A major change in the provision of post-compulsory education recently has been the incorporation of further education colleges following the

† This chapter is an edited version of an article in the *Scottish Educational Review*, 25(2), 123–131, 1993.

1992 *Further and Higher Education (Scotland) Act*. From April 1993 colleges moved out of local authority control and funding and were free to market their provision to their customers, either corporate or individual. The ideology behind such a commitment to competition rather than centralized planning stems from the writings of Hayek (1944) and others (e.g. Friedman and Friedman 1980), who have argued that the collective good can be properly realized in most cases *only* by private individuals acting in competitive isolation, pursuing their interest with minimal state interference. Distributive justice always imposes on some person or group someone else's conception of merit or desert, since it requires the allocation of resources by a central authority acting as if it knew what people should receive for their efforts or how people should behave. Hayek (1944) has therefore argued that only the free market, protected by a constitutional state, can provide a mechanism of collective choice which is dynamic, innovative and responsive to a multitude of individual choices. This ideology has generally been characterized as 'New Right'.

Adult education has been pushed into a more market-oriented situation in recent years, partly as a result of funding crises and partly as a response to this New Right thinking. As a result, it has come to be seen as a commodity like any other that can be marketed by the use of attractive presentation, effective publicity, market research and product evaluation, etc. In addition to this, deregulation in the distribution of education, as exemplified by the 1992 Act, has pronounced a climate of competition for access to whatever form of education is seen as having the highest exchange value, thus encouraging a move away from negotiated community-based education to more narrowly vocational provision.

## PARTICIPATION IN EDUCATION

The HMI report on the education of adults in Scotland (HMI 1992) states that there is no doubt that 'there are a wide range of opportunities available for adults and that there has been a marked increase in the number of adults participating' in education. There has, indeed, been an increase in participation; for example, according to Scottish Office statistics (Scottish Office Education Department 1993), there were over 14,000 adults in Scottish schools in 1991 compared with about 13,600 in 1989 and the age participation rates of students aged 20 or over in full-time vocational further education have risen from 3.2 per thousand population in 1988/89 to 4.4 in 1990/91. However, these statistics tend to hide the fact that the adults who participate in education come from a limited age range and socio-economic background. They tend to be under 35, from skilled, managerial or professional backgrounds and they have either positive memories of, or tangible achievements from, school. Put crudely, education is seen by this group as a positive good and more is sought. Non-participants, on the other hand, tend to be from older age groups, ethnic minorities, the long-term unemployed and those from semi- and unskilled occupations. In addition, those living in rural areas and women with dependent children tend to be under-represented. Similarly the range of opportunities on offer to such groups has decreased rather than increased as budgets for community-based provision have been squeezed.

Research into the extent and pattern of adult participation in education and training (Munn and MacDonald 1988) shows that non-participants have little or no knowledge of the educational opportunities available. There is also a probable link between social and community involvement and people's knowledge of educational opportunities. People involved in social and cultural activities are in information networks, and are therefore more likely to be aware of the existing educational opportunities. However, there is little evidence that simply knowing what is on offer leads to participation. What is necessary is a view that the purposes of education are relevant to identified needs, a positive image of education as well as information about what is on offer and how to access it.

The obstacle to participation most frequently mentioned by adults in American and British surveys is a lack of time, a constraint arising from family responsibilities and work schedules, with those people working part-time or doing shift work at unsociable hours reporting the most difficulties. However, unemployed people are least likely to take advantage of learning opportunities. Thus, an increase in leisure time does not necessarily lead to participation in adult education.

The financial costs of participation have been found to be a major perceived barrier by both men and women. However, it has frequently been found that non-participants who cite expense as an obstacle have little idea of the actual cost of learning activities. This has led some researchers to suspect that cost, like lack of time, may serve as a socially acceptable or face-saving reason for not participating which camouflages more complex and possibly unrecognized reasons (see Merriam and Caffarella 1991).

McGivney (1990) has pointed out that many adults do not participate, not because of low motivation but because powerful constraints arise from cultural and social class divisions. School creates (or reinforces) sharp divisions in society by conditioning children to accept different expectations and status patterns according to their academic 'success' or 'failure'. Through the use of imposed standards and selection, the education system traditionally rejects or excludes large numbers of people, many of whom subsequently consider themselves as educational failures. To a significant degree, adult education perpetuates the values and status patterns embedded in the school system, thus reinforcing inequalities that commenced early in childhood. People who have ostensibly 'failed' in the school system do not wish to repeat that failure. Many are consequently suspicious of education in any form, even informal learning opportunities specifically designed for them.

The 'social stratification' achieved, cumulatively, through the influences of family background, school and work results in education becoming part of the value system of some groups but not of others. The importance of peer or reference groups in shaping behaviour and attitudes cannot be over-estimated. It has been observed that whereas professional white-collar workers tend to be influenced by a much wider network than just their co-workers, manual workers form very strong peer pressure groups which have a determining influence on norms and behaviour. For example, a report on the Education and Training Scheme for Redundant Steel Workers at Consett (Holmes and Storrie 1985) observed that men returning to education which did not lead directly to employment found this difficult to justify to their co-workers.

Many people from working-class communities are reluctant to attend classes in non-traditional subjects because this makes them different. Hostility or disapproval can be particularly strong if participation is seen to threaten accepted gender roles. It could be argued, therefore, that certain sections of the community do not readily participate in education and training partly because of constraints arising from their personal circumstances, but primarily because voluntary learning is perceived to be part of the culture pattern of the middle class.

Attitudes and perceptions play a significant role in non-participation. Notably, these include perceptions of inappropriateness and lack of relevance; no awareness of learning needs; hostility towards schools; the belief that one is too old to learn; and lack of confidence in one's ability to learn.

A powerful psychological barrier to participation may be perceptions of powerlessness linked with the lack of a future perspective. Hedoux (quoted in McGivney 1990) argues that decisions to participate in education and training are intimately connected with a person's ability to control his or her own life and anticipate the future. Hedoux found that this ability was blocked, particularly for older people and married women, since their autonomy and freedom of movement were severely constrained by their partners.

Dispositional factors (attitudes, perceptions, expectations) would appear to constitute the most powerful deterrents to participation. When these are added to the numerous practical obstacles that prevent individuals from taking up educational opportunities, for example lack of time, money, transport, daytime facilities and childcare, the immense difficulties faced by providers wishing to recruit non-participant sections are clear. Non-participation, then, results from the combination and interaction of diverse factors rather than one or two obstacles which would be relatively easy to overcome.

Currently, therefore, those who benefit most from the public provision of education are not necessarily those in greatest need of it: they have often already benefited from the education system or they can actually afford the private market. A marketplace model then militates against providers who are trying to involve traditional non-participants because of the pressure on providers to become responsive to the 'market' and hence reduce costs.

## UNDERLYING VALUES

Behind a commitment to the market model is a particular set of values. MacPherson (1962) quoted in Martin (1992) has characterized these values as 'possessive individualism' which he defines as follows:

> the human essence is freedom from dependence on the will of others, and freedom is a function of possession. Society becomes a lot of free and equal individuals related to each other as proprietors of their own capacities and of what they have acquired by their exercise. Society consists of relations of exchange between proprietors. Political society becomes a calculative device for the protection of this property and for the maintenance of an orderly relation of exchange.
>
> (McPherson (1962) in Martin 1992)

Under this model no individual would be required to subsidize another's learning; this would be an infringement of the liberty of individuals not to avail themselves of opportunities for learning. Similarly, institutions compete with each other for customers and customers choose on the basis of their rational individual choices. One problem with this form of thinking is that, as Jonathan has pointed out:

> by delegating to individuals decisions which, in aggregate, have substantial policy effects, legislatures are not lessening the extent to which they direct policy but covertly changing its direction. Indeed freedoms, to make rational individual choices, when centralised policy pre-structures the options, and social reality largely determines which choices are rational, are not like the freedom to devise a game of one's own choosing, or one which reflects personal goals, priorities and values. They are much more like freedoms to compete in a game whose parameters are set in advance and whose finer details (and outcomes) are to be blindly produced as players make rational, self interested, non-cooperative decisions.
>
> (Jonathan 1990)

In effect changes in legislation are leading to the breakup of strategic planning and intervention on the part of the local authorities in favour of a market in which many of the players, if viewed as individual consumers, are disadvantaged.

If individuals are to secure the social prerequisites of real individual freedom, such as health, education, material substance and so on, then the liberty of others must be infringed so that such conditions may be created. The individual must have the material and cultural resources to choose between different courses of action in practice.

## PURPOSE OF EDUCATION

Currently much encouragement is being given to individuals to return to education. However, such encouragement is not politically neutral and has a particular purpose. Rogers (1992) has argued that there are four main clusters of ideas about the purpose of education:

1 That it has a *technical* function, to provide a trained labour force, to promote the skills and knowledge required by a modern industrialized society to acquire greater prosperity; education gives capabilities.
2 That it *establishes status*. Education is a process of jostling by which an individual achieves a role and thereby a set position which he or she occupies for the rest of life. In this 'meal-ticket' view of the function of education, the constant battles between groups to control different social and economic resources spill over into the schools and colleges. Education follows the changes in society.
3 That its main effect is to *reproduce* social structures and cultures, preventing change taking place so that the individual is adapted to the dominant social and cultural norms; education instils respect for the existing elites.
4 That if it is effective, it is a *revolutionary force* for both individual (providing mobility) and society (promoting development). It enables the learner to reflect critically on the reality around and to cooperate with others to change that reality.

Purpose (1), which is generally described in the rhetoric of politics as 'the creation of a flexible, adaptable workforce', has clearly been the priority as far as central government policy has been concerned. Individuals and educational providers have been encouraged to develop the ability to adapt to changing employment and technical demands through education and training. This might be an example of the state interfering to correct some anomalies in the system whilst purpose (2) might reflect a marketplace view of education where individuals maximize their resources by investing in education. Purpose (3) might be characterized as the way in which the hegemony of the dominant group is imposed and so becomes an acceptable, if hidden, reason for investing in education, whereas purpose (4) represents a countervailing ideology to that of the New Right.

## INDIVIDUAL CONSUMERS

The language of the marketplace speaks of customers and providers and, although the customer is rarely defined, it is clear that the customer is an individual. Edwards (1991) has argued that a philosophy of meeting individual learner needs contains an assumption that the learner has a particular identity and therefore needs a particular form of learning programme. He points out that it is no surprise that most people participating in adult education, and the majority of programmes provided, are overwhelmingly middle class. He suggests that whilst 'choice' and 'autonomy' are key words in the process of meeting individual needs, this means that practices are created which 'reflect and engender notions of equality of opportunity'. Edwards argues that:

> while this provides a pyramid of opportunity for the individuals who are able to compete within the educational market place, it condemns us all to structures of inequality and the subordination of groups continues. Unequal opportunity is perpetuated and legitimised within an ideology of equality of opportunity and individual escape, rather than social emancipation, is the learning project . . . Individual needs-based consumption of educational and training services in the market place and for the market have primacy. In focusing our practices on the individual, we are reproducing the fragmentation of collective experience and social relations which is part of the wider social, economic and political changes in our social information. The collective nature of experience, its foundation in unequal relations of power, is not addressed in programmes to meet the individual needs of individuals. Persons learn to experience themselves as autonomous from others as private consumers of goods. Meeting the learning needs of individuals can therefore be argued to contribute to the needs of the liberal capitalist state for a population which is disciplined to consent actively or passively to the inequalities of social formations.

(Edwards 1991)

Another of the difficulties of meeting individual learners' needs by adopting a marketing approach is that providers are likely to set out to attract particular groups of students in as easy a way as possible. Johnston (1992) has pointed out that there are dangers if the approach to learners is 'supply led'. Taking as an example the development of a long-term strategy for working with unwaged adults he has argued that only a token dialogue can be developed if resources are limited and time for consultation is short. This results in the unwaged adults being allocated

> a passive role in making a purely reactive choice from a limited menu of educational possibilities. In contrast, an outreach approach may be less concerned with finding a market for its potential educational provision (supp'y/institution led), than making education responsive to the prevailing concerns and interests of those in the local community (demand led). It tries to move away from ideas of educational consumerism and to view the educational process as much more of a dialogue.
>
> (Johnston 1992)

A key finding of Blair *et al.* (1993), in their study of adult participants in education and training, was that 35 out of 50 respondents effectively had no choice in deciding which provider was most suitable for their needs; 'either they knew of no other provider or their choice was determined by their personal circumstances'. They found that it was the *provider* that was chosen first and the *provision* second. Although in interview most adults were able to describe at least one reason for their choice of provider, usually related to the convenience of the provider's locations, or the attractiveness of the courses they offered, they were, in fact, often unaware of other providers. This finding means that there are likely to be situations where it is the provider who determines the provision, not the 'consumer'.

A marketplace definition of choice has to see the customer as an individual and there is also an assumption that individual customers have identical needs and will buy the same product if the quality and price are attractive. Clearly, these research findings have demonstrated that the customer does not have this kind of choice and that large numbers of customers are disadvantaged in this competitive situation.

Jonathan has argued that:

> when we consider the most popular justifications for the market model education game – the appeal to individual rights – we see that it is dubious in three principal respects. There is firstly the general moral objection that these rights constrain the broader autonomy even of those individuals on whom they appear to confer immediate benefit. There is secondly the egalitarian objection that some will exercise these rights more effectively than others, giving a further twist to the spiral of cumulative advantage and disadvantage. Thirdly, there is the fact that this procedural change in the policy mechanism brings about substantive changes in the nature and distribution of education, and in the general political economy and takes such changes out of the proper forum of debate.
>
> (Jonathan 1990)

## COMPETITION AND COLLABORATION

This chapter has considered the difficulties posed by assuming that an individual has 'choice' and 'autonomy' in securing access to educational opportunities. I will now go on to consider the provision made for adult learners and the effect that competition between providers may have. A key finding of Munn *et al.* (1993) was that collaboration between providers was an important factor in helping adults participate in education for the first time, and in sustaining participation, by enabling adults to move onwards and upwards to other provision. This finding was true across the range of national initiatives that were examined and of the in-depth study of one region. The research highlighted cooperation among departments in the same institution; among institutions in the same sector; across sectors and between education and industry. Although collaboration took time and effort it was clear that it benefited adult students and the institutions and professionals involved. A particular example cited was SWAP [the Scottish Wider Access Programme]. The report stated:

> Numbers of students on SWAP courses have risen steadily, from about 750 in its first year of operation 1988/89 to almost 2,000 in 1992/93 (SOED, 1993). It has been successful in attracting students from working class homes (Gallagher *et al.*, 1992) and students report high levels of satisfaction with their access courses (Munn *et al.*, 1993). A high proportion of students successfully make the transition from access courses to higher education and staff involved in FE and HE are very positive about the experience of teaching SWAP students.
>
> (Munn *et al.* 1993)

Marketplace provision, however, encourages competition not collaboration, in the interests of 'efficiency'. The justification for this is that changes in provision will be made in response to demand mediated through a price mechanism. If, however, as we have seen, many of the 'consumers' of education are unable to make rational choices and the provision offered to them is adversely affected by discouragement of collaboration then the marketplace model must be seriously inadequate. There is the added danger that if funding follows the individual student then providers will be less likely to seek or accept students who require support. This again will discourage the collaborative strategies already cited, many of which have been particularly innovative in ensuring that students moving from community-based provision into further education provision are supported through a network of collaborative links. It will also discourage providers in their efforts to encourage adult participation in education for the first time since, as we have seen, making such provision is resource intensive compared with making provision for those who are already oriented towards education.

## THE ROLE OF THE PROFESSIONAL

A final consideration is the implications for the role of the education professional in the light of these different models of provision. O'Hagan (1991) has suggested that there are three broad models of education which he has characterized as 'efficiency', 'enrichment' and 'empowerment'.

Under the 'efficiency' or marketplace model the role of the professional is to be 'an efficient manager, or service delivery expert'. Professionals become increasingly specialized either in working with particular groups such as the long-term unemployed or in specialist areas, such as basic education, but they remain impartial and neutral in relation to educational values. Changes are made to provision to make it more welcoming or responsive to demand in relation to perceived imperfections in the system.

Under the 'enrichment' model the professionals' role is to 'use whatever means are available to provide support for individuals and groups "targeted" as being in need'. A team-work approach is often used since it is assumed that the differences between the professionals' skills are less important than their common aim. Education addresses itself to 'social rather than industrial, economic or political issues. Education is essentially a social tool'.

Finally, under the 'empowerment' model, education is 'viewed as a means of intellectual liberation, but this is inextricably linked to action since there can be no intellectual freedom for the powerless, and no escape from exploitation without practical consciousness'. The professional therefore must see learning as a collective, rather than an individual, process which is not divorced from conscious action. This means that powerless groups have 'overall control of their own learning and therefore of the nature of the provision'. The professional is concerned with providing people with knowledge and skills which will allow them to struggle for and gain more power for themselves. 'Learning derives just as much from the experience of struggle as from structured teaching or reading.'

This way of defining empowerment is very different from the government's avowed commitment to empowering the public in its relationship with state bureaucracies. The government, as Ranson (1992) points out, sees market competition as the principal vehicle for public choice and accountability. He argues:

The market is formally neutral but substantively interested. Individuals (or institutions) come together in competitive exchange to acquire possession of scarce goods and services. Within the marketplace all are free and equal, only differentiated by the capacity to calculate their self-interest. Yet of course the market masks its social bias. It elides but also reproduces the inequalities which consumers bring to the marketplace. Under the guise of neutrality, the institution of the market actively confirms and reinforces the pre-existing social order of wealth, privilege and prejudice. The market, let us be clear, is a crude mechanism of social selection and intended as such. It will provide more effective social engineering than anything we have previously witnessed in the post-war period. The effect of the market mechanism in education can only be to create a social and selective hierarchy of institutions.

(Ranson 1992)

On the other hand, if the resources available to people through education (such as knowledge, skills, self-confidence and a sense of solidarity) are acquired through a process of social engagement then the balance of power between themselves and institutions will have shifted. As O'Hagan (1991) has pointed out, power 'is not something that can be given to the powerless' but professional educators have an important part to play 'in the process of educational engagement'. As long as people are treated as consumers whose only role is to pick from a range of objects chosen by others then there is little likelihood of them gaining the power to challenge and change the system. In the long run, therefore, polices which promote equity are more likely to produce 'efficiency' and 'effectiveness' for *all* than policies which distribute power and resources unequally.

## CONCLUSION

In this chapter I have argued that a marketplace model which assumes that education is responsive to a multitude of individual choices is seriously flawed. It is flawed from the point of view of individuals since they are not able to make 'rational' choices either because the education on offer and the system they are expected to enter does not cater for their needs or because they have insufficient or inappropriate information on which to base their choices. It is flawed from the point of view of the education providers because it discourages collaboration between providers and because it discourages initiatives designed to involve traditionally non-participant groups. It is flawed from the point of view of the educational professional who is no longer able to operate under an empowerment model of education which would shift the balance of power away from institutions and towards powerless groups. It is flawed from a point of view which seeks to develop equality of opportunity because the marketplace model actively discourages large sections of the community from participating in education because they see that it is not responsive to their concerns and interests. Finally, it is flawed because the marketplace model results in policies which perpetuate and multiply existing inequalities without subjecting such policies to the public debate which a democratic society should ensure.

# REFERENCES

Blair, A., McPake, J. and Munn, P. (1993) *Facing Goliath: Adults' Experience of Participation, Guidance and Progression in Education*, Edinburgh: SCRE.

Edwards, R. (1991) 'The politics of meeting learner needs: power, subject, subjection', *Studies in the Education of Adults*, 23 (1), April.

Friedman, M. and Friedman, R. (1980) *Free to Choose*, Harmondsworth: Pelican.

Further and Higher Education (Scotland) Act 1992, Edinburgh: HMSO.

Hayek, F. A. (1944) *The Road to Serfdom*, London: Routledge.

HMI (1992) *The Education of Adults in Scotland*, Edinburgh: The Scottish Office Education Department.

Holmes, J. and Storrie, T. (1985) *Consett – A Case Study of Education and Unemployment*, FEU.

Johnston, R. (1992) in G. Allen and I. Martin (eds), *Education and Community: The Politics of Practice*, London: Cassell.

Jonathan, R. (1990) 'State education or prisoner's dilemma: the "Hidden Hand" as a source of education policy', *British Journal of Educational Studies*, **XXXVIII** (2).

McGivney, V. (1990), *Education's for Other People: Access to Education for Non-Participant Adults*, Leicester: NIACE.

Martin, I. (1992) in G. Allen and I. Martin (eds), *Education and Community: The Politics of Practice*, London: Cassell.

Merriam, S. and Caffarella, R. (1991) *Learning in Adulthood*, San Francisco: Jossey-Bass.

Munn, P. and MacDonald, D. (1988) *Adult Participation in Education and Training*, Edinburgh: SCRE.

Munn, P., Tett, L. and Arney, N. (1993) *Negotiating the Labyrinth: Progression Opportunities for Adult Learners*, Edinburgh: SCRE.

O'Hagan, B. (1991) 'The Charnwood papers: fallacies in community education', *Education Now:* Ticknell.

Ranson, S. (1992) 'Towards the learning society', *Educational Management and Administration*, 20 (2).

Rogers, A. (1992) *Adults Learning for Development*, London: Cassell.

Scottish Office Education Department (1993) *Adults in Education*, Statistical review prepared for a conference on adult guidance, 12 March/0343/93.

## Chapter 11

# The learning society†

## Hendrik van der Zee

### CHARTING CRITERIA

Every community takes steps to ensure that its members acquire the different kinds of knowledge considered necessary for life. But societies vary considerably with respect to the importance given to learning, the specific aims that they try to satisfy through learning, and the way in which they attempt to support and reinforce learning. In the Jewish tradition learning occupies pride of place. Thus, in the twelfth century Maimonides wrote (according to Abram 1984: 64):

> Every Jew, whether rich or poor, healthy or sick, at the height of his powers or old and infirm, has the duty to study. Wood-cutters and water-bearers figured among their great scholars, even blind men. They studied day and night. (. . .) Until when should a person continue to learn? Until the day of his death. (. . .) Learning is the most important of all the rules of behaviour given in the Torah. Even stronger: learning is more important than all other rules of behaviour together. (. . .) Make learning a regular habit. Do not say: 'I'll learn if I have time'. You may never have time.

These words deserve noting in the light of the contemporary world-wide debate on educational standards.[1] The pedagogical assumptions on which present-day curricula are based are increasingly coming under attack. However defective we may consider our curricula to be, we should bear in mind that criticism of education is not new. In the last century, for example, Friedrich Nietzsche (1872: 133–152) complained that educational institutions, far from seeking to civilize men and society, teach people to be functionaries and make them marketable. The same and similar complaints can be heard today.

Criticism of the functioning of our educational system should be seen

† This chapter is an edited version of an article in the *International Journal of Lifelong Education*, 10(3), 1991, 210–230.

in the context of the societal forces that affect learning needs. These forces include:

- the explosion of knowledge and technology;
- automation in companies and institutions;
- attempts to make labour and labour organizations more flexible;
- the economic and political unification of Europe;
- the innumerable people who have to scrape an existence on the edges of the labour market;
- the tendency towards individualization;
- the increase in the amount of free time we have at our disposal;
- the ageing of the population;
- the variety in sorts of households and forms of cohabitation;
- changes in the relationship between men and women and parents and children;
- the co-existence of different ethnic and cultural groups;
- the revaluation of the environment.

Various suggestions are proposed to address the diverse and shifting learning needs which are emerging in response to the combined impact of these social and economic changes.

Some scholars seek the solution primarily in a *new approach to training and education*. Two different points of emphasis are discernible within this approach. In the one case, the introduction of a new or revised educational concept is stressed (self-directed learning, problem-oriented instruction, learning from experience, andragogy). In the other case, the emphasis lies on the methods that should be used in the design of instruction and for solving performance problems (instructional design, educational technology, course planning).

A second response to the new demands for education and training is the *effective school movement*. This research-driven movement takes the organization of education as its point of departure. It is maintained that such factors as strong management, regular testing of learning achievements, getting back to basics and a secure and well-ordered school environment have a vital influence on the achievements of the pupils.

A third innovation in educational thinking is the *open learning movement*. Client orientation and flexibility in the provision of learning opportunities are the main theme here. In practical terms this means the setting up of cafeteria-style arrangements for education, doing away with entrance requirements, the application of technology (television, video, telephone, computers), the use of self-instructional material, the development of a support system.

A more radical proposal for reform comes from the movement for the *de-schooling of society*. This movement, which was prominent in the 1970s, highlighted the side-effects of attempts fixated on promoting the extension and perfection of educational facilities. The de-schoolers argue that, little by little, a colossal learning factory has been created from which everything resembling education in the original meaning of the word has disappeared. Our schools have become instruments of repression: they reinforce social inequality, keep people dependent, stub out initiative and creativity, and impede common action. Moreover, what people most need to learn, schools seem least able to teach. However valid this criticism may be, it can be said that the de-schoolers have paved the way for a discussion about our educational priorities, in particular about what the basics are, about principles of self-organization, and about informal and non-informal modes of learning.

The final theme for change which I would like to mention is the idea of *recurrent education*. The term recurrent education refers to an overall strategy aimed at restructuring the educational system, so as to distribute periods of study over the total life span of the individual in a recurring way, i.e. alternating with extended periods of other sorts of activity such as work, leisure and retirement. Although recurrent education has been a political hobby-horse for many years in The Netherlands, statistics on participation and time-budget studies show that the idea has not been put to work.

Of course, the above is not an exhaustive catalogue of new directions for education. None the less the survey does give an impression of the variety of proposals for reform. It is clear that the changes in society's demand for education have produced divergent reactions.

The more miscellaneous the chorus of critics and reformers, the more dire the need for an overall score, a concept which stresses the importance of harmony between the multitude of separate approaches. A preferred score would provide room for a variety of initiatives to renewal, without justifying every proposal beforehand and so circumventing the need to choose. Rather it would act as a common source of inspiration. The metaphor of a *learning society* has the potential to fulfil this need.

However, at the present moment it is customary to sketch the society of the future as an *information society*. Why do I not take the availability of information (i.e. knowledge), but the acquisition of knowledge (i.e. learning) as the primary consideration? The reason is that an information society is still not an informed society. The evidence is otherwise. What is envisaged is a society in which the pressure from technology and the economy is so great that people, the users of the information, feel defeated. If we don't take action, an inhuman, highly technocratic society lies ahead of us (see, for example, Martin 1988 and Roszak 1986).

No matter how one regards an information society, one thing is missing in this metaphor: people. Kidd (1983: 530) maintains that an important linking operation is needed which enables us to make our own sense out of information. The word learning guarantees this sort of linking operation. It directs attention to the dynamics of the relations between information and information technology on the one side, and the individual and the community on the other.

'The learning society is growing because it must', is the opening of Patricia Cross's inspiring survey of literature *Adults as Learners* (1986: 1). This makes us curious about the characteristics of a learning society, or rather about the ideas and values to which the concept appeals. Defining a concept that has engendered a world-wide debate is tricky. Nevertheless, in this chapter five criteria (strategic issues) for the development of a learning society are pinpointed. These are:

1  The need to broaden the definition of learning (education as a dimension of society).
2  The need to redirect the goal of learning (growth towards completeness).
3  The need to go beyond learning and instruction (increasing collective competence).
4  The need to foster autonomy in learning (self-education).
5  The need to stress a political approach to learning (the right to learn).

## DIMENSION OF SOCIETY

A learning society stimulates and allows all its members and groups continually to develop their knowledge, skills and attitudes. Education is anchored in culture as a primary condition of existence. It is high on the agenda of many societal institutions. Besides the educational system proper, numerous other agencies are involved – the mass media, the unions, industry and commerce, the health services, travel organizations, public information outlets, prisons, and so on. This is what I mean by education as a dimension of society.[2]

Education can be described as the manner in which persons and groups gain skills, extend their knowledge, receive impulses, define their attitudes: in short, learn things. I believe that a comprehensive strategy, aimed at opening up new opportunities for people to learn, should consist of the following three steps. First it is necessary to chart the existing forms of learning. Then we should examine how the potential of the suggested types of learning can be further developed. Finally, we should take into account the unique contributions as well as the interdependencies of the many agencies of education and other learning resources. I will now discuss these three steps in order.

### Forms of learning

The bewildering variety of modes in which human learning occurs can be viewed from various angles. The context determines what constitutes a meaningful classification and terminology. Here the first priority is to clarify the possibilities for strengthening the educational dimension of society. From this point of view it is essential to distinguish between three basic forms of learning.

The first, but not necessarily most powerful, mode of learning is *guided learning*. By guided learning I mean all sorts of learning activities which involve a measure of instruction or tuition. This includes following occupational training, attending a management seminar, taking part in a course via the television or going to dancing lessons.

The second basic form can be referred to by the term *do-it-yourself learning*. It covers all activities people undertake on their own initiative, without the mediation of teachers or course-makers, with the intention of broadening their horizons or improving their capacity to accomplish some task. Ferreting something out in the public library, doing a job 'with the social sciences', cracking a computer with the aid of a manual and mastering a physical handicap with the support of a patients' association are examples of do-it-yourself learning. It should be noted that self-learners often do not regard their behaviour as 'learning', and that only a fraction of their initiatives take the form of learning projects.[3]

The third basic form is *spontaneous learning*. Like do-it-yourself learning, spontaneous learning, as a rule, takes place without organized instruction. However, whereas do-it-yourself learning is deliberately designed to cope with a problem or to summon inspiration, one bumps into spontaneous learning without meaning to, as in the case of a serious accident (through which daily worries are put in perspective), a conflict at work (through which scales drop from the eyes), and a love affair (through which we come to look at ourselves and to reassess old relationships). At other times learning happens by the way, as a by-product of an activity which is primarily guided by other motives. Watching television, starting an own company and practising a sport are examples of activities from which a lot can be learnt in an unselfconscious fashion.[4]

To say that much learning takes place without recourse to teachers or producers of instructional materials is to state the obvious. Everyone concerned with the training and education of young people and adults acknowledges this phenomenon.

Nevertheless, professional practitioners, policy-makers and researchers continue to regard the school system as 'too separate, too all-sufficient and too effective an organization of provisions' (Fletcher 1984: 406).

### Promoting learning

The forms of learning mentioned above offer us many points of contact for educational reform. With respect to the area of guided learning, at least three groups of initiatives deserve special attention.

1 Improving the quality of the existing school system. This category includes all activities which aim at more effective, efficient and appealing methods of instruction, improved instructional materials, greater differentiation, more skilful teachers, innovative management and better amenities.

2 Developing new programmes and types of education, especially around questions and needs for which the present range of educational facilities does not, or does not fully, provide.

3 Enlarging access to courses and training by getting rid of all sorts of impediments which prevent people from taking part. Examples of such impediments can be: irregular working hours, transportation problems, not being able to afford the registration fee, lack of self-confidence, ignorance of the opportunities, insufficient studying skills, not satisfying the entrance requirements.

The problem of how to cope with the two remaining types of learning is less easily answered. This is due to a lack of knowledge about the processes involved. A framework for examining the tasks facing us in our daily practices is needed before more conscious action can be taken. Which tasks question our ways of thinking and behaving? How do we respond to the difficulties and opportunities these tasks represent? What sort of competence and wisdom will help us move ahead? In what way can the required proficiencies be obtained? With regard to the last question, I advocate keeping the perspective as open as possible. A multitude of sources and means deserve consideration.

- Informal contacts: friends, neighbours, members of the family.
- The mass media: books, radio, television, newspapers, magazines, audio- and video-cassettes.
- Labour organizations: the place of work as place of learning.
- Cultural institutions: museums, libraries, theatres, cinemas, creative centres.
- Utilitarian facilities: trade fairs, labour exchanges, banks, do-it-yourself shops.

Uncovering this educational potential is a daunting task. Recent studies on learning in the workplace, the public library as an open-learning centre, learning through television, and the educational possibilities of museums indicate a basis upon which we may proceed.

**Harmony**

Let flowers flower everywhere. However, the situation in which the diverse 'agencies of education' only care about their own back yard must be avoided. As Houle (1972: 6) sketched:

The typical career worker in adult education is still concerned only with an institutional pattern of service or a methodology, seldom or never catching a glimpse of the total terrain of which he is cultivating one corner, and content to be, for example, a farm or home consultant, museum curator, public librarian, or industrial trainer.

The many sources and means available to learners must be brought into harmony. This requires cooperation, the formation of networks, the division of duties, a realization of the unique contributions one agency can make that other agencies cannot, continuous innovation and a common perspective. There may be no misunderstanding about who should judge the harmony: in the last analysis, the user of the facilities.

The fact that there is a negative side to teaching should never be forgotten. Resnick (1987: 13–20) has unravelled how knowledge gained at school relates to knowledge required in everyday life and at work. She discovered four differences.

1 At school individual achievements are tested, while in life you are judged by what you can contribute in a social context.
2 In school it is what is in your head that counts, while in life what matters is if you are good at using technology, aids and appliances and sources.
3 At school you learn to use meaningless symbols, while in life inventiveness in approaching meaningful problem situations is required.
4 At school you learn general skills and subject-dependent understanding, while in life you need knowledge and experience which is relevant to specific problem situations.

These findings may not be revolutionary. But it does not hurt to think about them once again. The failure of our schools to teach proficiencies that are essential for living challenges the pedagogical assumptions on which a lot of today's curricula are based.

It is a great mistake, however, to equate a society's broad educational goals with instrumental learning and an utilitarian bias. Genuine education teaches people to stand 'above the machine'. Moreover, schools share this responsibility with the media, literature and the arts, the public library, and many other institutions. This brings us to the second foundation of the learning society: education as the growth towards completion.

## GROWTH TOWARDS COMPLETION

Now we proceed from the ferment in the learning society, its sources, means and institutions, to the consideration of what is learnt. The creation of the opportunity to learn, irrespective of content, is not necessarily a positive virtue. At school and elsewhere we often learn things that do nobody any good, either directly or in the long run. Narrow-minded opinions, antiquated theories, ossified working methods, empty skills, disturbances of the motorial system, callous behaviour, ungrounded fears, docility – all are examples of the wrong kind of learning. In such cases education degenerates into, to use a word introduced by John Dewey, mis-education. But it is even worse than that. Much of the knowledge that would be most valuable to us no doubt goes unlearned, as Hirsch (1988) sets forth in his book *Cultural Literacy: What Every American Needs to Know*. How, then, do we settle our educational priorities?

Here it is only possible to talk about the direction in which I think the answer should be sought. I am not really happy about the wording but am as yet unable to do better: we learn to become a *complete* person. The justification for any educational activity, therefore, lies in the following question: in what degree does the learning contribute to a person's completeness? All learning objectives are subordinate to this ultimate test. The concern for completeness has far-reaching implications, as Abram (1984: 69), who has made an extensive study on the role of learning in the Jewish community, indicates:

> The permanent pupil does not learn to be able to practise a profession, not even that of rabbi, in order to obtain power or authority, but to improve himself and his behaviour and thereby the world. The purpose of his learning is, in other words, to become a complete person. (. . .) But what is 'a complete person'? There is no straightforward answer to this question. The answer depends on the picture of the world and especially of humanity in the mind of the permanent pupil, on what he studies and appreciates in the culture, on how he digests the past and sees the future. (. . .) Each pupil has his own learning journey to make and the true significance and personal implications of the desired result, completeness, can only be revealed to him in the course of the learning process. The Torah rejects imitation both of learning method and of learning result.

This – selective – description of what 'completeness' means, of course, can only be a starting point. A connection must be made with the formation of present-day opinion on the purpose of education. When we make this connection, we notice that the concept of 'completeness' consists of two components: it encompasses a double aspiration.

## Pursuit of quality

The first component is the pursuit of quality, an attempt to achieve improvement and ultimately excellence. In a certain sense this aim serves as a counterpoint to a point of view which dominated the discussion on the relations between education and society in the 1960s and 1970s: the ideal of equal opportunities. I am in no way advocating that the topic of social inequality and justice should disappear from the agenda. Further on the opposite will become apparent. [. . .]

The passion for quality is *in no way* connected with the formation of an élite and *hardly* with assessments and tests, inspection committees, diplomas and examinations. On the other hand, it is *very much* related to recognizing potential and the continuous search for conditions which stimulate potential.

## Pursuit of all-round development

There is a second side to the emphasis on 'completeness': the pursuit of all-round development. This striving can be seen as a counterpoint to another dominant educational trend, i.e. the concentration of attention on the cognitive development only of human beings. Other aspects of personality – including the aesthetic, social, moral, emotional, physical and even technical/manual – are regarded by western culture as more or less peripheral to education.

The British education philosopher, Louis Arnaud Reid, is one of those who has repeatedly denounced this one-sidedness. In *Ways of Understanding and Education* Reid (1986) stresses that there are two basic forms of knowledge. One form is discursive. It involves propositional statements of fact about the world around us. The other form, which covers the area of intuitive experience, is called non-discursive. The arts are excellently suited as media for expressing non-discursive knowledge. According to Reid, there should be an interchange between these ways of knowing, since the rational–intellectual and the intuitive–creative need each other. However, in western culture in general, and in curricula in particular, human knowledge is identified with what can be expressed in propositional statements. This has led to a separation of the world of the intellect, science and technology from the world of feelings, values, emotions and creativity. A disastrous schism, as Reid (1986: 2) writes:

> The life of personal subjects, the life of feelings and emotions, of the creative urges, of obscure symbolisms, of moral urges and intimations, religion, personal relations – all these, cut off, on this divisive assumption, from the critical purgings of thinking and intellect, remain raw, chaotic, often infantile. The personal self is split down the middle.

More attention for the training of 'eye, hand and heart' and more recognition of the importance of history, languages and literature will not, it is true, halt the increasing encroachment of specialisms, but it could nevertheless provide some counterbalance. To put it more positively, education is concerned with the whole human being and the whole culture. Does this mean that the medieval idea of the *homo universalis* is about to be reinstated? However much this ideal may appeal to us, circumstances are now very different to those of our distant forefathers. There is no demand for a *homo universalis* in the present day because of the abundance of collective competence constantly around us.

## COLLECTIVE COMPETENCE

The expression 'collective competence' is taken from De Zeeuw (1984, 1985). Put simply, collective competence is the ability to act, given the availability of support systems. What, then, is a support system?

In this context I take the concept of a support system in its widest sense. Support systems are of all times and are part of the human tradition. Cultural artefacts, such as songs, fairy stories, the Bible and a hammer, can be regarded as support systems. The same can be said of manuals, spreadsheets, self-help groups, planning procedures, consultancy bureaux, radar installations and data-banks. Thus, support systems are means, tools, sources, facilities, technology.

Some support systems augment our physical strength, others reinforce our senses or our thinking powers. Some support systems enable us to act collectively (forms of social organization), others inspire us and shake us awake (art, literature).

But all support systems have one thing in common: they embody the understanding, ideas and values of the past, and in this respect they are human projections. Thus, using a source or aid, or some other appliance, implies calling on experience which has often been built up painfully from generation to generation in tackling the problem with which the facility is intended to cope. [. . .] There can be no dispute that an approach to education which ignores today's support systems is out of touch with reality and, therefore, undesirable. A countervailing approach that stresses the importance of appropriating the human achievement embodied within support systems is badly needed. De Zeeuw (1984) suggests such an approach, and calls it the *participation model*. His model relies on the tacit knowledge that sources, tools and other facilities represent. We reveal this knowledge by using it, i.e. by participating in the culture in which we all have our stake.[5]

Currently there are, however, human, economic and technological obstacles to realizing this model. Let us look at some practical measures that could be taken to increase participation, thereby putting human achievement to work. These measures are centred around five critical points: (a) enriching the school environment, (b) redesigning the curriculum, (c) incorporating an educational element in the design of facilities, (d) making facilities more intelligent, and (e) removing restrictions on access to facilities. I do not have room to discuss these points at length here but will limit myself to a short explanation. In each case the explanation is confined to a single example of a support system: the community or office data-base.

## Enriching the school environment

The school is still too much of an island. The sources from which pupils learn for the most part remain restricted to material that has been specially designed for educational purposes, and to teachers and fellow-pupils. Facilities which are available in society still do not penetrate far enough into schools. However, here and there things are changing. For example, new technology is now welcomed enthusiastically in vocational training, as are simulations of practice. But the situation is still unsatisfactory in more generally orientated educational institutions. As society moves into the micro-electronic environment of the future, the installation of computers giving access to data-bases relevant to the subject being handled in classrooms would be a step in the right direction.

## Redesigning the curriculum

Redesigning the curriculum is even more vital than the mere presence of present-day technological facilities in the school environment. Students need to be taught how to work from and with facilities. So, no mental arithmetic, but a task performed with the calculator. No hand-written business correspondence, but straight into the computer. No prefabricated teaching material but 'real life' sources should be used.

The community and office data-base is such a source. As computerized knowledge systems become more accepted in educational settings, students will have to acquire new skills in order to cope with them. What can teachers do to help students in this respect? The solution which schools are beginning to develop is the provision of special programmes on subjects with names such as study skills, information skills, computer literacy, library skills and communication skills. An alternative is to integrate the training in the normal discipline-centred courses, which involves a different kind of pedagogy. In whatever way they are organized, the perspective – what are the lessons for? – must be clear. Explanation (of why), broadening (of the possibilities for application), coupling (of the various forms of computer applications in daily life) and recognizing 'the meaning of meaning' should be key areas of attention.

## Embedded training

Few individuals like to invest a lot of time and energy in learning how to use facilities such as libraries or computers. By incorporating an educational element into the design of such facilities it is possible to avoid forcing the beginner to struggle through all sorts of manuals and instructions, or even to attend training courses before being able to start off. It makes instruction available when and where needed, on the job, in everyday settings. Furthermore, building education into a support system ensures that actors keep on developing their skills to a 'professional' level. Indeed, embedded training can best be seen as a form of learning by doing.

What are the implications for our case study, the computerized knowledge system? First, the information offered and the retrieval procedures must be clear. Second, support must be available at critical moments when decisions have to be made and steps taken. Third, this support facilitates reflection on the user's actions and the development of an own perspective on the subject. Fourth, the data file must contain valuable information which is attractively presented and tempts the user to proceed further. Fifth, there should be room for several methods of working.

## Making facilities more intelligent

This measure lies in the extension of the previous one. However, here we are concerned not so much with the educational aspect, but rather with the desire for something that is referred to as 'user friendliness'. The criteria are, then, simplicity in use, accessibility, the appeal of working with the facility, efficiency. But there is more. The facility must not only be 'friendly' towards the user, it should also be designed from the users' perspective and not proceed from the demands of a specialized discipline or a programming language. There is even a further criterion. Most facilities are inclined to deteriorate over the years as, for example, when professionals come to dominate their use or when insufficient attention is paid to changing needs and circumstances. For this reason, facilities should be designed with mechanisms that ensure a permanent dialogue between the (projected) user and the professional.

Despite the fact that they may be regarded as wonders of sophistication by some, all the automated information facilities with which I am familiar seem depressingly inadequate with respect to the criteria just mentioned. Take one example from my own experience. I discovered part of the documentation for this study using the Online Public Catalogue which the Library of the University of Amsterdam recently installed. It had something to offer, undoubtedly. But, to begin with, the layout on the monitor was so primitive: no pictograms, far too many words and codes, no attempt at all at a pleasing graphical presentation. And to think that this is a relatively advanced system. Contrary to the shining visions of the computer enthusiast, it is obviously still a long time till the microelectronic era. Lessons on how to use information often deal chiefly with problems which would not exist if the system had been built more intelligently in the first place.

### Increasing the availability of facilities

Modern society is rich in facilities. But not everything is within everyone's reach. Wealth – and consequently opportunities to learn – is unevenly distributed. [. . .]

With regard to computerized knowledge systems there are signs that in the coming years increasingly more information on the most diverse topics will be (exclusively) stored in computers. But the public at large has no or no easy access to these electronic publications. It is a good thing that in several countries the public library is trying to do something about this problem. Two Dutch projects are worth mentioning, TACO (a national data-bank) and Biblitel (a local data-bank). However, the context in which a project such as TACO must function deserves more attention. Taking repercussions on existing ways of working, established responsibilities and hierarchies into account, there are three basic possibilities. First, the data-bank leaves everything as it is (and is probably hardly ever used). Second, the introduction of the data-bank requires some adjustments to be made in its environment (until a new equilibrium is reached). Third, the introduction of the data-bank leads to a restructuring of intelligence work and to adjustments at other levels of the institution and this, in turn, leads to special design requirements for the data-bank, and so on. Only in the last case can we speak of a true innovation, in the sense of a long-term increase in the collective competence embedded in public libraries.

So much for a number of measures connected with collective competence. I would add this: by regarding sources, equipment and other facilities as support systems, terms of reference are set within which a constructive discussion of our culture can be held. Such a discussion is constructive because it is directed to transforming our culture into a living possession with everyone participating in it. The notion of collective competence has brought the third premise for the learning society into focus. But more is involved in such a society.

## SELF-EDUCATION

The achievement of self-education is the fourth key to the advancement of a learning society. Although different writers mean different things when they use the word self-education, the insight that the concept contains two elements is gradually emerging. First, self-education is the objective aimed at: encouraging people to keep on learning of their own volition. A general heading that applies to this aim is *learning to learn*. Second, self-education is a recommended *way of teaching*, an approach for helping people to learn. In educational practice self-education can be both the objective and the vehicle. However, to avoid confusion, I have unravelled these two strands.

### Learning to learn

Learning to learn seeks to emphasize that, throughout life, human beings are what they are because of learning. The concept assumes a 'recursive framework', one that sees actors as potentially creative. At its heart is the achievement of autonomy: people taking the responsibility for their own learning.

Libraries could be filled with what has been written on these ideas, though not every writer goes under the same banner. Because of its utilitarian flavour, Smith (1982: 19) prefers the phrase learning *how* to learn. His effort to come to terms with the slippery concept starts from the following definition:

> Learning how to learn involves possessing, or acquiring, the knowledge and skill to learn effectively in whatever learning situation one encounters.

Such a general definition looks attractive, but it is not adequate in this case, since it ignores the fact that the concept can be approached from various angles. Thus, learning to learn is variously described as:

- acquiring skills in tracing and making sense of information;
- becoming proficient in solving problems in varying situations;
- obtaining a grasp of the principles of good research;
- reinforcing self-regulation in school and training settings;
- practising study techniques;
- developing 'higher order' skills;
- increasing one's ability to learn from experience;
- nurturing the desire to become a complete person.

Admirable as these goals are, instruction to increase people's competence in learning is usually simplified into courses or lessons in studying skills. Often such efforts are dominated by a school-bound mentality, by helping students to survive in the educational arena. The chief concern is about coping with the system: tricks on how to get through examinations, learning material by heart, doing homework, marking study texts, making notes.

In my opinion, the study-skills movement should broaden its perspective and shift its focus from the reproductive to the productive aspects of knowledge. For that a link should be sought with the other approaches to improving the capacity to learn.

In addition, it is necessary to emphasize the crucial importance of the environments in which the skills one has learnt are applied. What I advocate is an ecology of learning to learn. The ecological view may be premised with some thoughts on the problem of transfer, which is indeed a major deficiency in many study-skills programmes (Nisbet and Shucksmith 1986). But the ecology of learning implies more than simply taking care of transfer. It also involves being fully alive to the power relationships within the social structure. To paraphrase the Czech-born novelist Milan Kundera (see McEwan 1984: 26–32), we can say that in a world which has become a trap the struggle for inward independence (and against the monster within) should coincide with the struggle for outward independence (against the monster from outside).

How can this look at learning to learn be implemented in practical situations? Various suggestions have been made. Some, e.g. Boud (1988: 8), advocate changes in the regular curriculum: 'They believe that it is the responsibility of all teachers to ensure that they construct their courses to foster autonomy and that this goal is compatible with the discipline-centred goals which often predominate'. Others take the existing curriculum as a fact of life but think that it should be enriched with supportive lessons, optional or otherwise, on subjects such as coping with self-instructional materials, working through projects, writing a thesis, using a library, and 'reading' media constructions. A third group maintains that measures outside education are also needed; there is a task for broadcasting organizations, museums, libraries, publishers and creativity centres.

As I see it, a learning society will explore all possible avenues of promoting learning to learn. With one reservation, I have very little faith in initiatives determined from on high which do not take the day-to-day experiences of those involved into account. Emancipation – meaning inner and outer independence – is not granted, it has to be fought for and won.

## Way of teaching

As I said, the word self-education stands not only for something to strive for, but also for a means, a way of teaching. This is another topic which has fuelled a lot of controversy and, again, polemicists do not all share the same background. This is expressed in the variety of concepts denoting the principles of good practice. Perhaps the issues at stake can be clarified by identifying two basic ways of helping people to increase their knowledge and improve their qualifications. I have labelled these contrasting views the 'school approach' and the 'adult approach' (Table 11.1).[6]

Table 11.1 Basic ways of increasing knowledge

| The school approach | The adult approach |
| --- | --- |
| Transmitting a given body of knowledge | Developing an own perspective on a subject |
| The teacher decides | The learner decides |
| A semantically poor context | A semantically rich context |
| Learning without facilities | Learning with facilities |
| Learning as drilling | Learning as a conscious activity |
| Experience as condition | Experience as foundation |
| Directed to subject-matter | Directed to problems |
| Evaluation as a check | Evaluation as a means of improving |
| Compulsion and duty | Voluntary basis, pleasure in learning |
| Directed at achievement | Directed towards completion |
| Closed tasks | Open tasks |

It has to be admitted that this scheme is full of crass contradictions. But the descriptions help us to cut out the proverbial rigmarole that is so typical of the age-old discussion about the most appropriate ways of meeting learners' needs. It goes without saying that the approach advocated here is the adult approach. Its principles characterize the spirit in which pupils – of any age – and teachers deal with each other in a learning society.

For clarity's sake: an adult approach is also possible outside general forming and development work and group teaching. Its principles are viable everywhere: in study at a distance, in computer-assisted learning, in mathematical education, in in-house company training programmes, in occupational training, at universities, in museums, in public libraries, and elsewhere.

## RIGHT TO LEARN

As a social issue education is the responsibility of the community. In a learning society, therefore, learning should be a right and not a privilege. All citizens – regardless of social status, income, initial training, descent, sex and affiliations – should be given equal opportunities to develop themselves and to improve proficiencies throughout their lives.

This goal is music to democratic ears. Is it then any wonder that since the 1960s terms such as lifelong learning, permanent education and recurrent education have occurred regularly in the introductions of official educational documents? Enough rhetoric to sink a ship.

But what are the implications for educational practice? Which attitude should the government adopt? What is entirely private domain, and how far should state interference reach? Kidd (1983: 530) sketches the alternatives:

> Is there a basic education that a citizen should have as a birthright and would the provision of such constitute the main conditions of a learning society? Or would something more be needed, such as national declarations or laws, or an ethos of learning, or an environment for learning?

It seems that, as far as the right of learning is concerned, the Dutch government does not wish to commit itself to more than guaranteeing a sort of minimum programme and even that is under review. The most important policy instrument is the general-proficiency schooling for 12- to 15- or 16-year-olds. In addition there are plans for an educational voucher system.

## General-proficiency schooling versus basic education

According to the Scientific Council for Government Policy (1986: 8) general-proficiency schooling is concerned with:

- *basic* skills: proficiencies (knowledge, attainments, understanding) that are vital to be able to function as a member of society and which are the essential foundation and nucleus for further development;
- education for *everyone*: in principle, the contents of the basic forming are the same for all groups;
- *common* education: in principle, the schooling is directed to the common acquisition of the contents of a curriculum that is equally valid for all. Forms of differentiation between pupils in anticipation of their further education are, in principle, to be avoided.

How does this renewed interest in the myth of 'the common school, common programme, common core' (Holmes 1988: 246) fit in with the notion of a learning society? Getting back to basics, in keeping with the diversity of tasks that life has set aside for people, seems to me a viable idea, provided that general schooling allows for differential educational provisions to accommodate inequalities in pupils' capacities and backgrounds. As far as the belief in common public education appeals to the idea of equality as a principle of justice it cannot possibly mean equality of treatment. Rather it has to come to terms with the principles of equal consideration and equal opportunity (Fletcher 1984).

Whatever general-proficiency schooling may mean, my greatest fear is that we may claim to be achieving quality if everyone in the Netherlands can neatly answer a barrage of pre-set questions drawn up by experts in different fields. We will then be even further from the mark. Our educational system will not be truly worthwhile until schools succeed in motivating youngsters to keep on learning and asking critical questions about the world.

Another point which prompts criticism and concern is that adult education has been left out of the discussion. It is an obvious step to give not only young people but also adults the opportunity to acquire and cultivate basic proficiencies. The State Regulation on Adult Elementary Education could be applied to this end. In addition to higher priority for this branch of adult education, a more differentiated package of lessons with more choice, more quality and less utilitarian bias is needed.

A third issue is also important. It must be recognized in word and in deed that it is not just schools that enable citizens to function in contemporary society. The involvement of companies, television, newspapers, museums, public libraries and other 'socializing contexts' is essential. A *national newspaper literacy day*, an American initiative, could be held up as an example.

### Educational vouchers?

The second policy instrument that is expected to strengthen the right to learn is the educational bond. The idea has been broached that all young people should be presented with an educational bond at the end of their compulsory schooling at sixteen. The bond would consist of a fixed number of vouchers which would entitle each holder to the same number of years of full-time day education, to be filled in as they choose. The personalized vouchers would remain valid indefinitely, but when they are used up, that is it. Precursors of such a voucher system exist already. We only have to think of the time limits in higher education.

Much as support must be given (with reservations) to the idea of general-proficiency schooling, so the idea of an educational bond is hopeless. The introduction of a voucher system does not lead to an enlargement but to a contraction of the opportunities for learning. Will schooling soon only be available to ticket holders? Whatever ends this regulation meets, it certainly does not serve that of lifelong learning, even leaving aside the question of practicality. Social security has proved to be beyond our reach in many ways; would educational security fare better? (Not to mention the containment of the expectations roused by the voucher system.) Should government credulity be trusted this time?

## Looking further

A government which takes the right to learn seriously cannot limit its actions to seeing to it that skills 'which are an essential foundation and form the nucleus for further development' are taught. Attention must also be given to the quality of the learning environment. For this is often the difficulty, as can be seen from research into the background and reasons for (non-)participation in educational activities. Lists of the large number of barriers to learning have been drawn up time and time again. However, we are still waiting for a plan of campaign for tackling these obstacles. Unless it is accompanied by free access to the relevant sources of learning, the right to learn is just so many words.

## CONCLUSION

The disturbing question of the future of education led an American government commission in 1983 to shake the American people awake with the report *A Nation at Risk*. The typical Dutch reaction was to conduct a 'trial investigation to establish if a periodical assessment study into the level of education in the Netherlands' was feasible. This unsentimental attitude appeals to me. But at the same time, I hope that a more creative answer will be found based on a sense of direction concerning the future of our culture and not on mourning for a lost past. An answer, moreover, which takes learning human beings and not educational institutions as its starting point.

The concept 'learning society', a society in which learning is the whole of life and the whole of life is learning, is a powerful stimulation to the formation of opinion. In this chapter I have outlined what the cornerstones of such a society could be. I realize the risks involved in working with an abstract, even Utopian, idea such as that of a learning society. On the other hand, it has to be said that it is impossible to work without a perspective – without sources of inspiration, aims, guidelines and norms.

A lack of commitment is one of the risks of the approach proposed above. Dimensions of society, growth to completeness, collective competence, self-education, right to learn – all good publishers' blurb. But what are the practical implications of this way of thinking? The values to which the notion of a learning society appeals will indeed have to be embodied in the various situations in which people can learn. This is precisely the strength of the chosen concept: it enables us to gather a variety of approaches and social initiatives together at a higher level of abstraction, beyond immediate self-interests and parochialism.

Time is of the essence. The general climate has not become more hospitable to human learning in the last twenty years. Today the criterion is the return from educational institutions and not the contribution made to stimulating potential. Training courses increasingly benefit ambitious men in senior and top functions, while the training chances for those with only elementary education, for the unemployed and for women are decreasing. The school approach to learning and teaching is gaining the whip hand. Consumerism and cafeteria-style education is encroaching on all sides. But the cause for most concern is probably that the discussion about such a crucial public issue as educational reform is being conducted by the civil service, industry and commerce and educational specialists; there are no organized counterforces. Is this the culture we want?

## NOTES

1 Here I am concerned with the organization principle, without the restrictions on contents. For a Jewish believer the sources are fixed (the Torah); he only has to dig things out. In this chapter, on the other hand, the selection of sources is under discussion.

2 As defined here, the *educational* dimension coincides with the *cultural* dimension (Zijderveld 1983) and the *moral* dimension (Etzioni 1988). Politics and the economy are examples of alternative perspectives for viewing societal processes. My position is quite close to that of Fletcher (1984).

3 The concept 'learning projects' has gained some popularity through the writings of Penland and Tough (see, for example, Penland and Mathai 1978, and Neehal and Tough 1983). But two related terms are increasingly found now: self-directed learning and independent learning. Strictly speaking, the phrase 'learning project' refers to sustained, planned and voluntarily chosen major efforts to learn something that is fairly well defined. This meaning has been eroded. The idea that people are the active agents of their own education has led to a plethora of empirical studies. Yet the findings are still very modest. Cross (1986: 199): 'So far, most pioneer researchers on self-directed learning have left what happens during the learning project virtually unexplored territory. Whether one wants to know how to facilitate learning or how to present information to adults, more in-depth study of how learning takes places in everyday settings is a necessity, one that should receive first priority in the 1980s.' Cross has put her finger on the sore spot. But more work has to be done. There is also a pressing need for clarity about the theoretical basis of this line of thought and practice.

4 The unintentional lessons which accompany taking part in training programmes and courses are a special case of spontaneous learning. Asserting yourself in a group, waiting your turn, getting used to discipline, and experiencing company culture are examples of this phenomenon. The occurrence of such side-effects, whose importance should not be underestimated, is called the 'hidden curriculum'.

5 A theoretical framework that has kinship with De Zeeuw's ideas is Donald Schön's concept of *knowing-in-action*. Schön (1987) uses this term to refer to the sorts of know-how skilled practitioners display in their judgements, decisions and other complex actions, usually without being able to state the rules or procedures they followed. The knowing is part of the action.

6 There are many other terms in circulation at the moment which denote the

polarization of ways of (thinking about) teaching. To name but a few: pedagogy versus androgogy (Knowles), the dissemination orientation versus the development orientation (Hodgson c.s.), the didactic model versus the communication model (Laurillard), the behavioural paradigm versus the normative paradigm (Pask).

## REFERENCES

Abram, I. (1984) 'Permanent leren in de joodse samenlevina' (Lifelong learning in the Jewish community), in H. Van der Zee (ed.), *Volwasseneneducatie: dilemma's en perspectieven* (Adult Education: Dilemmas and Perspectives), Meppel: Boom.

Boud, D. (ed.) (1988) *Developing Student Autonomy in Learning*, London: Kogan Page.

Cross, K. P. (1986) *Adults as Learners: Increasing Participation and Facilitating Learning*. London: Jossey-Bass.

De Zeeuw, G. (1984) 'Verborgen vaardigheden' (Hidden skills), in H. Van der Zee (ed.), *Volwasseneneducatie: dilemma's en perspectieven* (Adult Education: Dilemmas and Perspectives), Meppel: Boom.

De Zeeuw, G. (1985) Problems of increasing competence. *Systems Research*, 2(1): 13–19.

Etzioni, A. (1988) *The Moral Dimension: Toward a New Economics*, New York: The Free Press.

Fletcher, R. (1984) *Education in Society: The Promethean Fire*, Harmondsworth: Penguin.

Hirsch, E. D., Jr. (1988) *Cultural Literacy: What Every American Needs to Know*, New York: Vintage.

Holmes, M. (1988) 'The fortress monastery: the future of the common core', in I. Westbury and A. C. Purves (eds), *Cultural Literacy and the Idea of General Education*, Chicago: University of Chicago Press.

Houle, C. O. (1972) *The Design of Education*, London: Jossey-Bass.

Kidd, J. R. (1983) 'Learning and libraries: competencies for full participation', *Library Trends*, 31(4): 525–542.

Martin, W. J. (1988) 'The information society: idea or entity?', *Aslib Proceedings*, 40(11/12): 303–309.

McEwan, I. (1984) 'Een gesprek met Milan Kundera' (Talking to Milan Kundera), *De revisor*, 6: 26–32.

Neehal, J. and Tough, A. (1983) 'Fostering intentional changes among adults', *Library Trends*, 31(4): 543–553.

Nietzsche, F. (1872) *Waarheid en cultuur* (Truth and Culture), a selection from Nietzsche's early work, issued by the publishing house Boom in 1983.

Nisbet, J. and Shucksmith, J. (1986) *Learning Strategies*, London: Routledge & Kegan Paul.

Penland, P. R. and Mathai, A. (1987) *The Library as a Learning Service Center*, New York: Marcel Dekker.

Reid, L. A. (1986) *Ways of Understanding and Education*, London: Heinemann.

Resnick, L. B. (1987) 'Learning in school and out', *Educational Researcher*, 16(9): 13–20.

Roszak, T. (1986) *The Cult of Information: The Folklore of Computers and the True Art of Thinking*, New York: Pantheon.

Schön, D. A. (1987) *Educating the Reflective Practitioner: Towards a New Design for Teaching and Learning in the Professions*, London: Jossey-Bass.

Scientific Council for Government Policy (1986) *Basisvorming in het onderwijs* (Basic Forming in Education), The Hague: State Publishing House.

Smith, R. M. (1982) *Learning to Learn: Applied Theory for Adults*, Milton Keynes: Open University Press.

Zijderveld, A. C. (1983) *De culturele factor: een cultuursociologische wegwijzer* (The Cultural Factor: A Cultural/Sociological Guide), The Hague: VUGA.

# Chapter 12

# Investment

## Adding value through lifelong learning†

### *Commission on Social Justice*

We are inspired by a vision of national renewal, where everybody is engaged in creating a better society and a dynamic economy. At the heart of that vision is the extension of opportunity: the opportunity for us all to learn, to earn and to care for our families.

Equality of opportunity is often dismissed as a weak aspiration. But if every child and every adult is to fulfil his or her potential, we need a social and economic revolution. We have to create an economy that generates new jobs and businesses faster than old ones are destroyed. Instead of an inefficient and divided labour market, we need fairness and flexibility to allow men and women to combine employment, family, education and leisure in different ways at different stages of their lives. In place of the old conflict between better protection for working people and lower profits for employers, we need new social standards designed to raise the contribution which workers can make to the productivity of their organizations. Above all, we will have to transform our old education system, designed to serve an academic élite and to fail the rest, into a means for lifelong learning.

Deregulators argue that the less government does, the more opportunities there are for individuals. But opportunity does not depend only on individual effort. That is why investors argue for collective action and above all collective investment – whether it is public, private, voluntary or a partnership of all three – to promote individual opportunity. The first and most important task for government is to set in place the opportunities for children and adults to learn to their personal best. By investing in skills, we raise people's capacity to add value to the economy, to take charge of their own lives, and to contribute to their families and communities. 'Thinking for a living' is not a choice but an imperative (Marshall and Tucker 1992).

† This chapter is an edited version of a chapter from Commission on Social Justice/ Institute for Public Policy Research (1991) *Strategies for National Renewal*, London: Vintage.

## THINKING FOR A LIVING

Lifelong learning is at the heart of our vision of a better country. A good education is the most effective way to overcome inequalities of birth and status, to enable people to create and seize new opportunities, and to promote social improvement and mobility. As new technologies transform what is possible, a high level of skills, constantly updated, will increasingly be the passport to satisfying leisure as well as to a decent job. 'Empowerment' is a politician's word: but it is absolutely real to the women we met at Handsworth College in Birmingham, whose vision of what they could do with their lives had been transformed by a 'women-into-management' course.

The social benefits of learning have been central to civic life since the ancient Greeks. The *economic* centrality of education and training is also now widely accepted.[1] It is absurd to believe that economic success can buy us the 'luxury' of lifelong learning. Only lifelong learning can win us the prize of economic success.[2]

The mass-production economy did not need a well-educated mass of workers. All that was required of most employees was that they obediently followed the orders of the small group of planners and supervisors who did the thinking for everyone. But new high-performance organizations – with flat hierarchies and team-working – depend upon a high level of skill and creativity throughout their workforce. Management layers disappear as front-line workers become responsible for many of the tasks – from quality control to production scheduling – that their 'superiors' used to do.

For individuals as well as companies and countries, education and training are the foundations of economic security. The Organisation for Economic Co-operation and Development (OECD) estimates that one in ten jobs in the industrialized world will disappear every year (OECD 1994a). People starting work now can expect to change jobs and employers half a dozen times or more during their working lives, with the risk that every change could mean a move down and not up. As one 38-year-old software designer in Norwich told us: 'I'm already out of date, compared with the kids coming up behind me.' According to the USA's Labor Department, half of the skills acquired today will be out of date within three to five years. Yet only two decades ago, the average worker's skills lasted between seven and fourteen years (US Department of Labor 1989). Education and training alone cannot solve the problem of unemployment, although the bankers, Kleinwort Benson, have gone as far as to estimate that there would be one million fewer people unemployed in the UK if our standards matched the best in the OECD.[3] In the modern economy, individual security no longer stems from a job for life, but from skills that last throughout life.

Education and training are already undergoing enormous change in the UK. Some reforms are widely accepted as beneficial: the National Curriculum was long overdue, though its details are very controversial. The delegation of some financial power to schools makes sense. But some of the changes have made things worse, rather than better, notably the creeping return to selection at eleven years old, and the accumulation by central government, in the person of the Secretary of State for Education, of hundreds of new powers since 1979. Although this country is a market leader in the development of distance learning, largely thanks to the Open University, the present government has not begun to grasp the extraordinary possibility offered by modern technology – that we will be able to learn almost anything, anywhere, at any time. Assumptions about who learns, when and where need to be fundamentally rethought. Mobility between and flexibility within institutions of learning will become the rule, rather than the exception.

[. . .] But to revitalize our education system on the basis of high standards and high performance, there are six priorities that need to be highlighted.

- A universal system of pre-school education for 3- and 4-year-olds and new investment in childcare.
- An attack on the problem of inadequate basic skills.
- An end to the divide between education and training for 14- to 19-year-olds, in order to promote high achievement.
- A minimum training investment by all employers.
- Expansion of higher education, with a new and fairer system of funding.
- A 'Learning Bank' to extend to every adult the opportunity of learning throughout life.

Deregulators see investment in education and training as a burden on government coffers like any other; investors see it as an investment in people unlike any other.

## FIRST GOAL: UNIVERSAL NURSERY EDUCATION AND A NEW INVESTMENT IN CHILDCARE

We learn more and develop faster in our first five years than at any other time in our lives. If we want to be serious about investing in people, we must start at the beginning. But the investment we make in babies and young children is wholly inadequate:

- Parents' entitlement to time at home with young babies is less than in almost any other EU country: there is no statutory paternity leave, a shorter period of paid maternity leave, no parental leave, and no subsequent family leave available to either parent in emergencies (Cohen and Fraser 1991).

- Investment in education for under-fives in the UK is 4 per cent of the education budget compared to 11 per cent in Norway and 10 per cent in France.[4]
- Childcare services are scarce, fragmented and inequitable. Although 47 per cent of UK mothers of children under five go out to work, there are publicly funded daycare places for less than 1 per cent of under-fives (Cohen and Fraser 1991). Eighty-six per cent of childcare services in the UK get no funding from the public purse.[5]

This country urgently needs a coherent, comprehensive approach to the needs of under-fives and young schoolchildren. 'Daycare' has traditionally been separated from 'pre-school education', the former the responsibility of social services departments and the latter of local education authorities. The 1989 *Children Act* requires local authorities to review all their provisions for children under eight every three years, but there is no requirement to provide pre-school education and they are only required to provide daycare services for children 'in need'. This produces nursery schooling which ignores children's needs for care; publicly funded care services limited to deprived families and communities; and the development of separate and thereby often stigmatized services for children with working and non-working parents, instead of an integrated approach to the needs of children, their families and others who look after them.

## A NATIONAL STRATEGY FOR THE UNDER-FIVES

The UK needs a new strategy that simultaneously meets the needs of growing children and extends their parents' choices:[6] under-fives provision is good for children, good for parents and good for the economy and society. Although government should take the lead in developing this new strategy, it is not and cannot be the job of government to provide every service itself. Government should set targets for a wide extension of high-quality pre-school education and childcare services, and create a clear national framework of objectives and responsibilities, better training, and publicity for best practice. The UK must not go the way of the USA, where a recent large-scale study has found that more than half of under-threes are being cared for in ways that damage their development and educational potential.[7]

Because babies and very young children need continuous, individual care, consistently given by adults whom they know, the first element in any strategy must be time for parents who wish to care for children themselves. But whatever changes are made to working patterns, many parents need and will continue to need part-time or full-time childcare provision, for infants as well as older children. Some parents may need collective childcare starting immediately after maternity leave, whereas others may prefer to have children cared for individually, in their own home or in that of the carer. Such private arrangements should not exclude children and their carers from community resources; as well as effective registration and inspection procedures, all local authorities should be encouraged to do what the best already do in offering support to childminders and other carers. Good-quality nursery education, with extended care where it is needed, should be offered to three- and four-year-olds; we should also aim to extend out-of-school and holiday care for under-elevens. Collective provision of care and education should not be seen as a substitute for parenting, but as a support for it and an enrichment of children's lives.

The second step should be to build upon the review of services to under-eights which local authorities already have to make, by requiring social services and education departments to work together and with parents, community organizations, businesses and schools to draw up an effective local strategy. As a start, every local authority should be expected to develop a comprehensive information and advice service. North Tyneside Council already offers parents and employers such a service through its 'childcare shop'. Local authorities should be encouraged to develop integrated services brought together in centres that make the full range of services flexibly available to all children and carers. Manchester City Council's children's centres, for example, provide part-time and full-time day nursery care, informal parent-and-toddler sessions and out-of-school care for older children, but the council bears the £12 million cost on its own, with no help from central government.

## UNIVERSAL PRE-SCHOOL EDUCATION

Following a succession of reports from the House of Commons Select Committee on Education, Science and Arts, the Royal Society of Arts and the National Commission on Education, the support for universal education for three- and four-year-olds is overwhelming (Select Committee on Education 1989; National Commission on Education 1993; Ball 1994). Studies in several countries, including a recent one from the Republic of Ireland, have shown that early-years education has positive effects that last well beyond the primary school years and affects much more than children's academic performance (Kellaghan and Greaney 1993). At sixteen-plus, young people who have had pre-school education are more likely to undertake further education or training than those who have not, *irrespective of their measured success in school.*

In the 'High/Scope' study, the most detailed of its kind, American researchers monitored and costed the effect of pre-school education on the fortunes of children from poor African-American families in Ypsilanti, Michigan, tracking them through to twenty-nine years of age. Children who had pre-school education were considerably more likely to complete high-school or further education, three times more likely to own their own homes, four times more likely to earn a good income and five times less likely to have been in repeated trouble with the law. Every $1 invested in nursery education produced a payoff of over $7 – partly because of the savings on police, prisons and probation services, partly because of the taxes paid by those former nursery school children when they became adult earners (Schweinhart and Weikart 1993).

We endorse the target of the National Commission on Education (NCE) that the UK should aim to provide 85 per cent of three-year-olds and 95 per cent of four-year-olds with pre-school education. If we can achieve the target by the year 2000, as opposed to the target of 2005 set by the NCE, so much the better. [. . .]

## PAYING FOR CHILDCARE AND NURSERY EDUCATION

Good-quality care and education does not come cheap. The costs of near-universal provision are estimated by the NCE at £860 million (NCE 1993); the Department for Education (DFE) put the figure for doubling take-up in England among three- and four-year-olds to 90 per cent at over £1 billion per year (DFE 1993). In either case, it will take several years to achieve universal provision. So great is the importance of this investment, however, that we would make it one of the highest priorities for government investment over the next decade. [. . .]

Nursery education, like statutory schooling, should be free to parents. It is simply not feasible, however, to aim to provide all child*care* facilities, including additional care for children in nursery and primary education, free at the point of use. Where a child is being cared for outside the family, whether privately or in publicly funded facilities, charges for that care should continue for those parents who can afford them. In Australia a federal government system of daycare fee relief applies to private and community, as well as public, daycare services and has led to a rapid expansion in the number of high-quality places available. Since much UK provision is private, we should consider applying a common system to all registered services, including childminders and playgroups provided they meet nationally agreed standards. The aim would be to enable service providers to raise standards while the service remains affordable to all. Playgroups, for example, could increase the number of sessions available to each child to five per week, and offer extended days to those requiring them.

Some local authorities have already developed a sliding scale of charges, so that parents on low incomes pay nothing while those who can afford it pay a full fee. Whereas means-testing traditionally causes poverty traps for people on low incomes, this problem can be overcome if the charges start for people earning a reasonable wage. In order to avoid the problem of very different charges in different parts of the country, national government should establish an advisory fee-relief system for local authorities' use.

In developing early-years services, local authorities will also need to establish public/private funding partnerships designed to tap new resources, including subsidies from employers towards childcare places for their employees.[8] Local partnerships will also be able to apply for and receive EU structural funds, particularly in areas of industrial decline and in deprived rural communities. In some areas, the capital costs of developing a new nursery or children's centre could be partly or wholly met by 'planning gain' (where planning permission for a new development includes the building of social facilities). National government itself should also aim to increase public funding for childcare services, for instance by earmarking a budget available for local programmes which can provide models of best practice. Investment in childcare services can also provide a return to government, as well as families and children. [. . .]

## SECOND GOAL: BASIC SKILLS FOR EVERY CHILD

There is much to admire in our education system. In classrooms up and down the country, we have seen enormous commitment and high performance from teachers and pupils alike. The number of students staying on at school has risen, partly as a result of the recent recession but also because of the positive effects of new methods of teaching and learning at GCSE level and beyond. We need organizations designed to bring out the best in every individual. The crude testing of individuals initiated by the government has given attempts to assess school effectiveness a bad name, but more sensitive, 'value-added', school-based measures – designed to measure the progress pupils make – can help schools focus on their own performance, and their own success in adding value. Greater choice for parents is meaningless if there are not enough good schools, and those which are oversubscribed end up choosing which children they want to admit.

We know from detailed academic research what makes a good school: strong leadership from the headteacher, continuous staff and curriculum review, parental involvement, and a culture of high expectations, among other things (Brighouse and Tomlinson 1991). An effective, successful local school, which increases the knowledge and skills of all pupils, should be the birthright of all children. At the end of the twentieth century it is intolerable that an advanced country should have citizens with problems of basic literacy and numeracy. Yet in the UK one in five 21-year-olds has problems with basic maths, one in seven has problems with basic reading and writing (ALBSU 1993), and reading standards among 11-and 15-year-olds have not significantly improved since 1945 (Foxman et al. 1994).

Illiteracy and innumeracy are an economic disaster: young men and women with poor basic skills are more than twice as likely to be unemployed as the average, and on average they are out of work for five times longer than those who communicate well (ALBSU 1993). Men without basic skills suffer particularly from unemployment; they are twice as likely to be unemployed as women with the same problems (ALBSU 1993). Traditionally, girls have shown earlier aptitude for reading, writing and verbal communication; partly because of highly stereotyped assumptions about the proper role of women, they have also been powerfully encouraged to develop their personal skills. There is now disturbing evidence that boys are falling even further behind in schools, with six boys to every girl in special units for children with behavioural or discipline problems (Hymas and Cohen 1994).

Basic skills should be learned young, when they are most easily acquired. Given adequate educational opportunity and investment, almost all children can learn to read fluently by the age of seven and it is essential that they should do so. Because children who cannot read find it hard to learn anything else, they are more likely to be bored or disruptive, or to play truant. Government and local education authorities should therefore commit themselves to the target of ensuring that every seven-year-old can read. [. . .]

A Literacy Guarantee should be matched by a 'Numeracy Guarantee' at the same age. In both cases, intensive tuition for six- and seven-year-olds needs to be followed up by careful monitoring, and perhaps further guarantees, at eleven and fourteen, to prevent pupils slipping behind again, and to ensure that they start secondary education with the essential skills. [. . .]

We also need to tackle the problem of missing basic skills amongst adults. A good starting point would be programmes targeted at those of the long-term unemployed with basic skills problems; it would be part of the process of reconnecting this group with the labour market. It is also essential that we build on the work being done by the Adult Literacy and Basic Skills Unit (ALBSU) in the area of family literacy:

educating mothers not only enhances their life-chances, it improves the skills of their children.

In Rathcoole, Belfast, the Commission saw 'Bytes for Belfast', an innovative project housed in a youth centre and supported by the Belfast Action Team. Modelled on a similar and highly successful programme in Harlem, New York, the scheme offers disaffected young people the opportunity to apply their aptitude for video games to a wide range of sophisticated information technology programmes. In the process, they gain the skills and self-confidence they so desperately lack.

## THIRD GOAL: HIGH ACHIEVEMENT FOR EVERY YOUNG PERSON

An education system appropriate to the demands of the twenty-first century must be designed to establish a foundation of knowledge and skill for all children and to nurture the particular talents of each child.[9] But that is exactly what our system is failing to do. Only just over one in four English students attains two or more A-levels, with about 10 per cent achieving the vocational equivalent (Green and Steedman 1993), while the French government is on target to get 80 per cent of school-leavers to *baccalauréat* standard by the year 2000. Although participation rates among sixteen-year-olds are improving rapidly, the qualifications system blocks progression. Beyond the age of seventeen, fewer than half our young people are in full-time education. The talent is there, the demand is there, but both run up against the buffers of a system designed to select an élite rather than educate a majority.

The twin tracks of the English and Welsh education and training systems – academic A levels on the one hand and vocational training on the other – are both flawed. Whereas A levels are too narrow and force early specialization, the vocational track lacks intellectual rigour and economic status. In the past, graduates from the government's Youth Training Scheme have had a lower chance of getting a job than those with no qualifications at all (Unemployment Unit 1993). The government introduced General National Vocational Qualifications (GNVQs), with strong general education components, in an attempt to bring vocational training up to A-level status; but this is more a practical recognition of the problem than a remedy for it.

The division between education and training is damaging because it polarizes knowledge and skill into separate courses rather than combining them to promote understanding; it splits theory and practice when the demand from the economy and from society is that they be combined; it reduces the motivation of most young people because it condemns them to a 'silver'- and 'bronze'-level vocational education while the minority are allowed on to the prestigious academic track; and it forces a false choice between general and vocational education when it is a combination that we all need as preparation for a life of change and continuous learning. The requirement is to discover and develop the talent of every young person and deliver to them all a balance of intellectual and practical study.

The traditional approach to reform is to argue that the top third of pupils should take five subjects at A-level standard rather than two or three, and that the quality of the vocational alternative must be improved. Both steps would be helpful. But we agree with the NCE that a far more radical approach is needed. We must start where the problem starts, with the division between education and training. We must develop a unified qualifications system, broadening the A-level and vocational experience, and incorporating and replacing today's divided pattern. Its components should be organized as modular units, tailored to the pace at which individual students can learn, encouraging them to forge ahead where they are strong and consolidate in areas of weakness. Although students would be based at school or college, they could also study some work-based options.

The present system of qualifications drives our education system towards selecting a few and failing the rest. Reform of qualifications is needed to drive an integrated education and training system towards participation and progression for everyone. The details of a unified system obviously need to be worked out, though models already exist (Finegold *et al.* 1990; Royal Society 1991; NCE 1993). The aim must be to allow the diversity of talent that already exists to flourish. The basic principles we support for this country are:

- the creation in the long term of a single qualification to be awarded on graduation from secondary education – a 'British Baccalauréat' – broadening the A-level experience and providing general educational rigour for those currently in specialized vocational options;
- the development of a credit-based system of learning, so that students have a wide choice of courses;
- a review of the status of the GCSE examination at sixteen-plus; England and Wales are now the only industrialized countries except Russia with a 'school-leaving' exam at sixteen;
- a combination of continuing assessment of coursework with final assessment through exams;
- a commitment to high-status and high-quality work-based learning.

## YOUTH TRAINING

However rewarding the new programme of learning options, some young people will still decide to leave education. There are currently

270,000 sixteen- and seventeen-year-olds on Youth Training and a further 80,000 who are neither in work nor in education nor on youth training. Some of them are homeless; all of them are vulnerable to long-term unemployment and low-paid, insecure work. Raising the school-leaving age is not the way to deal with young adults sick of school.

The government has announced a 'modern apprenticeship' scheme to provide in-work training up to NVQ Level 3 for 150,000 sixteen-and seventeen-year-olds. Although new apprenticeships may have a place, especially in the short term, courses and qualifications should be integrated with mainstream education and training.

Some young adults leave school for a job. But too often their employers fail to train them in the 'learning to learn' skills that are the basis of future employment security (Courtney and McAleese 1994). We strongly agree with the CBI's Taskforce on Vocational Education and Training, which emphasized that employers should not be allowed to dodge their responsibility to provide training for young workers (CBI 1989). Part-time training, at a standard equivalent to A levels, should therefore be compulsory for all sixteen- and seventeen-year-old employees. Employers who do not provide the training themselves should fund it at a further education college. Training and Enterprise Councils (TECs) and, in Scotland, Local Enterprise Councils could provide advice, organize some training themselves and monitor employers. Because of the costs to employers, they should be allowed to pay sixteen- and seventeen-year-olds a 'training wage' at a lower rate than our proposed national minimum wage. [. . .].

## FOURTH GOAL: TRAINING FOR EVERY EMPLOYEE

This country can only achieve the productivity improvements it needs to create a high-skill, high-pay economy if employers invest in workers' skills and their ability to add value to the company. Although business spends an estimated £25 billion a year on training, according to CBI Director-General Howard Davies, our record is not impressive (Davies 1993). Nearly two-thirds of UK employers invest less than 2 per cent of payroll costs in training; three-quarters of French employers invest more than that level (CBI 1989).

Under-investment in training is one of the major weaknesses of neo-liberal economics. Companies are reluctant to train, fearing that staff in whom they have invested will be poached by competitors. The most successful market economies have taken a simple step to cure this market failure by setting minimum standards for all employers. In Germany, businesses contribute nearly 3.5 per cent of payroll towards training, employment and unemployment programmes. In France, the minimum training investment, initially 1 per cent of payroll, is now moving to 2.5 per cent. In Singapore, employers contribute 1 per cent of payroll to a national skills development fund, and Japanese companies invest the same proportion into a national employment insurance fund which provides training as well as unemployment compensation.

The last attempt by the government to tackle this problem – through a training 'levy-grant' system – was, however, bureaucratic and widely evaded, and therefore resented by the employers who did follow the rules. All firms had to pay the levy, and those carrying out satisfactory training gained rebates. Instead of this system, all but the smallest organizations should be required to invest a minimum proportion of each employee's earnings in training, and only required to pay into common funds if their training investment does not reach the specified level. The initial figure could be set at 1 per cent or 1.5 per cent of payroll, moving gradually to at least 2 per cent. Employers unable to provide that level of training themselves would be required to put the difference towards training, either through collective provision at TEC level, or through the Individual Learning Accounts of their employees set up via the Learning Bank, described below.

Training opportunities are unequally divided within firms and between them. The Institute for Fiscal Studies argues that the growth in skills differentials is primarily due to a polarization between high-pay jobs in skill-intensive plants and relatively low-pay jobs in low-skilled plants (Chennels and Van Reenan, in press). Compulsory payments into Individual Learning Accounts by firms that do not provide training will allow people to move from low-skill workplaces to high-skill ones much more easily.

Some of the UK's most far-sighted companies are investing much more than our proposed minimum in creating a learning culture at the workplace. As part of its strategy to overtake the Japanese, Rover invests £200 per employee through a separate company, Rover Learning plc, allowing employees to take up almost any course, from metalwork to French to computer science. But Rover and other employers who make the same investment are only allowed to offset the costs of *job-related* training against tax. A small but important reform would be to allow businesses to deduct all the costs of helping their employees to learn. Rover, Ford and other companies that have given employees new rights to education and training have been astonished by the take-up. We need to think of the skills of a company's workforce as an asset like any other and – as the OECD suggests – reform accountancy practice so that human capital is a recordable asset which can be considered by investors (OECD 1994b). People want to learn, our country needs them to learn, and government must help provide the opportunities for them to do so.

## FIFTH GOAL: EXPAND HIGHER EDUCATION THROUGH A FAIR FUNDING SYSTEM

British universities have always provided a world-class education for a small number of students. But the challenge for the twenty-first century is to extend these high standards to far more people. The growing number of people taking degrees is good news; the proportion of eighteen- to nineteen-year olds entering higher education rose from one in eight in 1979 to one in four in 1992. It now stands at three in ten. Many more mature students are also entering degree courses. But the present structure and funding of universities simply cannot cope. Staff are overwhelmed by a bureaucratic paperchase caused by the introduction of an internal market; they lack the critical mass of support necessary to a thriving research base; and support staff, libraries and laboratories are being squeezed. Unless we make fundamental changes, the expansion of our system will be a botched job.

The present government, which wants to see one in three eighteen- to nineteen-year olds entering higher education by the end of the century, is rationing resources through a freeze on tuition fees in order to hold down numbers. This is economic madness. The CBI, among others, argues for a target of 40 per cent by the year 2000 (CBI 1994). But if standards are to be maintained, more students must mean more resources.

But the present funding system is not only inadequate; it is grossly unfair.

- Because higher education is still dominated by students from well-off families, student grants and tuition fees for students living away from home are worth ten times as much to the richest 20 per cent of families as they are to the poorest 20 per cent (Evandrou *et al.* 1993). Financed in the main by taxpayers who never went to university and whose children do not do so either, student funding is neither fair nor efficient. As Figure 12.1 makes clear, there is a link between education and lifetime income.
- Part-time students – who include many mature students and many of those from poorer backgrounds – have no right to the free tuition which is given automatically to full-time students in higher (but not further) education.
- Because many courses – from professional law to dance – only qualify students for discretionary awards from local authorities, geography may determine whether someone can afford to learn. Across the country, local government spending on discretionary awards was 8 per cent lower in 1993/4 than three years previously, and in Inner London fell by more than a third.[10]

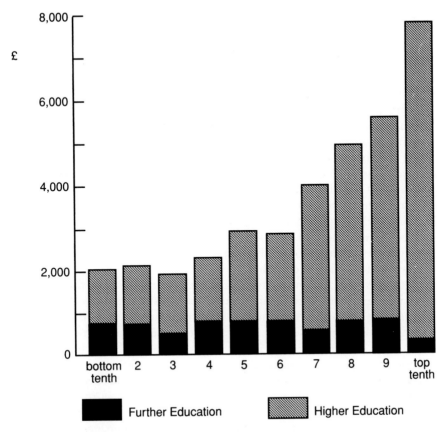

*Figure 12.1* Rich pickings: expenditure on further and higher education by decile of annualized lifetime net income
*Source:* Nick Barr, Jane Falkingham and Howard Glennerster (1994) *Funding Higher Education,* (London: BP/LSE)

- Many full-time students are extremely poor. The current combination of student loans and a grant frozen in real terms does not provide an adequate income. The removal of benefits for vacations and reduced temporary employment prospects have exacerbated the problems.

A new funding system must be created to finance the necessary expansion of higher education, maintain high standards, end student poverty and treat people fairly – and all this without breaking the bank. Like the NCE, we believe that the way forward is to ask graduates themselves to contribute towards the cost of their higher education once they have graduated and entered the labour market. Both retrospectively (in their family background) and prospectively (in terms of their potential earnings), higher education graduates are better off than the average.

Like the NCE, we support a new system of higher education contributions, sensitive to the need to ensure that people can participate in
higher education on the basis of their ability to learn, not their ability to
pay. By asking the graduates who benefit from higher earnings to make
a contribution to the cost of the investment made in them, we can offer
high standards of higher education to far more people.

There are, of course, real worries that anything other than free tuition
and full grants will discourage students from poor backgrounds. A fair
system of student contributions would, however, increase the number of
places and therefore allow far more of the people who are now excluded
to enjoy higher education. In Australia, a sensitively designed Higher
Education Contribution Scheme appears to have had no impact on
university entry rates of less affluent students (Tracey 1992). The real
barrier to the expansion of higher education in this country at the
moment is not the cost of entry but the supply of places, and raising
money from students once they have graduated from university into
employment could help cure this.

Once the principle of a student higher education contribution has
been accepted, two more detailed questions must be settled. The first is
whether the contribution should relate to maintenance, tuition fees or
both. The current obsession with maintenance support for full-time
students in higher education is in various ways misplaced: it is on the
funding of tuition that most of the money – four-fifths – is spent, and
from which the greatest inequity, between full-time university students
and the rest, stems. The present Government's policy is to ignore the
inequities in tuition funding while weaning students off maintenance
support and on to loans. But the funding of maintenance is itself a
product of the peculiar assumption in this country, much less true in
Scotland, that universities should continue the boarding tradition of
public schools. And as more and more mature and part-time students
enter the system, the proportion dependent on the full maintenance
grant will fall.

The burden of expansion in higher education will have to be borne by
people who do best out of the current system – above all, full-time
university students living away from home. Maintenance support should
be increased to take students out of poverty, but turned entirely into a
payment repayable on an income-related basis. In order to raise sufficient
funds to expand the system, we also support the proposal of the NCE
that a proportion of tuition fees – they recommended 20 per cent –
should also be paid back on an income-related basis. Decisions in this
area must also take account of developments elsewhere in Europe.

The second question is how graduates should pay back the maintenance payment and share of tuition fees. Since the new system must not
compromise the commitment to participation based on ability to benefit

rather than ability to pay, graduate contributions should be based on post-graduation income. In any of the three schemes outlined below, the higher education contribution would only last until repayment had been made; this is not a proposal for a graduate tax. There are three main options.

- A monthly payment by all who reach a certain income (under the Government's current scheme for maintenance, 85 per cent of the average income). The problem with this 'mortgage-style' loan is that repayments are high in the early years, when graduates have the least income, and smaller later when they can probably pay more.
- A surcharge on National Insurance, until the repayment has been made. Although this would mean the government recouped a higher proportion of the support given out, it would also mean graduates started to repay money while their earnings were as low as £57 per week – the level at which National Insurance is first paid.
- A rising surcharge on National Insurance which only applies to those who reach a certain earnings level, for instance starting at or above average earnings. This would remove the burden from people on below-average earnings, but would bring in less money.

The NCE estimated that once higher education contributions for maintenance and 20 per cent of tuition were fully in place, the savings to government would amount to about £1.5 billion a year. The levels of saving, impact on individuals, and overall levels of repayment will depend on which of the different repayment schemes is adopted. Piloting, modelling and costings would be necessary before deciding on the specific repayment method. Once the principle of student contibutions is accepted, detailed studies and public consultation will be required to settle the most efficient and fair option.

## SIXTH GOAL: A LEARNING BANK FOR LIFELONG LEARNING

Expansion of higher education and new opportunities for adult training (goals 5 and 4) are essential to our future. But reforms in these areas fall into the conventional mode of reforming education and training separately. Instead of starting from where we want to end up, they start from where we are now. To make a reality of the rhetoric of lifelong learning, the long-term goal must be radically to transform the funding structure of post-compulsory learning: higher education, further education and vocational training.

The key to this expansion of lifelong learning is the creation of a unified system of funding for adult education and training. Our vision is of a national *Learning Bank* which enables everybody to have access to lifelong learning. Expanding higher education is important – but lifelong learning is much broader and includes adult further education, currently the Cinderella of education and training policy. In the 20th century, a minority have always been confident that compulsory schooling would be followed by A levels and three years' higher education.[11] In the 21st century, we must make the entitlement to extended education across the life-cycle the expectation of everyone – regardless of whether or not they choose the traditional route of A levels followed by an undergraduate degree.

Our aspiration is nothing less than the creation of a learning society: and the Learning Bank would provide a framework for funding it. At the moment the Learning Bank exists only as a concept. Its organization, and the details of its funding, structure and other matters, need to be developed more fully. But the main features of the Bank would be:

- funding adult learning on an equitable basis, with no discrimination between different types of learning;
- building on a credit-based system of learning, allowing mobility and choice;
- providing the flexibility of Individual Learning Accounts to fund education and training;
- promoting partnership in the funding of learning, between the state (including the 'leveraging' of private finance), employers and individuals.

Figure 12.2 illustrates the basic concepts of the Learning Bank.

## Equity

Instead of the traditional emphasis on young academic students, the Learning Bank would be available to people throughout their lives. Instead of the present discrimination in favour of full-time education, the Learning Bank would equally help people studying part time. Instead of favouring higher over further education and vocational training, the Learning Bank would fund them all on the same basis. This would allow individuals to learn *when* appropriate to them, and in the *form* appropriate to them, without the current discrimination between a thirty-five-year-old part-time and a nineteen-year-old full-time student, and without the enormous division between funded 'academic' learning and unfunded 'vocational' training.

## Building on credits

The precondition for a new flexible funding system is a shift in the organization of learning to a modular system of credits. Courses would

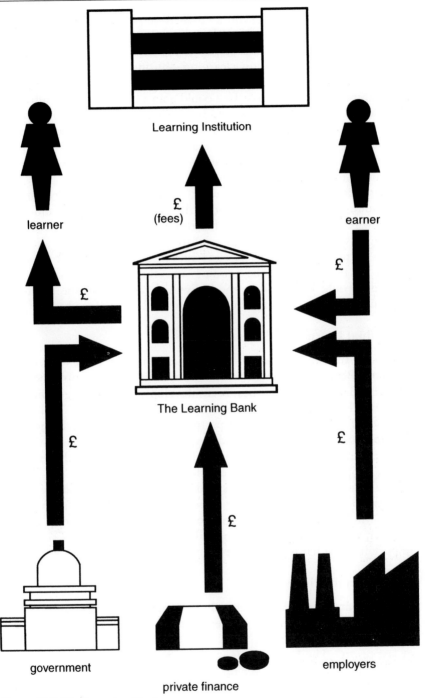

*Figure 12.2* The Learning Bank

be broken down into units and a credit framework established to cover all institutions where recognized learning takes place. The accumulation of credits by students would drive the system. The credits would form the building blocks of lifelong learning, shifting the focus from teachers to learners, from a national curriculum to an individual's curriculum. For example, a classroom assistant could gain a credit from a combination of in-work training and home study, adding to that through part-time study at the local further education college or a distance-learning course, and building up to a degree in primary education. Already, 80 per cent of universities and higher education colleges have introduced or are committed to developing credit-based courses.

These credits would create what David Robertson, Professor of Continuing Education at Liverpool John Moores University, and author of a new report for the Higher Education Quality Council, calls a 'ladder of progression' through further education, higher education and vocational learning.[12] A credit-based achievement structure of this kind would be the basis for the funding structure of the Learning Bank. Funding would be based on the individual rather than the institution, allowing people more choice in the subject and place of study.

## Individual Learning Accounts

Everyone should have an Individual Learning Account (ILA) at the Learning Bank, to which government, individuals and employers could all contribute. This idea has been developed by, among others, Sir Geoffrey Holland, Vice-Chancellor of Exeter University and former Permanent Secretary at the Department of Education.[13] Some TECs and, in Scotland, LECs are already experimenting with ILAs and credits for Training for Work. ILAs would provide enormous flexibility, by giving people control over their entitlement to learning.

The other strength of ILAs is that they would overcome the current impasse between employers, government and individuals over who should finance training, and provide a mechanism for sharing the cost between them. Investment in the national learning effort is simply too important to be left to any single party.

## Partners in funding

Government clearly has a lead role in funding education and training. But there is no reason why government should be the only source of investment in adult learning, even if the public purse has to be 'guarantor of last resort'. The Learning Bank, while wholly accountable to government, would therefore be set up separately from the Treasury, both to attract private finance and to ring-fence contributions from individuals and employers.

The Learning Bank would build on and extend the principles for funding higher education outlined in the previous section, with individual learners who go on to be successful earners putting something back into the system from which they have benefited. For those living at home, or studying part-time while in employment, or supported by their parents or a partner, maintenance may not be a problem. But adequate maintenance must be available so that people could choose to move from full-time employment to full-time education or training.

Public money could lever private money into investing in learning. In a study of income-contingent loans for higher education, Dr Nicholas Barr of the London School of Economics estimated that the overall payback from graduates would be about 80 per cent (Barr and Falkingham 1993). If this level of payback was realized for payments made by the Learning Bank, the Bank could – in theory – raise £1 billion of private sector money for every £200 million provided by the public sector, although in the early stages the Treasury would need to underwrite a higher proportion of the risk.

Of course, interest would have to be paid to investors. And the balance between affordability for students and attractiveness to private capital is a fine one. It would take detailed studies to produce reliable costings, but we are clear that the Treasury has a role – through the Learning Bank – in bridging the gap between fair interest rates for graduates and sufficiently attractive rates for investors. The use of the National Insurance system and, if possible, other EU social security systems to collect contributions would add to the Bank's financial credibility and keep its administrative costs down (fewer than 2 per cent of employees default on National Insurance).

Where employers were unable to provide the minimum training investment we proposed earlier, the balance would also be paid into the employee's Individual Learning Account. Once the Bank was established, employers could also offer payments into an employee's Individual Learning Account as part of their remuneration package, over and above general employer-provided training. An employee might choose this over membership of a private medical scheme or a company car and, unlike other perks, support for government-accredited learning could attract full tax relief.

## Setting up the system

It would clearly be impossible to offer the whole existing adult population immediate rights to the equivalent of three full-time years of education and training, even with the partial repayment system described. The new system would have to begin for a generation which turns eighteen in its first year of operation. It would, however, be desirable to extend the Learning Bank to priority groups of adults, starting with people who have been out of employment for a long time and moving on to employees without educational qualifications. One of the strengths of the Learning Bank is that it would enable government to target specific groups with entitlements to training and education.

There are a number of practical issues to be resolved in relation to the Learning Bank, in particular, the treatment of longer courses, such as Scottish or medical degrees; whether – in the long run – all post-sixteen education should be covered by the Bank, including sixth form study; what courses should be eligible for funding; how postgraduate study should be funded; and what controls on numbers would be required.[14] [...]

However, the idea behind the Learning Bank is both sound and exciting. Once fully functional, it would allow individuals, government and employers to fund lifelong learning in a way which attracts private capital, allows individual choice and flexibility, and promotes equity of access. There are of course many issues which still need to be worked out. But in the future, the Learning Bank could be sponsoring new opportunities for millions of people. The prize of a learning society would be in view.

## CONCLUSION

If an education system were improved by the number of reports written about it, British education would be the best in the world. Since the Royal Commissions of the mid-nineteenth century, august bodies have repeatedly bemoaned the failings of our education system. There are more than enough policy ideas in the education field; and some teachers and parents are sick of reforms and just want a period of stability. But the desire for continuity in children's learning should not become an excuse for condoning underperformance; and underperformance, relative to potential, marks our system today. There is no more important investment than that in our own education.

Educational improvement is a social and economic mission central to our vision of a more inclusive, productive and cohesive society. In this chapter, we have been keen to add to and build on what exists, rather than subtract and tear down. We have sought at all stages ways of lowering the barriers to high achievement, and improving the incentives for high performance. Out of the current muddle, we have sought coherence and clarity. These reforms could not be implemented over-night, but in time they would reshape our system around fundamental goals – high standards at the beginning, choice in the middle, and investment throughout. They are central to our vision of national renewal.

## NOTES

1  The German *Technische Hochschule* (Technical High Schools) were created over 100 years ago.
2  For a recent review of the literature, see Roland Sturm (1994) *How Do Education and Training Affect a Country's Economic Performance?*, Santa Monica: Rand Corporation.
3  Kleinwort Benson Securities *Economic Comment*, August 1991.
4  Report in *The Independent*, 9 December 1993.
5  Moss, P. 'Daycare and pre-school education in England: an overview', paper presented to the Institute of Education Conference 'Daycare for Under-8s in England: The Children Act', 23 November 1993.
6  A recent study showed the particular problems faced by shiftworkers – from broadcasters to factory workers – in juggling family and work responsibilities. (See Kozak, M. (1994) *Not Just Nine to Five*, London: Daycare Trust.)
7  Carnegie Corporation of New York (1994) *Starting Points: Meeting the Needs of Children*, April.
8  Many models exist and are summarized in Pugh, G. (1992) *Investing in Young Children: Costing an Education and Daycare Service*, London: National Children's Bureau, with the Association of Metropolitan Authorities and the Association of County Councils.
9  England and Wales have a similar system of secondary education. Scotland has a different – and more successful – system, whereas in Northern Ireland, the 11-plus remains in place. Although our proposals focus on the situation in England and Wales, the principles apply throughout the UK.
10  National Foundation for Educational Research survey reported in *The Guardian*, 7 June 1994.
11  Scottish degree courses are in general four years in length.
12  Robertson, D. (1994) *Choosing to Change*, London: Higher Education Quality Council. In Professor Robertson's system, 30 credits are broadly the equivalent of one year's full-time study from A level/NVQ Level 3 upwards. One hundred and fifty credits would therefore take a student through a sixth form/further education college, into university and through to an undergraduate degree.
13  Sir Geoffrey Holland, 'The challenge: making it happen', at 'University for Industry' conference, 16 June 1994.
14  The IPPR is establishing a research project to work through the details of the Learning Bank.

## REFERENCES

Adult Literacy and Basic Skills Unit (1993) *The Basic Skills of Young Adults*, London: ALBSU.
Barr, N. and Falkingham, J. (1993) *Paying for Learning*, London: LSE Welfare State Programme Paper 94.
Ball, C. Sir (1994) *Start Right: The Importance of Learning*, London: RSA.
Brighouse, T. and Tomlinson, J. (1991) *Successful Schools*, London: IPPR.
Chennels, L. and van Reenan, J. (in press) *The Rising Price of Skill: Investigating British Skill Premia in the 1980s Using Complementary Datasets*, London: Institute for Fiscal Studies.

Cohen, B. and Fraser, N. (1991) *Childcare in a Modern Welfare System*, London: IPPR.

Confederation of British Industry (1989) *Competing with the World's Best*, London: CBI.

Confederation of British Industry (1994) *Thinking Ahead: Ensuring the Expansion of Higher Education into the 21st Century*, London: CBI.

Courtney, G. and McAleese, I. (1994) *England and Wales Youth Cohort Survey: Cohort 4: Young People 17–18 Years Old in 1990*. Report on Sweep 2, London: Employment Department.

Davies, H. (1993) *A Social Market for Training*, London: Social Market Foundation.

Department for Education (1993) *The Government Expenditure Plans 1993–4, 1994–5, 1995–6*, London: HMSO.

Evandrou, M. *et al.* (1993) 'Welfare benefits in kind and income distribution', *Fiscal Studies*, February 1993.

Finegold, D. *et al.* (1990) *A British Baccalauréat: Ending the Division between Education and Training*, London: IPPR.

Foxman, D., Gorman, T. and Brooks, G. (1994) 'Standards of literacy and numeracy', in NCE, *Briefings*, London: Heinemann.

Green, A. and Steedman, H. (1993) *Education Provision, Educational Attainment and the Needs of Industry: A Research Review for Germany, France, Japan, the USA and Britain*, London: National Institute for Economic and Social Research.

Hymas, C. and Cohen, J. (1994) 'The trouble with boys', *Sunday Times*, 19 June 1994.

Kellaghan, T. and Greaney, B.J. (1993) 'The education and development of students following participation in a pre-school programme in a disadvantaged area in Dublin', Studies and Evaluation Paper No. 12, Bernard van Leer Foundation.

Marshall, R. and Tucker, M. (1992) *Thinking for a Living: Education and the Wealth of Nations*, New York: Basic Books.

National Commission on Education (1993) *Learning to Succeed*, London: Heinemann.

OECD (1994a) *Employment Outlook*, Paris: OECD.

OECD (1994b) *Jobs Study*, Paris: OECD.

Royal Society, The (1991) *Beyond GCSE*, London: Royal Society.

Schweinhart, L. and Weikart, D. (1993) *Significant Benefits: The High/Scope Perry Preschool Study through Age 27*, Michigan: High/Scope Press.

Select Committee on Education, Science and Arts (1989) *Education Provision for Under-fives*, London: HMSO.

Tracey, H. (1992) *Financing of Higher Education in Transition*, Canberra: Department of Education and Training.

Unemployment Unit (1993) *Working Brief*, Issue 42, February/March 1993.

US Department of Labor (1989) *Labor Market Problems of Older Workers*, Washington, DC: Department of Labor.

# Chapter 13

# Toward a career-resilient workforce†

*Robert H. Waterman, Jr., Judith A. Waterman and Betsy A. Collard*

People mourn its passing: the long-time covenant between employee and employer. We remember fondly the days when IBM could offer lifetime employment. And even if we didn't work for the likes of IBM, most of us understood that respectable companies would offer at least a measure of job security in exchange for adequate performance and some exhibition of loyalty. No longer. While a few prominent companies argue that the old covenant still exists, most people – and most companies – now hardened by downsizings, delayerings, right-sizings, layoffs, and restructurings, have concluded that the old covenant is null.

But what will take its place? Some management thinkers are arguing that instead of the traditional focus on *employment*, the focus should now be on *employability*. In other words, we should forget about clinging desperately to one job, one company, or one career path. What matters now is having the competitive skills required to find work when we need it, wherever we can find it.

Is that it? A workforce of loners roaming corporate halls, factories, and E-mail systems? What responsibility, if any, does a company now have to employees? Ought management be concerned only about staying lean to keep up with competition and not about acting mean? Should management be satisfied with employees whose only loyalty is to their own careers? How can an enterprise build capabilities, forget empowered teams, develop a deep understanding of its customers, and – most important – create a sense of community or common purpose unless it has a relationship with its employees based on mutual trust and caring? And how can an enterprise build such a relationship unless it commits something to employees and employees commit something to it?

The answer is by entering into a new covenant under which the employer and the employee share responsibility for maintaining – even enhancing – the individual's employability inside *and outside* the company.

† This chapter is an edited version of an article which appeared in *Harvard Business Review*, July–August, 1994.

Under the old covenant, employees entrusted major decisions affecting their careers to a parental organization. Often, the result was a dependent employee and a relatively static workforce with a set of static skills. Under the new covenant, employers give individuals the opportunity to develop greatly enhanced employability in exchange for better productivity and some degree of commitment to company purpose and community for as long as the employee works there. It is the employee's responsibility to manage his or her own career. It is the company's responsibility to provide employees with the tools, the open environment, and the opportunities for assessing and developing their skills. And it is the responsibility of managers at all levels to show that they care about their employees whether or not they stay with the company. The result is a group of self-reliant workers – or a *career-resilient workforce* – and a company that can thrive in an era in which the skills needed to remain competitive are changing at a dizzying pace.

By a career-resilient workforce, we mean a group of employees who not only are dedicated to the idea of continuous learning but also stand ready to reinvent themselves to keep pace with change; who take responsibility for their own career management; and, last but not least, who are committed to the company's success. For each individual, this means staying knowledgeable about market trends and understanding the skills and behaviours the company will need down the road. It means being aware of one's own skills – of one's strengths and weaknesses – and having a plan for enhancing one's performance and long-term employability. It means having the willingness and ability to respond quickly and flexibly to changing business needs. And it means moving on when a win–win relationship is no longer possible.

A workforce that is constantly benchmarking and updating its skills is one that not only responds to change but anticipates it. Competitiveness – keeping close to customers, staying on top of technology and market trends, and striving to be ever more flexible – becomes everyone's responsibility, not that of just a handful of executives. All employees become involved in shaping the company's strategy, in shifting the company's collective eyes from navels to market forces. By looking out for themselves, employees look out for the company.

Sound far-fetched? Some companies are already moving in this direction. Not surprisingly, many of them are located in Silicon Valley, where the struggle to cope with the ever-faster pace of change has long been a way of life. These pioneers include Apple Computer; Sun Microsystems, the workstation manufacturer; Raychem Corporation, a manufacturer of specialized industrial products; and 3Com Corporation, a maker of computer-networking products. These companies are in various stages of implementing programmes to create a career-resilient workforce. While their approaches may differ, they share a common aim: to give employees the power to assess, hone, redirect and expand their skills so that they stay competitive in the job market. In return, they expect employees to make a bigger contribution to the company. 'Companies must shift from using and then harvesting employees to constantly renewing employees,' says Robert J. Saldich, president and CEO of Raychem and an ardent proponent of the new covenant.

This approach requires a sea change in attitudes and values. First, the traditional definition of loyalty must go. Companies can no longer take the view that talented employees who jump ship are betraying them. Nor can individuals take the view that they have been betrayed when a company no longer needs their skills. On the other hand, employees must feel like valued, trusted, and respected members of the corporate community while they are a part of it.

Second, the usual view of a career path must change. In the old days, it pretty much meant sticking with one company and rising in one specialty area. These days, both companies and employees are healthier if employees have multiple skills, if they can move easily across functional boundaries, if they are comfortable switching back and forth between regular duties and special projects, and if they feel comfortable moving on when the right fit within one company can no longer be found.

Third, all employees – not just bosses – must be much more aware that the purpose of the organization is to provide goods and services that customers value, and that if the organization does not do that, nobody in it will have a job. The corollary is that the organization has room only for people who contribute to creating such goods and services.

Fourth, a new relationship must be established between the organization and its employees. The traditional parent–child relationship must give way to an adult–adult relationship, and this applies to the organization's way of dealing with all employees, not just those on the fast track. Assignments that provide an opportunity to grow and to acquire new skills should be available to everyone.

Over the long run, companies have a lot to gain from encouraging career resilience. But there is also an immediate reason to adopt this approach: employees are beginning to demand it, say corporate leaders. People are angry these days when they find that they lack the skills needed to get another job. People are angry when their employers break the old covenant and offer nothing to take its place.

Awareness of that anger, plus an obsession with creating a 'nimble organization' and a fervent belief in treating employees as respectworthy adults, prompted Sun to establish its career-resilience programme in 1991. Like many Silicon Valley companies, Sun was in the midst of rethinking its businesses, reorganizing its manufacturing operations, and re-examining the make-up of its workforce. The result was little change in the overall number of employees but a big change in the composition of the workforce. While Sun added hundreds of sales representatives, it 'redeployed' hundreds of manufacturing employees. That meant that their jobs were being phased out and they had to find other jobs in the company, if they could, or accept a severance package, which was what most had to do.

'We became convinced that we had a responsibility to put employees back in control of their lives,' says Marianne F. Jackson, who was a human resources director at Sun when she came up with the idea for the career-resilience programme. Jackson, who is now at another high-tech company, believes that organizations that replace the old covenant with one based on career resilience will have a dramatic edge. We do too. They will have an edge in attracting and retaining the best people. And they will have an edge in the struggle to develop the capabilities needed to compete tomorrow.

Today the handful of pioneering companies with career-resilience programmes are still feeling their way forward, learning what works and what doesn't. But from the progress they've made so far, we can discern some basic ingredients all programmes should include and some pitfalls to avoid.

## THE BASICS OF CAREER RESILIENCE

One ingredient of a successful programme is a system that helps employees regularly assess their skills, interests, values, and temperaments so that they can figure out the type of job for which they are best suited. Another is a system that enables employees to benchmark their skills on a regular basis. These systems help employees understand both themselves and the work to be done so well that, ideally, they routinely find their way into the right jobs and routinely update their skills. These systems help prod, awaken, and galvanize so that square pegs and round pegs find their way into the right holes. Imagine how productivity would soar if most people had jobs that turned them on!

By self-assessment, we mean a systematic process of taking stock of those attributes that influence one's effectiveness, success, and happiness. Unless individuals understand the environments that let them shine, the interests that ignite them, and the skills that help them excel, how can they choose a company or job where they can make their greatest contribution? Unless they understand how their personal style affects others, how can they function with maximum effectiveness? Knowing yourself is the first step toward becoming career resilient. [. . .]

Companies certainly can encourage employees to assess themselves and can help them by providing the necessary tools. For some, self-assessment can be as simple as digesting a career-development book like

Richard Nelson Bolles's *What Color Is Your Parachute?* or articulating their strengths and the value they can bring to a job. But most people will profit from a more thorough process. This may include tests – or 'assessment instruments', as career-development professionals call them – designed to reveal an individual's motivations and interests [. . .].

As we mentioned, the second step in the process of becoming career resilient is ensuring that one has competitive skills. Companies need to give employees the tools to benchmark their skills and experience with what the job market inside and outside the company is demanding.

We are not saying that a company should relinquish its right to judge what skills it needs in its workforce in order to be competitive, and what training that involves. What we are saying is that, *in addition*, all employees should have the right to demand the training and challenging work experiences they need to update their skills. They have a right to minimize the risk of winding up stuck in a dead-end or vulnerable job. In other words, employers and employees should be partners in the continuous process of benchmarking and updating skills.

## THE COMPANY'S OBLIGATIONS

To enable employees to benchmark their skills, companies will have to be much more open with them than most have traditionally been. Management must maintain a continuing dialogue about the company's business direction and what is happening in its markets. How else can employees determine which skills the company will need down the road? How else can they decide whether they want to develop those skills – or prepare to leave? Managers have an obligation to give employees as much time as possible to prepare for the future. Sun's management has promised workers that when it comes to strategic decisions that affect jobs or careers (like outsourcing a function), 'as soon as we've decided something, you'll know'.

At 3Com, most departments hold weekly discussion sessions on the status of the business and its implications. Those sessions helped most of the forty people in the MIS department who supported 3Com's computer network to make the transition smoothly when 3Com changed the network operating system in April from 3+Open to Netware and Lotus Notes. They had long known that such a change was in the offing, that it would require them to get new skills or leave, and that the company would give them the time and resources to obtain the new skills. 'The large majority were excited about making the change and getting the new skills,' says Debra Engel, a 3Com vice-president whose responsibilities include MIS and human resources. 'Only a few departed – those who didn't want to make the change or didn't feel they could.'

A company must help people explore job opportunities, facilitate lifelong learning and job movement, and, if it comes to that, support no-fault exits. Raychem, for example, has created an insiders' network of more than 360 people throughout the organization who are willing to take the time to talk with any employee who wants to learn about the nature of their work and the requirements of their jobs. Their names and backgrounds are in a computerized database called IIINsiders (for Internal Information Interview Network). Apple lets people sample jobs by filling in for those taking the sabbatical that is available to all employees.

Most of the companies we studied make information on job openings inside and outside the organization available to all employees. In addition, they provide reference materials and training to help employees develop plans for professional growth and hone their résumé-writing and interviewing skills. They also bring in experts to speak about market trends. Such support, which can be made available at a 'career centre' or through a computer network connecting the company's operations, is essential. It not only helps employees find new jobs inside or, if need be, outside the organization but also enables them to benchmark their skills.

Companies and individuals often fail to realize that benchmarking without self-assessment may cause an employee to make the wrong choices. The experiences of an electrical engineer at a progressive high-tech company that lacked a bona fide career-resilience programme demonstrate why. Through benchmarking, the engineer learned that the road to modest riches lay in project management. He took that road and was successful. But at the end of his typical twelve-hour day as a project leader, he was completely stressed out. At home all he wanted to do was to curl up in a corner and read. 'When I got home, I just didn't want to be with people,' he says, adding that this situation certainly didn't help his marriage, which ended in divorce.

The problem was this: by nature he was something of a perfectionist who enjoyed working alone. Constantly having to work with others was simply not a good fit. He finally realized this after working as a project leader for six years and decided to go back to straight engineering. But he'd been away from it for so long that he needed to go back to school to catch up. His company fully supported his move; it even paid the tuition. The engineer is now much happier, and, at least in this instance, a company was able to keep a valued employee.

Besides facilitating self-assessment and benchmarking, a company must make it easy for employees to learn and to become flexible. Workers should have the right to obtain ongoing training. Managers must be receptive to lateral transfers and even to employees' taking a step back to broaden their experience or to be happier and more productive. Indeed, an employee should have the right to switch jobs within the company, provided there is a need and he or she readily qualifies to fill it. An employee's manager should not have the power to block such a move unilaterally.

If an employee is not qualified for a desired job, then the company and the employee should jointly try to make the necessary training available. In some instances, the employee might take an in-house course on company time. In others, the company might help to pay for courses at a college or vocational school that the employee takes during his or her personal time.

For most companies, supporting each employee's need for lifelong learning will entail a greater commitment of time and resources to education. Raychem's Saldich passionately believes that it's not enough for an organization's leaders to make more resources available; they must campaign to get employees to use them. 'I started out saying to people throughout Raychem that it's now okay to spend more time, money, and energy on learning,' Saldich says. 'After a year of that, I realized that saying it's okay is not good enough. Our philosophy now is that learning is mandatory and that every one of our people should have a learning or development plan.'

Leaders elsewhere seem to agree. Executives from Motorola, who estimate that the company reaps a return of $33 for each dollar it spends on education, think that at least 5 per cent of each employee's time should be spent on training or education. In his book *The Age of Unreason*, published in 1989, Charles Handy says that 20 per cent is reasonable for managers. The 'correct' percentage isn't important. (How do you measure it accurately? What about the value of special assignments that are both training and real work?) The point is that continuous learning is imperative, and the organization must be seen by its employees as committed to their development.

But employees must be aware that a shift in the company's direction may mean that the company, for justifiable reasons, suddenly will no longer need their skills. Similarly, people who decide to leave the organization should be able to depart with their heads held high. 'The new covenant is about empowering people so they have job choices when circumstances change,' says 3Com's Engel. 'That's a lot healthier than the traditional blame relationship.' Last and far from least among the company's obligations is to provide for no-fault exits.

Whether a departure is voluntary or involuntary, the company must support the affected employee in managing his or her transition. Kenneth M. Alvares, vice-president for human resources at Sun Microsystems, puts it this way: 'Companies ought to be able to figure out a way to manage all aspects of an employee's career with class or dignity. We do a great job of recruiting people. We also ought to do an equally great job of helping them to manage their careers while they're here. And when people find out it's time to leave this organization, we ought to handle that process with as much class as we do the recruiting process.' Alvares does not just mean providing employees with the resources to make and implement a decision to leave. He also means continuing to treat them as valuable people. A company might even emphasize to departing employees that they will be welcomed back should their return serve the company's and their interests in the future.

## CONTROLLING THE RISKS

Creating a career-resilient workforce in the manner we have described is obviously easier said than done. 'How can a company realistically give employees much greater freedom to demand new jobs and training?' sceptical managers will undoubtedly ask. 'Won't it result in chaos? Isn't there a big danger that it will undermine productivity rather than increase it? Isn't it absurd to think that a company can put the career interests of an individual employee ahead of, say, getting a key product under development to market? And the notion of an insiders' network that will enable people to explore new jobs or careers might sound dandy, but how can we expect already overworked people to spend endless hours talking about what they do with employees in search of themselves?'

All those risks are real. But the short answer is that tomorrow's managers may have no choice. In this age of mobility, companies face even greater dangers if they do not commit themselves to developing self-reliant workers. They risk losing talented people who decide that the drawbacks of staying at such a company outweigh the rewards. This is already a big problem, managers tell us.

Consider the following story, which is replayed every day at scores of Silicon Valley companies. A gifted software engineer is an important member of a team that is developing a major new release of a workstation company's operating system. The engineer, who has been at the company for eight years, has worked on three previous releases and feels stale. In hunting around for a new challenge that will allow her to expand her skills, she discovers an opening in the division that is working on a decoder that the company hopes will give it a foothold in the emerging interactive TV market.

The head of the division says he'd be thrilled to have her. But the manager of the release project doesn't want to let her go. Her departure will only make it more difficult for the team to meet its ambitious deadline. While interactive TV may be the big market of the future, there won't *be* a future if the workstation business continues to lose ground, he tells her. A month later, the engineer quits to join a start-up that is developing software for interactive TV. When the company's president learns about her departure, he is dismayed. 'I would have overridden the project manager,' he says. 'If only I had known.'

There is another element of our model that we know can make executives nervous: sharing sensitive information with employees. For example, conventional wisdom holds that a company has much to lose and little to gain by telling employees as soon as it has decided to exit a business or shut down an operation. The assumption is that morale and productivity will suffer, people will abandon ship, and the performance of the operation will quickly deteriorate, hurting the company and reducing the operation's value to a potential buyer.

But executives at companies such as Sun, Apple, and 3Com don't think there is a choice. By not sharing such information, a company perpetuates the traditional parent–child relationship with employees, which is no longer tenable, they say. Companies that do share information say that employees have appreciated being treated as adults and have responded in kind. That is what happened with 3Com's buildings-management function, which the company outsourced last year.

In 1992, when 3Com decided to analyze whether it should outsource the function, the company immediately informed the unit's 35 employees. 3Com told them that the decision would take about nine months to make, invited their input, and promised to give them monthly updates. The company also said that if it did decide to go with outside vendors, the employees would have two weeks to decide whether to take two months' severance pay or a temporary position that would tide them over until they found another job inside or outside 3Com. Most of the employees stayed until the end and took the severance pay. But even the few who didn't stick it out kept 3Com informed of their plans so that the company had time to figure out how to manage without them. 'It is no coincidence that we were very open with them and they were very open with us,' Engel says.

Once organizations accept the inevitability of change, there are systems they can put in place to minimize the risks involved in adopting career-resilience programmes. At 3Com, for example, when an employee deemed critical by his or her current manager requests a transfer to an available job, the transfer cannot be denied but the date of the transfer can be negotiated. 'If managers resist,' says Engel, 'they're reminded, "You'd find an answer if that employee quit tomorrow." There's always an answer.'

Raychem and Apple have devised a way to prevent their information networks from consuming much of the time of valuable, overworked employees. They ask people throughout the company to volunteer to give informational interviews. When someone signs up, he or she agrees to do a certain number. Afterward, the person has the option of doing a certain number more or dropping out.

In fact, managers themselves have a lot to gain by participating in such networks. Informational networking enables them to get a look at a broader set of people than they otherwise would in the normal course of their work. As they form task forces or look for people to fill vacant slots, they have more potential candidates. And this process can help their organization achieve something that is increasingly hard to do in this era of churning workforces: build a sense of community.

## GAINING CREDIBILITY

Unless employees are convinced that a career-resilience programme truly is there to serve their interests, they simply won't participate in it. Establishing a career-management centre helps a programme gain credibility. Sun, Raychem, and Apple have set up such centres as havens where employees can go to work on self-assessment, receive counselling, and attend seminars on, say, how to conduct an effective job interview or how to network. They are places where employees can obtain career reference materials, check on internal and external job openings, contribute to discussions on business strategy, and, most important, learn how to think strategically about their own careers.

The centre's location is very important. By making it highly visible and easily accessible, the company sends the message that it is not only acceptable but desirable for employees to use it. The opposite message may be sent by locating it off the beaten track. Raychem and Sun are considering opening satellite centres for employees at other operations who cannot easily use the companies' single centres. Another idea is mobile centres that can serve several sites.

Sun and Apple also use their centres for outplacement. But before doing so, companies should carefully consider the trade-offs, according to several executives. The advantages are that the skills and resources needed for career development and outplacement overlap, and that the dual role makes the centre easier to justify financially.

The disadvantage is that, especially in the beginning, employees might infer that the career-resilience programme is an outplacement programme in disguise – and misinterpret the message when management encourages them to use the centre. For that reason, Raychem does not use its centre, which opened in September 1993, for outplacement; its sole mission is to enhance career resilience.

To allay employees' initial fears, several companies urge managers to encourage their employees to use the centre, but they make it clear that managers do not have the right to know if they have gone there, let alone what happened. Also, to assure employees that the purpose of the programme is to help them manage their careers and not to help their superiors manage them, these companies believe that the career-management process must be separate from the regular performance-appraisal process.

The human dimension is perhaps the most crucial element of any career-resilience programme. It is hard to imagine a successful programme without counsellors and career-research specialists to add a personal touch. Without them, many employees will not be able to use the information effectively; many probably won't even bother to try. Sun, Raychem, and Apple seem to understand that. At their centres, as soon as people walk in, they encounter specialists whose job is to teach them how to use the facilities.

But employees have to believe that the counsellor represents their interests. Confidentiality is an obvious concern for people thinking about changing jobs or employers. It is difficult but not impossible for a staff counsellor to gain an employee's trust. But as one manager who uses outside career counsellors puts it, 'Employees often believe that the human resources department represents management's interests, not theirs.' Use of outside career counsellors can help convince employees that the programme really is there to serve them.

There is another advantage to the use of outside counsellors: it can be more cost-effective. Several pioneers in developing career-resilient workers have taken this course.

Sun, Apple, and Raychem have turned to the Career Action Center, a non-profit organization in Palo Alto, California. Formed in the early 1970s to provide career advice to women in Silicon Valley, the centre has become a major institution in the area, serving thousands of Silicon Valley workers. Whilst Sun's, Apple's, and Raychem's career centres are headed by their own employees, the staffs include career-research specialists and counsellors from the Career Action Center. The mix of insiders and outsiders makes a powerful combination: the insiders know the company's culture, networks, and operations, and the outsiders bring special expertise, objectivity, and cost flexibility.

Taking the idea of partnership a step further, several mid-size Silicon Valley companies led by 3Com are studying the idea of forming a consortium to provide career-resilience services to all their employees. There are several reasons why this idea appeals to them. One is that the consortium could afford to provide more services than each company could on its own. A second is that the companies could learn from one another. Finally, an operation relatively immune to the politics and financial ups and downs of any one company might be better able to serve its customers: the employees. The flip side is that it might be harder to integrate such a shared centre into each company's mainstream operations.

Some companies, most notably Apple, are using technology to make career-resilience programmes widely available and part of the mainstream. Apple is placing large amounts of career information on its 'electronic campus', the computer network that ties together its operations. By strolling the right digital paths on the campus, individuals can find a 'resource and referral' section that includes lists of books, professional associations, conferences, courses, articles, and other information that Apple employees recommend to their co-workers.

The big advantage of an electronic network over a career centre is, of course, accessibility. All employees in Apple's far-flung global operations will have equal access to career-related information. Moreover, computer systems are private, available at the convenience of the user, and easy to update. The danger is that companies and people will become so absorbed by the technology that they will lose sight of the importance of the human dimension. Computer networks may be a superior way to make data widely available. But for individuals trying to remain employable and for executives trying to keep the organization competitive, the patterns and analysis that give meaning to the data are the most valuable tools. And it usually takes personal interactions for them to emerge.

## SUPPORT FROM THE TOP

It almost goes without saying that a career-resilience programme won't even get off the ground without visible support from the top. Without the backing of top management, it is implausible to think that managers down the ranks will consistently share with employees their knowledge about strategy and market conditions so that employees can anticipate the company's needs and make career decisions. Nor is it plausible to assume that most managers will automatically buy into the notion that employees should be the eyes and ears of the company, that all employees can and should help shape strategy. There is still too much tradition to be overcome.

Among the companies we studied, Raychem stands out in terms of top management's visible commitment. At the opening ceremony for the career centre Harry O. Postlewait, the company's executive vice-president, spoke, and he made sure the audience knew that the CEO, Bob Saldich, would have been there, too, had he not been at home in bed with the flu. Several senior executives, including Saldich, are in the database of people who volunteered to be interviewed by anyone in the company seeking career information.

Saldich and other senior Raychem executives seem to realize that to cultivate a sense of community in a company, management must show that it genuinely cares about its people – even those who have left. That is why Raychem's policy is to try to find places inside the company for those in dead-end jobs or in need of development, to use outplacement only as the last resort, and to tell talented people who leave that they will be welcomed back if possible. This type of caring approach is the only way an organization can get employees to believe that its fate is their responsibility, not just that of top management. It's a new basis for loyalty in today's transient world. Potentially it's a great competitive advantage.

But for a company to reap the full benefits of a career-resilience programme, the programme must be consistent with and supported by the other elements of the company's business and human resources strategies. There must be systems to support the approach – like a pay system that rewards flexibility, not position in the hierarchy, and flexible work arrangements so that employees have time to improve their skills.

Contrast Raychem with another company we know of that has attracted a lot of naturally self-reliant people. Its top management has yet to prove that it is genuinely committed to helping employees become career resilient, however. While the company generously supports education and training, many of its employees feel that top management doesn't really care whether they stay or leave. And top management gets poor grades on keeping employees informed about the company's business direction and enlisting them in shaping strategy. No wonder employees, when surveyed, cited career development as their main concern.

At some companies, the conviction that helping employees become career resilient should be a top priority still seems largely confined to the human resources department. That's a good start. But the responsibility for building a career-resilient workforce is too important to be relegated to any one department over the long run. That is why the early converts must include top management – so that the conversion process will continue down the tanks until everyone in the company is a believer. This is the approach that has been taken at Raychem. Its human resources department, the original champion, sees itself as a partner with operating management in the effort to create a company-wide career-resilience programme.

Of course, we realize that many operating managers are lamenting that their jobs are already impossible. On the one hand, the manager is supposed to be the coach, the coordinator, the conductor, and the team leader who supports, advises, and cheers on others so *they* can carry out the task. On the other hand, the manager is still the one held accountable for the final results. 'How can you heap even more contradictions and uncertainty on us?' some have said in reaction to our ideas.

The answer is that this is an age of perhaps unprecedented uncertainty. Those managers who excel at juggling all the contradictions and uncertainties – who figure out how to harness the potentially awesome power of today's mobile workforce – will be the ones whose organizations will prevail in the marketplace.

On a less lofty level, managers have much to gain personally for two reasons. First, the career-resilience approach gives them a way to deal with an increasingly common phenomenon: the employee who is extremely distressed about his or her job – because the job is vulnerable, because it is no longer challenging, or because it offers no advancement opportunities. Second, career resilience is for managers too! Understanding themselves will help them be more effective managers. And by understanding themselves and benchmarking their own skills, managers – like all workers – will be better equipped to manage their own careers.

More than ever, the manager is responsible for creating an environment in which all employees have opportunities to develop so they do not hit a dead end, so their skills remain competitive. This means three things: keeping employees fully informed about the direction of the business; helping each employee understand that the responsibility for ensuring that he or she has competitive skills is ultimately the employee's; and abiding by the employee's right to be a free agent.

The switch from career dependence to career resilience is not only imperative but also inevitable. The company that recognizes this sea change and rides the waves has a huge strategic advantage. Such a company can be swift without being ruthless. It can encourage people to grow, to change, and to learn, and in doing so it becomes better at those things itself. Career resilience replaces a covenant we can no longer keep with one that is in everyone's best interest.

# Chapter 14

# Who really benefits from employee development schemes?

*John Payne*

## THREE EXAMPLES OF EMPLOYEE DEVELOPMENT

Employee development (ED) is the term used to describe training and education initiatives in the workplace which focus on the personal development of employees. They may include elements of job-related training but are typified by their broad approach to the education and training requirements of employees.[1] The employer almost invariably foots the bill for ED, but there are wide variations in organization. Most ED takes place in employees' own time, but some takes place within working time; most ED is organized by management alone, but trade unions (TUs) will be seen to play a key role in each of the schemes described in this chapter. Two characteristics which distinguish ED from job-specific employer training are that employees take part on a purely voluntary basis, and that development is seen as a process over time rather than the typical one-off company training session.

### Ford Employee Development and Assistance Programme

I want to begin by describing briefly the Employee Development and Assistance Programme (EDAP) run by the Ford Motor Company (UK). Ford employs 30,000 workers on twenty-two sites in the UK, the main plants being those at Halewood (Merseyside) and Dagenham (east London). The early history of ED is in a number of schemes set up in the USA in the early 1980s. These were joint initiatives between the management of Ford and the United Auto Workers (UAW) in response to industrial restructuring in the US car industry, and included both employees and 'displaced' (i.e. redundant) workers (Toronto 1993: 21–22). The commitment to develop an equivalent scheme in the UK was included in the 1987 pay-bargaining round at Ford. From 1989 it has developed as a leader in ED activities in the UK, with a remarkably high rate of participation – 34 per cent of all employees in 1991/2. Characteristics of the scheme include:

- the high percentage of EDAP participants not previously involved in continuing education. Moore (1991) puts this figure at 70 per cent;
- the inclusion of health-related activities as a major part of the programme. Metcalf (1992) gives this figure as 18 per cent of participants;
- the insistence that activities *must not* be 'work-related'. The 'Top Ten' courses are Bricklaying, Computer Literacy, German, French, Spanish, craft courses, academic subjects, Music, BTEC courses and Art. Leisure courses are encouraged as ways of returning to learning for adults with unsatisfactory previous experience of education and training;
- the employment of Local Education Advisers who are independent of Ford management and who promote the scheme within the company and offer educational guidance and counselling to employees;
- the involvement of TUs in monitoring the scheme at a local level, through the Local Joint Programme Committees;
- a balance between courses held on site and those held off site (43:57 per cent in 1991/2). On-site courses are particularly successful in meeting the requirements of shift-workers who have traditionally found it very difficult to participate in such 'normal' adult education activities as evening classes;
- courses are taken in the employee's own time, but fees and costs are paid up to £200 per employee for off-site courses while on-site courses are provided free of charge.

The introduction of the Ford/EDAP scheme has coincided with a remarkable transformation in industrial relations at Ford. A company once notorious for confrontational industrial relations now loses very little time through industrial action. Is this because of Ford/EDAP or is Ford/EDAP an outcome of improved industrial relations? This question is impossible to answer, particularly as there has been no external, objective evaluation of Ford/EDAP, but must certainly be placed in the context of legislation which has curtailed the power and influence of TUs by the use of continuing high rates of unemployment by successive Conservative governments (1979–present) to discipline the labour force. But while it would be naive to ascribe to ED magic powers to revolutionize industrial relations, it would be equally misguided to ignore the enthusiasm which the success of EDAP has produced in management, unions, employees and adult educators. Although such schemes do little for part-time workers in the peripheral labour force (McGivney 1994), many adult educators recognize their success in reaching out to groups who have often been reluctant to participate in adult education – unskilled and semi-skilled manual workers.

One final point that needs to be made in relation to Ford/EDAP is that while its success has encouraged other large manufacturing firms, such as Lucas, Rover, Peugeot, to develop ED schemes, it is not an effective role-model for all employers. The reaction of smaller firms is often that such schemes are 'all right for the Fords of this world, but what about us?'. The Leeds Report on ED (Forrester *et al.* 1993a: 41) referred to research findings that:

> At the end of 1989, 95% of UK businesses employed fewer than 20 people, and accounted for 35% of employment outside central and local government,

and argued that public support was necessary if small and medium-sized employers (SMEs) were to be able to emulate the success of larger firms.

## BAXI Partnerships

Baxi Partnerships manufactures central heating boilers and other heating appliances at three neighbouring sites in Bamber Bridge (Preston) in Lancashire. Since 1983, all shares have been held in trust on behalf of employees and a profit-sharing scheme is run.[2] As the ED organizers note:

> The Partnership Council looks after the interests of the shareholders and is in great demand from other companies both in the UK, Europe and eastern Europe for guidance and advice on employee participation and ownership schemes.
>
> (Baxi Heating 1993: 69)

In 1993 there were 1,050 employees. The firm is unionized, and the TUs have played an active role in promoting ED. Indeed, it was TU contact with Workbase,[3] a north London-based non-profit consultancy specializing in basic skills work with less skilled and manual workers which first introduced the idea of non-job-specific training (now referred to by the less cumbersome title of ED!) to the firm in 1989.

The development of the ED programme was based on partnership between management, unions, Workbase and Runshaw College (the local Further Education college). It is significant that in attempting to implant a 'learning culture in the firm', particular emphasis was placed on those employees – semi-skilled in the main – who had had least access to education and training in the past. Lack of opportunity and low self-esteem and self-confidence were identified as major barriers to development (including promotion) for this group (Baxi Heating 1993: 70). The ED was concentrated on an Open Learning Centre set up within one of the plants. Unlike Ford/EDAP, where employees are expected to study in their own time, release at Baxi is on the basis of 50 per cent employee time and 50 per cent employer time. Educational facilities within the Open Learning Centre cover individual educational guidance and counselling, group tuition and self-study.

Basic skills is interpreted in a broad way to include not just English and Maths but also modern European languages and Information Technology. This covered approximately 150 employees in 1993. Further, the Open Learning scheme is now seen as part of a wide strategic approach to education and training which includes job-specific training, the accreditation of prior learning, and a voucher scheme which allows employees to enrol on both vocational and non-vocational courses within the Runshaw College Adult Education programme within their own time (130 employees in 1992/93).

TU representatives are active in monitoring the scheme and bringing problems to the attention of management. There are both formal and informal ways of bringing pressure on managers and team-leaders who are more reluctant than others to release workers for study in the Open Learning centre in working time. Cultural change can thus be seen not just in terms of modifying the attitudes and behaviour of shop-floor workers, but also those of supervisory management.

Two important issues implicit in Ford/EDAP arise in an explicit form in the case of Baxi Partnerships. They are introduced here within the specific context of one employer, and referred to more generically later in the chapter.

*Learning and new working methods*

The year 1990 saw the introduction at Baxi of a flatter management structure, team-working and Total Quality Management (TQM). ED is integral to the success of new working methods:

> To maintain our competitive advantage and remain market leader, we need to develop our existing staff in order to meet these demands. As our turnover is practically nil, for professional and shop floor staff, we cannot rely on new entrants coming straight from school or college and being armed with the necessary skills. The company therefore feels that the responsibility for training and retraining its Partners rests with the company. The long-term objective is to have an educated and adaptable workforce and to create a learning environment in which basic skills education is just the beginning. Having rediscovered the joy of learning and the satisfaction of knowing that one is not just a pair of hands and thereby boosting confidence, encourages our employees to take up other training opportunities, both vocational and non-vocational.

*Learning and participation*

Learning is seen within Baxi as not just related to quantitative ('bottom-line') issues of profitability, but as being related to the quality of working life – the partnership organizational form of the company:

> The development of workplace education is perceived by the Company as being an essential part of its Partnership culture – the employees "own" the business and therefore have a right to be able to contribute their best to it.
>
> (Baxi Heating 1993: 71)

Although this might suggest that the Baxi experience is of limited currency, it nevertheless reflects an important trend within the conventional, for-profit sector towards participative forms of management and the concept of social partnership in general use in a number of European Union (EU) countries.

## Humberside County Council

Humberside County Council is responsible for a wide range of public services on both sides of the Humber (the 'Yorkshire' and 'Lincolnshire' sides). It includes the major ports of Hull and Grimsby as well as widely scattered rural communities. As in many parts of the country, the County Council is a major employer throughout the area.

ED in Humberside County Council appears at first sight to operate in a rather different way from the two cases referred to above. This is partly because its most public face relates to an older debate around 'Paid Educational Leave' (PEL) which flourished (or rather flickered) in various western European countries in the 1970s and 1980s.[4] The Humberside PEL course is a two-year day-release course based at the University of Hull which began, in 1989, for low-paid manual and clerical workers with few if any educational qualifications. There is a strong emphasis in the early stages on study skills, but later stages of the course take on more specific academic content: Industrial Relations; Local Government; Employment Law; Politics and Sociology. Most students take (and pass!) the University Certificate of Extension Studies, which potentially gives them access to university undergraduate courses. Students are selected to achieve a proportion of women : men similar to that in the council as a whole (3:1), and balance across departments, north and south of the River Humber, union and non-union. Since more apply than there are places (18 each year), final 'selection' is random, with unsuccessful applicants being given priority the following year.

However, 'PEL' is only the tip of the iceberg or the icing on the cake of ED on Humberside. The County Council also supports employees to

ED + OL ?are they for the lower social
classes what about professionals ??

226   The learning society

attend Basic Education skills classes (up to ten in their work-time, others in their own time) and operates an Open Door scheme which pays fees and other costs for employees to study work-related (but not job-specific) subjects in their own time.[5] This can include confidence building, assertiveness or returning to study. One hundred and sixty-five grants were taken up in 1992/93 with a further sixty applicants unsuccessful because of budget restraints being given priority for 1993/94. All these initiatives are coordinated at corporate level.

Just as private sector schemes are subject to unpredictable shifts in market conditions for the firm's products, or decisions on relocation, redundancy and so on, so public sector schemes are also subject to external forces. The probable abolition of Humberside County Council by the government places large question-marks over whether current ED arrangements will continue. It is also important to recognize that such a loss will not be evenly distributed within the workforce, because of the integration of ED with the Council's Equal Opportunities policies. This involves not only a stress on the development of manual workers but also a specific concern for women employees. Most of the workforce is female, but as in most organizations the proportion of women decreases in more senior positions. Thus, the various initiatives mentioned above need to be seen in the context of positive action to improve the position of women within the authority, and within the broader context of equal opportunities policies. This explains the importance of the extension of opportunities to clerical workers, by definition non-manual, who often earn less than manual male employees. Women clerical workers may have done relatively well in compulsory education but, having traditionally looked at employment in terms of a 'job' rather than a 'career', seldom have much in the way of post-compulsory education and training. Positive action reflects social change and the greater aspirations of women, but also helps create motivation among women employees.

If we now return to the wider field of ED and look for evidence of equal opportunities within schemes, the outlook is not good. One of the more depressing findings of the Leeds University team (Forrester *et al.* 1993a: 25) was that only 25 per cent of employers prioritized unskilled workers against 39 per cent prioritizing management: many respondents simply failed to respond to a questionnaire item on priorities. Humberside County Council was the only employer visited by the researchers which was immediately able to provide figures detailing participation rates for men and women. The absence of such information was normally justified by the notion that ED was 'for everyone', which ignores the widely different experiences of education and training for women and men, for different social classes, and for black and ethnic minority employees.

## EMPLOYEE DEVELOPMENT AND TRADE UNIONS

Of the ED schemes outlined above two (Ford/EDAP and Baxi) have substantial trade union involvement. This is not the case with most ED schemes, and indeed the Leeds University researchers saw the development of policy and practice on ED as an urgent priority for unions (Forrester *et al.* 1993b). Where unions are not actively involved, there is usually, though not necessarily, a lower level of participation than was identified at Ford and Baxi. In one firm, which is written up in the literature as a successful example of ED, the Leeds researchers found at the time of their visit that only one shop-floor worker was studying under the scheme. Unions may also actively oppose an ED scheme which they identify as contrary to their interests. We shall see later how closely ED is identified by the new demand for 'flexibility' in the workforce. In practice this can mean changes in working practices which threaten:

- job demarcations and the interests of highly unionized skilled workers;
- the sense of security of individual workers who perceive any change as being change for the worse, even where it may be intended to enrich jobs;
- the jobs themselves, through redeployment and redundancy.

Additionally, these same changes bring hard-pressed union branches and shop-stewards plenty of negotiating work without going out to look for more.

Trades unions are generally sympathetic towards ED but nevertheless are not actively promoting ED schemes at a local level. Personal development tends to be seen as something of a side-issue compared with formulating demands for a deeper involvement in industrial training matters. However, at a national level, the Trades Union Congress (TUC) and several large unions issued well-developed policy statements shortly before the 1992 general election, which placed personal development alongside improved vocational education and training (VET) as legitimate union demands. There has also been increasing trades union involvement with local Training and Enterprise Councils (TECs), including a joint project between the TUC Education Department and South London Training and Enterprise Council (SOLOTEC) in 1992/93 aimed at placing training much higher up the agenda of trades unions (Sherriff 1993).

The motives underlying the reluctance of management to concede management prerogative on any kind of training are complex (Forrester *et al.* 1995). Even the willingness of Ford to concede joint control over EDAP is balanced by its insistence on management prerogative over the actual training budget which is, of course, very much larger than the

EDAP budget. In part, management prerogative is simply a straightforward reflection of other aspects of management ideology, in which workers are viewed as a cost, and organized labour as a device for increasing labour costs. Yet it was clear from interviews conducted by the Leeds researchers (Forrester *et al.* 1993a: 27) that ED was deeply associated in management minds with the notion of Human Resource Development (HRD), which represents a strong progressive tendency within management practice. HRD sees labour as an investment and its development as a priority to increase productivity, competitiveness and so forth. It might therefore be expected that union involvement would be welcomed as a way of stimulating education and training at the grassroots, especially as evidence from both the Leeds study and an earlier Labour Research Department (1990) study suggests that union involvement in both training and ED leads to greater rates of participation. It is a similar logic which has led managers in other EU countries to adopt a social partnership approach to vocational education and training (VET).

If the predominant EU version of HRD represents an incorporation of organized labour, initially expressed in the Social Chapter of the Maastricht Treaty, the UK version enshrined in the UK Government's opt-out from the Social Chapter represents a clear attempt to marginalize organized labour. Whereas those UK employers who are reluctant to concede management prerogative over VET see their approach legitimated by their government's attitude, those who are prepared to concede an element of jointism can produce the EU to vindicate their position. For the former group, ED can be seen as an integral part of the thrust of HRD to open direct lines of communication with the workforce, sideline the unions and increase management control over the labour force. However, there is no particular evidence that this strategy is likely to succeed, in contrast to the clear evidence produced by employers, such as Ford and Baxi, of the crucial role played by unions in developing and sustaining ED schemes.

## POST-FORDISM: THE ARGUMENT OVER 'FLEXIBILITY' AND 'MULTI-SKILLING'

In the absence of any single in-depth evaluative study of the relationship between ED and innovations in production methods, this section will be brief and at a high level of generality. This is not to say that it is unimportant, since it has a clear bearing on the reluctance we observed in the previous section both of employers to concede management prerogative over developments in this field, and of unions to commit time and effort to their implementation.

Post-Fordism represents a new stage in production in advanced industrialized countries (Wood 1989). The term is used to represent the shift from mass-production methods characterized by semi-skilled work on a production line to multi-skilled employees working in teams to produce a diversified range of products.[6] Murray has summarized these new working methods as involving

> a core of multiskilled workers whose tasks include not only manufacture and maintenance, but the improvement of the products and processes under their control ... In Post-Fordism, the worker is designed to act as a computer as well as a machine.
>
> (Murray 1991: 63)

It follows that the value of an employee to an employer is incremental as the employee gathers experience and skills. It also follows that the ability and attitudes necessary to acquire new skills, with the knowledge and understanding that underpin skills, are just as important as the possession of a specific skill at a particular moment.

In international terms, the new economic arrangements involve the concentration of sophisticated production and services with high value-added in the core of industrialized countries, and the use of peripheral low-wage economies for routine production. This new division of labour is paralleled within the industrialized countries by a fracture between a core of full-time, well-qualified employees with access to continuing education and training, and a periphery of part-time or fixed-term employees with few rights and low wages merging into the twilight world of permanent unemployment and the informal economy. Within and beyond the peripheral labour force, women, black people and those with disabilities are over-represented in proportion to their share of the total population.

The ambivalence of trade unionists to workplace education and training reflects a deeper ambivalence in the world of work. The words flexibility and multi-skilling both have positive connotations for workers, yet in practice can imply job intensification linked to a narrow view of skills based on the concept of competence and the questionable assumptions of functional analysis. In this scenario, employees can be moved from one job to another at will, and are expected to turn their hands to an ever wider range of low-skilled tasks. In other words, flexibility can mean job intensification and multi-skilling comes to stand for multi-tasking.

However, these developments are not intrinsic to post-Fordism as a way of organizing production. The identification of these terms as new forms of controlling the work-force is a product of the fact that profit and capital accumulation, rather than the production of socially useful goods and services, are seen as the ultimate rationale for economic activity. Further, both positive and negative evaluations of post-Fordism rest on the assumption that individual employers correspond to a capitalist ideal type. In practice, employers (both private and public) recognize that treating core employees as an investment rather than a cost has advantages for both employee and employer, as we saw earlier. In the same way, most employees would rather be busy than have time hang heavy on their hands, would rather have a variety of activities rather than one monotonous task, and would rather receive narrow training than no training at all.

What is certainly the case is that flexibility and multi-skilling have both contributed to the massive decrease in recent times of the core labour force that large firms employ. Handy (1989: 73) mentions that as early as 1982–85, General Electric in the USA cut its labour force by 25 per cent from 400,000 to 300,000, with an increase in turnover. The Leeds team quote the example of a bulk steel-maker which produced 3.35m tons in 1995 with 4,700 employees, where in 1980 23,500 employees had produced 2.2m tons (Forrester *et al.* 1993a: 34). Indeed, the Leeds team surveyed a number of large firms employing together 1m employees in 1991; by 1992 that figure had shrunk to 800,000. This was only in part due to economic recession. A major cause was changing production methods linked to the introduction of information technology at all levels. Traditional tasks, the workers who performed them and the skills they used have all become redundant. It is this fact that those who look for an upturn in the economy to 'solve' unemployment ignore: it is not going to happen.

## WHO BENEFITS? EMPLOYEE DEVELOPMENT AND PUBLIC POLICY

The question of who benefits from ED schemes can be answered in different ways according to the context within which it is framed. It is a matter, in C. Wright Mills' phrase, of using the 'sociological imagination'[7] to see how employees' experience of ED relates to both the possibilities and limitations of ED: its ability to transform the lives of individual workers or even individual workplaces but its inability to transform social and economic structures which sustain and legitimate inequalities of opportunity and outcome. In the empirical evidence quoted below, we shall see social actors striving to come to terms with the world outside the immediate control of self (Giddens 1987: 221). Clearly, it is through a process of self-development that such an awareness grows. It is also clear that such knowledge and understanding is more likely to be obtained via programmes of broadly based education than by job-specific training (however essential that may be for limited day-to-day purposes within an enterprise). Where job-specific training has a present perspective, ED has a future perspective. Individual life in late modern society has, characteristically, to be lived in present and future simultaneously.

It is axiomatic that the chief factor that influences adults' participation in adult education is previous successful experience of education and training (Courtney 1992). Thus a crucial question that must be answered is whether this pattern is reproduced or transformed by ED. The answer is both! On the one hand, participant adults will take advantage of ED schemes to obtain employer support for courses which they would probably have attended in any case, although it must be stated that at a time of increasing fee levels, some at least have been able to continue with studies who might otherwise have opted out. Yet as we saw earlier, where employers are prepared to establish some kind of priority within schemes, very different kinds of employees are enabled to take part in education, often for the first time since leaving school. This is clearly the case at Baxi, with its emphasis on basic skills, at Lucas where the Continuing Education and Training (CET) scheme includes an innovative 'return to learn' provision and in the Humberside PEL scheme which targets manual and clerical workers with few if any educational qualifications.

One major group who stand to gain from ED are shift-workers. This explains more than anything the success of Ford/EDAP in attracting manual workers and also the substantial proportion of courses taking place on Ford premises to fit in with shift work. At Baxi, employees work 10–6 and 2–10 week on, week off, and can change shifts one day per week to allow attendance. Fully flexible working helps to make this possible. A team leader interviewed by the Leeds researchers admitted it took a lot of juggling to make it work, but since he was also involved in a sponsored evening class, he had a clear interest in making it work! It is practical questions of this sort, as well as attitudes of managers and shop-floor workers, which can produce a 'learning culture' in a workplace. A plant operator in a chemicals firm studying for a supervisory qualification through open learning found the three-shift system worked in his favour:

> I must admit, people who've been doing the course who've worked days have found it a lot harder than I have working shifts, actually getting the time to do it, 'cos they finish work at 4 o'clock, they find it difficult to get started on a night [ = in the evening], where being on shifts I could do a couple of hours in the afternoon or in the morning before I came to work. So they had trouble fitting it in. But having the time that I had, I got ahead rather quickly (. . .) It's one of the benefits of working shifts (. . .) I find it hard to adapt to days. (Plant Operator, chemicals firm)

Employees participating in ED schemes are almost embarrassingly grateful for the educational opportunities they are receiving. The question of women and confidence-building is a key example. Women are especially likely to have succumbed to pressures to leave school early or not continue school after the minimum leaving age. For some employees, confidence building has a direct impact on their ability to do their job:

> The course has given me the confidence to ask questions at work. (Woman Home Care Assistant, City Council)

> Before (. . .) I'd just sit and get on with my work. I mean, I give opinions now. (. . .) And obviously for the company's sake, if I am more confident, I'm working a lot better (. . .) I get involved a lot more now, whereas probably before I'd just come in and do the job. Now I want to get involved, I want to see things happening. (Woman clerical worker, chemicals firm)

Some men also lack confidence in themselves and their abilities, and identify confidence-building as a gain from participation in ED:

> Confidence with people, to do the job. You're picking up some of your shortcomings, like my spelling. If I'm writing reports, it'll be done better, you know, and I'm constantly writing reports, incidents in the hostel at night, I've got to leave for management in the morning. (Man hostel assistant, City Council Housing Department)

In each of these three cases, confidence is socially enacted through a sense of changed social relations with other people in the workplace. But in a wider sense it is intimately connected with people's self-esteem and sense of what is possible in all spheres of their lives:

> Speaking personally, it makes you realize that you're probably capable of doing more than what you have done. I mean, coming here, I don't say we necessarily think of ourselves as being thick or anything like that, but you come here and you realize probably you've got a bit more going for you than what you thought you had. (Man library caretaker, County Council)

Changes in the economy are linked to generational issues. Many of the workers who take part in ED schemes grew up (as did the author) in the 1950s and 1960s when jobs were plentiful. Qualifications were not thought essential. As one interviewee put it:

> I was one of those that left school when there were jobs round, so it didn't really matter (. . .) Qualifications on paper didn't matter so you just wanted to get out and go to work and earn some money, and there were jobs around. (Assembly worker, manufacturing firm)

It is precisely the point at which sociological theory and personal experience meet that such an employee is most 'at risk' as technologies change. Restarting education begins the process of individual employees adjusting to a world which is no longer the one they grew up in. They may live in the same town, their children may go to the school they themselves went to, they may meet old school-friends at the bus-stop, in the doctor's surgery, at the local pub, but the forces that mould that society into particular shapes at particular times are omnipresent in their lives. In the world of late modernity, the repositioning of individuals, groups and whole societies, and the role of education and training within those processes, are crucial. Personal development can be experienced as an insurance policy in an uncertain world: 'You never know, do you?' (Operative in a manufacturing firm studying Car Maintenance).

For some employees, the uncertain future confronts them directly in the form of redundancy. At a food manufacturing firm in Lancashire, education and training were provided for 400 workers due to lose their jobs because of plant closure. They were provided with guidance, a job search skills course and a communications skills course in the firm's time, and courses in Catering, Caring and Computing at the factory on Friday afternoons but in their own time. Additionally they could enrol on courses at the local college and have their fees paid. Jean Hewitt (real name), a machinist, sums up some of the possibilities and obstacles in the way of personal development:

> While many people took advantage of the courses, others held the attitude that they were a waste of time or they lacked the confidence to try them . . . At one time the Friday afternoon classes clashed with the overtime and it was difficult for people to choose between the two . . . The result of all this activity for me, is that I have gained confidence, learnt new skills, learnt to deal new situations and now the future holds more promise than it did two years ago . . . I think that on shop floors all over Britain there are workers who have talents that lie dormant because they are not given the opportunity to find out what their capabilities are.
>
> (Hewitt 1992: 8)

Redundancy impacts particularly on less skilled workers and those who experience problems with basic skills.[8] The choice for the future may not be between low-paid work requiring few skills and higher-paid work requiring more advanced skills. It is more likely to be between paid work and long-term unemployment.

At the heart of ED lies an enormous social problem. Those in the labour market, however dull their jobs or poor their pay and conditions, are almost always better off than those excluded from the labour market. In arguing for the growth of workplace ED schemes which support the ongoing, future-oriented personal development of employees, I am also arguing for an extension of the rights of all citizens to access to education and training throughout their lives. Thus employer support for those in employment must be matched by public support for those excluded (for whatever reason) from the labour market. In both cases, those with least skills and qualifications should represent a clear priority in public policy development.

## NOTES

1 For a longer discussion of the definition of ED, the reader is referred to Metcalf (1992: I: 3) and Forrester *et al.* (1993a: 3).
2 For further details, see Baxi Heating (1993). The ED scheme is summarized in Metcalf (1992: I:4). There is also considerable material on Baxi in Frank and Hamilton (1993) and by Baxi employees in Frank (1992).
3 The history and perspectives of Workbase are outlined in Bonnerjea (1987).
4 The interested reader is referred especially to Mace and Yarnit (1987).
5 Lucas Continuing Education and Training (CET) employ a similar definition of CET. The contrast with Ford/EDAP should be noted, although in practice there are broad similarities between the range of courses studied.
6 This section summarizes material in chapter 3 of Forrester *et al.* (1995). For a more detailed discussion the reader is referred to Wood (1989).
7 'The sociological imagination enables its possessor to understand the larger historical scene in terms of its meaning for the inner life and the external career of a variety of individuals' (Mills 1959: 5).
8 The most accurate estimate of this problem is the 13 per cent of adults who had experienced problems with English and/or Maths either at home or at work; see Hamilton (1987).

## REFERENCES

Baxi Heating (1993) 'Employee development in Baxi Heating', in K. Forrester, J. Payne and K. Ward (eds), *Developing a Learning Workforce. An International Conference*. Conference Proceedings, Leeds: University of Leeds Department of Adult Continuing Education, 67–73.
Bonnerjea, L. (1987) *Workbase: Trades Union Education and Skills Project*, London: ALBSU/Workbase.
Courtney, S. (1992) *Why Adults Learn: Towards a Theory of Participation in Adult Education*, London and New York: Routledge.
Forrester, K., Payne, J. and Ward, K. (1993a) *Adult Learners at Work*, Final research report, Leeds: University of Leeds Department of Adult Continuing Education.
Forrester, K., Payne, J. and Ward, K. (1993b) *Learning in the Workplace. A Report for Trade Unions on Employee Development Schemes*, Leeds: University of Leeds Department of Adult Continuing Education.
Forrester, K., Payne, J. and Ward, K. (1995) *Workplace Learning: Perspectives on Education, Training and Work*, Aldershot: Avebury. (Provisional title.)
Frank, F. (ed.) (1992) *Not Just a Number. Writings about Workplace Learning*, Lancaster: Lancaster University Centre for the Study of Education and Training.
Frank and Hamilton (1993)

Giddens, A. (1987) *Social Theory and Modern Sociology*. Cambridge: Polity Press.

Hamilton, M. (1987) *Literacy, Numeracy and Adults. Evidence from the National Child Development Study*, London: ALBSU.

Handy, C. (1989) *The Age of Unreason*, London: Business Books.

Hewitt, J. (1992) 'A chance to work', in F. Frank (ed.) *Not Just a Number. Writings about Workplace Learning*, Lancaster: Lancaster University Centre for the Study of Education and Training, 8.

Labour Research Department (1990) 'Training', *Bargaining Report*, January 1990.

Mace, J. and Yarnit, M. (eds) (1987) *Time Off to Learn: Paid Educational Leave and Low Paid Workers*, London: Methuen.

McGivney, V. (1994) *Wasted Potential: Training and Career Progression for Part-time and Temporary Workers*, Leicester: NIACE.

Metcalf, H. (1992) *Releasing Potential: Company Initiatives to Develop People at Work*, Sheffield: Employment Department, two volumes.

Mills, C. W. (1959) *The Sociological Imagination*, New York: Oxford University Press.

Moore, R. (1991) *Employee Development and Assistance Programme (EDAP)*, TURU occasional paper No. 101. Oxford: Trade Union Research Unit.

Murray, R. (1991) 'Fordism and post-Fordism', in G. Esland (ed.), *Education, Training and Employment*. Vol. 1: *Educated Labour – The Changing Basis of Industrial Demand* Wokingham: Addison-Wesley/Open University, 57–69.

Sherriff, C. (1993) *Working in Partnership for Quality Training*, London: TUC.

Toronto, R. (1993) 'The UAW–Ford Life/Education Planning program: an eight-year perspective', in K. Forrester, J. Payne and K. Ward (eds), *Developing a Learning Workforce. An International Conference*. Conference Proceedings, Leeds: University of Leeds Department of Adult Continuing Education, 19–31.

Wood, S. (1989) 'The transformation of work?', in S. Wood (ed.), *The Transformation of Work? Skill, Flexibility and the Labour Market*, London: Unwin Hyman.

# Chapter 15

# The idea of the university in the 21st century
## A British perspective†

*Peter Scott*

## INTRODUCTION

The university as an institution has escaped restriction by the university as an idea. If it had not been able freely to adapt to succeeding socio-economic orders, to radical shifts in science and intellectual culture, it would have long ago passed into history. That it has not done so, that in the late twentieth century the university remains a powerful and pervasive institutional form, not just in the West but throughout the world, is a tribute not so much to its transcendent virtue but its ceaseless adaptation. So, attempts to impose some over-arching idea, or principle, that describes the university can be dangerous. Either they are irrelevant, failing to capture the historically determined diversity of university practice; or, if successful, they limit the university's capacity to adapt and survive.

Fortunately therefore, most attempts have failed. John Henry Newman's (1976, originally published 1853) classic account, *The Idea of a University*, was an attempt to define an ideal type which he did not recognize in the booming universities of Victorian Britain. These, he argued, were mere professional schools, producing provincial lawyers, doctors and schoolteachers, their embryonic research efforts determined by the technological demands of industrial society rather than by any ideal conception of knowledge itself. His university would eschew professional training and research. No such university could have survived in the circumstances of the nineteenth century; nor under the conditions of the twentieth. High-minded reference to Newman may have been incorporated into the universities' rhetorical tradition, but his project was rejected.

More recent attempts to provide the university with a fundamental text, an authoritative constitution, have encountered similar difficulties.

---

† This chapter is an edited version of an article which appeared in the *British Journal of Educational Studies*, (1993), 1: 14–25.

Each has been a prisoner of its own time and categories. Ortega y Gasset's (1946) effort to place the (unproven) civilizing effects of the university at the centre of its mission, re-echoing both Newman's concerns and the preoccupations of American educators, such as Hutchins between the wars, did at least recognize that some response was needed to the collapse of European civilization in the mid-twentieth century, in which the university was implicated.

But Karl Jaspers' own *The Idea of a University*, published ninety years after Newman's, was a careful restatement, and so deliberate rehabilitation, of the Humboldtian ideals which had inspired German universities at their 19th-century climax (Jaspers 1963, originally published 1946). Despite world war, despite revolution, despite the Holocaust, no correction was required, although historians have argued that the passivity of the German universities in the face of the Nazi challenge demonstrated the infirmity of these philosophical ideals. Universities seemed to have been betrayed by their high-minded ideals more than by their practical engagement. [. . .]

## EUROPE AND AMERICA

Philosophical incantation about the mission of the university has fallen out of fashion — certainly in Europe. America's rhetorical public culture, commitment to moral educability, deep distress caused by student revolt and more radical transformation of post-secondary education, have all stimulated a lively tradition of writing about first principles. Motives have been various. Clark Kerr was preoccupied by the phenomenon that in Europe would be labelled massification (Kerr 1963); Edward Shils by threats to the integrity of both the university and the scientific tradition (Shils 1989, 1992).

But there has been little echo of this in Europe. Certainly, Allan Bloom's (1987) notorious *The Closing of the American Mind*, a best-seller in the United States, failed to have a similar impact in this country. Instead, the Newman tradition, entailing exploration of the university's fundamental values, has been absorbed into four different kinds of literature. First is the literature of reminiscence, rectors, vice-chancellors and other university leaders reflecting on their experience; or, in the case of the influential conservative thinker, Michael Oakeshott, the literature of regret (Oakeshott 1989). Not all this literature has been retrospective, of course. Both Asa Briggs and Albert Sloman in his notable Reith lectures attempted to articulate a distinctive philosophy for the new universities established in the 1960s and, by implication, to influence the direction and ethos of the wider university system. [. . .]

Second is a literature of policy-making and public administration. In Britain the most famous example is the Robbins Report (Robbins 1963), which managed to be both philosophical (in a common-sensical English way), so continuing the Newman tradition, and practical because it tackled real political issues. A succession of White Papers, policy documents and other public reports in Britain has been written in the spirit of Robbins, although to increasingly degenerate effect. During the 1980s public agencies took a more active role in stimulating debate about the future of higher education. At first the initiative lay with the newly established National Advisory Body for Public Sector Higher Education (NAB) because of the need to articulate a mission for the polytechnics and colleges of higher education distinct from that of the universities and of further education out of which these institutions had emerged (NAB 1984). Even the University Grants Committee (UGC), once the most private of public bodies, engaged in a wide-ranging consultation exercise on future prospects for the universities (UGC 1984).

Third is the literature of policy studies. To the extent that there has been fundamental thinking about university aims in recent years in Britain it has been refracted through discussions of the structure of the system and the management and funding of institutions. A good example was the two-year Leverhulme Inquiry into the future of higher education in the early 1980s (Society for Research into Higher Education, 1981–83). But, although a final report was produced, no grand vision emerged from the process (Shattock 1983). This set the pragmatic, even technocratic, tone for subsequent policy research in Britain (with the possible exception of pamphleteering by the right-wing think-tanks which flourished during the Thatcher years). In the rest of Europe a similar pattern prevailed, although the Studies of Higher Education and Research programme initiated by the Swedish National Board for Universities and Colleges was certainly an exception. In it broader intellectual themes were explored alongside more familiar managerial topics (Björklund 1991).

Fourth is the literature of broader social and cultural analysis. In it higher education features as the producer of cultural capital, engaged in the formation of national, professional and technical élites, the agent of modernity and in similarly theorized forms. There are important examples of such macro-analyses relevant to the purposes of universities in the United States too, which can be set alongside the tradition of rhetorical incantation. A serious example is Daniel Bell's work; both his major books, *The Coming of Post-Industrial Society* (Bell 1973) and *The Cultural Contradictions of Capitalism* (Bell 1976) speak to these broader themes. And Talcott Parsons took the American university as the theoretical focus of one of the best-known expositions of his functionalist theories (Parsons and Platt 1973).

But this literature has perhaps developed more sophisticated forms in Europe, often under the influence of Marxism (whether for or against).

Jürgen Habermas has written specifically about the place of universities in the culture of modernity and the process of modernization (Habermas 1987, 1990), whereas knowledge institutions play a key role in Anthony Giddens' theories of globalization (Giddens 1990). Margaret Archer's account of the origins of educational systems also covered universities, although from a broad sociological perspective (Archer 1979). But the detailed aims of universities, as understood in the rhetorical tradition that stretches back to Newman, do not figure in these broad social and cultural analyses, although a recent attempt has been made to apply Habermas' theories to a rewriting of these aims (Barnett 1991).

## EXPANSION AND TRANSFORMATION

The idea of the university, therefore, must be explored in different terms in Europe, both more empirical and more intellectual than the rhetorical discourse familiar in the United States. This chapter will try to build up to the idea of the university by considering both the external and internal dynamics that are shaping the system. In Britain this approach is unavoidable. For higher education the present moment is as decisive as that of Robbins a generation ago. In the past decade expansion has been rapid. Between 1980–81 and 1989–90, despite a dip following the severe budget cuts imposed by the UGC in 1981, the number of full-time students in universities increased by 17 per cent, from 306,000 to 357,000. The growth of full-time student numbers in polytechnics and colleges was even more impressive during the 1980s; they increased by 47 per cent from 228,000 to 339,000 over the same period. Since then expansion has accelerated.

Across the system as a whole the equivalent of 20 average-sized institutions has been added since the end of the 1970s. [...] This expansion has been accompanied by a radical transformation of the system. The binary system has been abandoned – and with it the idea that, within higher education, the 'open' tradition inherited from further education and represented by the polytechnics and colleges and the 'academic' tradition, represented by the universities, should be kept distinct. The number of universities has been almost doubled at a stroke by the 'promotion' of the polytechnics.

The Universities Funding Council (the UGC's successor) and the Polytechnics and Colleges Funding Council (which followed the NAB) have been abolished in turn and replaced by a single Higher Education Funding Council for England. At the same time separate funding councils have been established for Scotland and Wales, creating a much stronger regional, or sub-national, dimension in the organization of higher education. The funding of teaching and research have been separated, the former being determined by student head-counts and the latter by assessment exercises. The effects on the mixed academic economy typical of British higher education are likely to be profound as institutions and departments within them are pushed either in the direction of mass teaching or of research excellence.

All these phenomena [. . .] will transform the character of higher education in Britain and so possible definitions of the university in the 21st century. Yet they are taking place without serious consideration [. . .] Consequently there is no choice but to discuss the idea of the university in pragmatic terms. The approach of this chapter therefore, is the opposite of that generally taken by investigations of this topic. Its aim is not to impose from above a generalized theory about the 21st-century university, but to build up the idea of the university from the bottom, by considering, first, the environments – demographic, socio-economic and intellectual – in which higher education finds itself and, secondly, its likely response to these new challenges. Out of higher education's detailed accommodation to these new environments and, more broadly, the synergy between the socio-economic and academic systems, it may then be possible to construct an 'idea of the university' that is rooted in practice but has normative force.

## THE 21ST-CENTURY ENVIRONMENT

The idea of a university hard-wired into wealth creation is among the most pervasive ideas of the late twentieth century. At times this seems to have become the university's primary justification, as a key player in a post-industrial economy where knowledge itself is the primary resource. For others the near-market university is a more ambiguous phenomenon. Higher education, they fear, will become the servant of those who define 'wealth' and oversee its 'creation'; and these key players are still more likely to be found outside than inside the academic system.

However, it seems to be common ground that a qualitative change is taking place in the relationship between the academic system and the socio-economic order. But universities have always been profoundly functional institutions. Most, whatever their formal antiquity, grew up alongside the industrial revolution in the nineteenth century. The former polytechnics and colleges, of course, were deliberately designed to meet the demand for intermediate and high skills. Nor can the importance of the war-time alliance between science and the state, which produced the tight-knit networks between Oxbridge and Whitehall that dominated the political culture of mid-twentieth-century Britain, be exaggerated. In the 1960s a direct link between higher education expansion and economic growth was routinely assumed. [. . .]

The case for arguing that in the past two decades the rules of this engagement have been radically rewritten rests on the credibility of those all-too-familiar accounts of 21st-century society. Theories of post-industrial society, the new information age, the fourth industrial revolution, the super-symbolic economy and similar catch-phrases, of course, are commonplace. The most impressive account of these trends remains Daniel Bell's *The Coming of Post-Industrial Society* (Bell 1973), published a generation ago, but similar (and derivative?) interpretations have proliferated since. They all place greater emphasis on the production of knowledge, which appears to reinforce the centrality of higher education, the ultimate source of many of the new processes that power the modern economy – as it is, too, of the new ideas and intellectual structures which shape our understanding of the modern world.

But this impression of post-industrial hegemony has to be qualified in four crucial respects. First, most of these accounts place as much emphasis on consumption as on production – and so, more fundamentally, on instinct as on reason. [. . .] In late capitalist society advanced information systems offer unprecedented opportunities for social control and economic standardization; in that sense its capacity for constraint is greatly enhanced. Yet its reliance on mass markets in consumer goods, which materially represent life chances, demands a sensitivity to individual choice which has the opposite effect – of increasing its potential for emancipation (Berman 1982).

Post-industrialism is more than simply a pervasive version of an already familiar industrial society of large manufacturing and service conglomerates and extensive public bureaucracies. Rather, it is a radical departure from Fordist and welfare-state paradigms. The redundancy of these large-scale structures is likely to increase the volatility of social and economic relations undermining conventional distinctions between, for example, investment and consumption. Conventional accounts of the university's potential contribution to wealth creation, inherited from the mid-twentieth century, may no longer adequately encompass these new configurations.

Second, even in the most advanced economies only a small proportion of people will be engaged in so-called 'symbolic production' (whether the 'symbols' are computer or cultural codes). Mass higher education systems will be concerned not simply with the élite engaged in 'symbolic production' but also with the mass, some of whom may be deskilled by the spread of complex 'black-box' technologies. The university of the 21st century, therefore, will have to straddle both the old and the new orders, a key player in the post-industrial game, but rooted more deeply than ever in the far from residual routines of Fordist–Weberian society.

Third, the 'knowledge' in which the knowledge society will trade is not simply, or mainly, the sophisticated knowledge with which higher education is primarily concerned – theories, concepts, elaborate interpretative frameworks, high-grade skills, meta-knowledge. Rather, it is the massive flows of data through computers and other electronic media. The focus of this fourth industrial revolution, of 'symbolic production', therefore, is unlikely to be found within the academic system, however broadly defined. Instead, it will be located in the territory of sophisticated engineering processes, advanced information systems and the mass media.

Fourth, post-industrialism may actually undermine the university's authority. Established skills and received wisdoms are likely to be remorselessly undermined by the acceleration of a science-led economy. As a result the very notions of expertise, authority, discrimination, hierarchy, key characteristics of all higher education systems, may also be weakened. Even the scientific tradition may be compromised. The assumptions that 'knowledge' begins in the laboratory and ends in the factory, that its purest is necessarily its earliest form, have been increasingly challenged. Instead, it is argued, innovation can occur anywhere along the chain, perhaps most often where science and the market meet. All this has grave consequences for the university's authoritative position in the creation of knowledge.

There will be even less room for Great Traditions in the intellectual culture of the 21st century. The problem is not only poststructuralism, deconstruction, post-modernism and similar theories which have had limited impact outside literary criticism, philosophy and some of the social sciences. More responsible for the waning of the university's intellectual authority is the myopic reductionism of much of modern science, natural and social, a reductionism that also afflicts the humanities. Indeed, to the extent that postmodernism and its allied movements are an attempt to raise big questions once more, even if the answers they offer tend to be obscure and negative, they offer a basis for the reintegration of intellectual life which a strictly circumscribed scientism can never offer (Lyotard 1984).

It is this intellectual confusion that forms the back-drop to the stage on which the drama of the difficult transition, in Britain's case, from an élite and binary system to a mass post-binary system will be played out, and against which the idea of a 21st-century university must be defined. Yet how true an impression is it of the deeper currents of intellectual life? The playfulness of postmodernism may simply be a reaction, an antidote, to the inexorable reductionism of modern science. A truer description of academic life in the 1990s would emphasize instead its solidity, rigidity, ever finer divisions of intellectual labour, quasi-industrial quality.

The difficulty with this interpretation, of course, is that, as Max Weber and subsequent social theorists acknowledged, the rational as defined (curtailed?) by the scientific tradition fails to take into account the instinctive, the affective, the erotic, so excluding from its territory some of the most important aspects of the human condition. In late-capitalist or post-industrial society, at once more technologized and, paradoxically, less reasonable, the latter aspects are more significant than ever. And mass higher education systems, no longer aimed at élites with disciplined codes of thought, also have to give greater weight to these extra-scientific aspects. [. . .]

The intellectual forms of the 21st century are difficult to predict. Will there be a lurch towards ever greater relativism – or a collapse into ever more complete reductionism? No doubt that is too stark a contrast. Yet it is important, at any rate, to guess at its trajectory. A reasonable guess is that, while in the 1990s, the dominant impression is one of the decay of intellectual order, in the next century we are likely to be more aware of the emergence of new shapes, novel configurations of knowledge, recombinations of disciplines which may eventually come together to form a new intellectual culture.

The implications for the university of both postmodern and post-industrial change (to adopt two shorthand labels, for convenience rather than accuracy) are hard to exaggerate. The conventional curriculum will appear increasingly problematical and also its underlying intellectual values will be undermined. Either things are moving so fast it is difficult to catch at their truth, or it is impossible to say that they are true – or rather, the search for truth of any but the most relative kind is naive. The university as an institution, not just as an idea, may also be at risk. Like all large structures in a post-industrial society, whether Fordist industries or welfare-state bureaucracies (and the university has elements of both), it is threatened with redundancy.

## A MASS STUDENT MARKET

Higher education will be transformed by the need to adjust to this new 21st-century environment. Nowhere is this transformation likely to be more radical than in Britain. Because of the comparative under-development of the British system, the expansion of student numbers, which began in the mid-1980s and has accelerated in the early 1990s, is more rapid than in any other European country (OECD 1992). Because of its 'backwardness' (i.e. Britain's attachment to academic traditions abandoned a generation ago elsewhere), the swift transition from élite to mass forms of higher education is likely to have radical consequences for teaching and learning styles, and also the make-up of disciplines. It even has the capacity to upset the delicate equilibrium of British higher education which earlier expansions left undisturbed, perhaps irreversibly to alter its ethos.

Several explanations of this growth in demand for higher education, which has surprised those who expected instead a demographic slump in the 1990s, are possible. One is that the sons – and especially the daughters – of the Robbins generation are now reaching the age of higher education entry. Research has shown that graduate parents are very likely to have graduate children. A second is the success of comprehensive schools in increasing staying-on rates beyond sixteen and raising motivation levels (if not always standards of achievement). Another is the drying-up of job opportunities for school-leavers, whether at sixteen or eighteen. A fourth is upward occupational drift: there are more jobs for the highly skilled and fewer for those with more limited skills. Closely linked is inexorable credentialization; higher qualifications are needed to do the same jobs, not always because skill levels have been raised.

But, powerful as these forces are, they are not enough to explain the rising tide of demand for higher education which overleapt the demographic troughs of the 1970s and now the 1990s with ease (DES 1978 and 1979). Here is a deep-rooted secular trend. Larger social forces are clearly at work. And the vital connections may have as much to do with social, even cultural, aspiration as economic advancement. [ . . . ]

Because the real causes of student demand are woven into the fabric of an entire society, today's assumption that higher education will never again face serious supply difficulties may be premature. [ . . . ] Demand rises or falls at the margin. It is these marginal students, without a family tradition of higher education nor academically among the-best-and-the-brightest, which universities and colleges have been so successful in recruiting in recent years. To be educated in an also-ran school may disappoint or the lure of an immediate job may deflect their shallow-rooted academic amibitions. The motives of part-time students, likely to form an increasingly significant component in a post-binary system, are often more fragile and unfathomable than those of full-timers. Then there are postgraduate and continuing education students, different economies of expectation again.

Mass entry by school-leavers is likely to be complemented (and complicated?) by the increased enrolment of mature students (UCACE 1991). Again, growth has been rapid (DFE 1992). Not all of these, however, will be mature students in the classic sense, people seeking a 'second chance' higher education. Instead, many are people in their mid to late twenties who have taken some time to find their intellectual or social bearings or have realized how meagre the job prospects are for non-graduates in a high-skill society (especially in a time of recession). The mass and mature markets, therefore, will tend to merge. But if some mature students are likely to be younger, others may be older, perhaps squeezing out the mid-career and middle-aged. The balance of population is tilting inexorably towards the elderly. More people are retiring earlier. At some stage institutions are going to have to come to serious terms with the so-called 'Third Age'.

The reasons for increased demand from mature students are straightforward. In a rapidly changing economy demands for skills upgrading, professional updating and retraining will increase, so making continuing professional development a more central activity in the university. More value is now placed on experiential learning; the balance between theory and practice, cognitive and non-cognitive elements, is being rethought in many subjects; and traditional boundaries between education, work and life are being renegotiated. Finally, as student support becomes less reliable, there may be more 'worker students', older students who are less than full-time. The rapid growth of part-time masters' courses to match the changing economic circumstances of potential students, already a well-established trend by the end of the 1980s, may well be reproduced on an even larger scale at the undergraduate level.

The consequences of wider access are far-reaching. Most significant perhaps is that for many people the effective choice will no longer be to go to higher education, but not to go. Opting-out will replace opting-in as the key social dynamic of the system. So the nature of its input will be transformed. The same will happen to the system's output; there will be proportionately far fewer élite jobs for graduates, so breaking the old links between higher education and the formation of national élites. Higher education will become a democratic enterprise, part of the lives of ordinary people, not simply of a privileged minority. In Britain this represents a cultural sea change – from exclusion to inclusion as the basis for access to educational opportunities and all they represent in terms of life-chances.

## TOWARDS A NEW CURRICULUM

Curriculum is an uneasy term in higher education. It is seen by many as a schools-based concept that cannot properly be applied to the university. There are courses, delineated in terms of their academic content and of their structure and organization (these two aspects are not always well integrated). There is also a body of expertise concerned with the delivery of these courses, through teaching, learning and assessment strategies. Increasingly, new technologies are recognized as having a key role in the more effective (and economical?) delivery of courses. But these different aspects remain discrete. Several of the new universities established in the 1960s made efforts to draw new maps of learning, an intellectual project. During the 1970s and 1980s, the former polytechnics, influenced by the ex-Council for National Academic Awards, struggled to improve course organization and delivery, essentially a managerial and pedagogical project.

The need to respond to new socio-economic and intellectual environments and the creation of a mass student market are likely to oblige the

21st-century university to 'invent' the idea of a university curriculum. But, bound up in the curriculum, overt or covert, are many of the most fundamental values of those who participate in the system: that students must learn for themselves more than they are taught; that over-prescriptive organization of undergraduate courses is incompatible with the open-endedness of higher education; that high-level teaching, scholarship and research are inevitably ingrown activities; and so on. If the idea of a university curriculum is recognized and renegotiated, as seems inevitable, these value systems may be radically disturbed.

As the number and variety of students increase, it will become more difficult to maintain a common academic purpose, based on a set of intellectual assumptions which underlie all university courses, whatever the subject. Those destined to be engaged in 'symbolic production' will demand a curriculum that emphasizes high-level abstraction, now derived, sadly perhaps, from the world of advanced engineering and information systems rather than, as in the past, suffused with cultural references. Those who will form the cadres of experts that dominate employment in the most dynamic sectors of the economy, probably the largest group of tomorrow's graduates, will need to be drilled in high-grade technical and professional skills.

Finally, those who, either because they have been marginalized by the labour market, or deliberately chosen to stand askance from these post-industrial developments, may demand a higher education that re-emphasizes older academic values or engages new, even 'alternative', modes of learning. The motives of this last group, far from insignificant in a mass higher education system in a late capitalist society, are perhaps better explained in terms of patterns of cultural consumption rather than of theories of human capital.

So post-industrialism's impact on the university of the 21st century is likely to be ambivalent, even disintegrative. On the one hand, it will encourage a ruthless reductionism as old theories and processes are ceaselessly deconstructed and replaced by new ones. State-of-the-art knowledge and skills will become increasingly expert. A moment's lapse and an industry, institution, individual will be out of the knowledge game. On the other hand, there may be renewed emphasis on meta-languages and interpretative frameworks, which are the key to 'symbolic production', and also the synoptic skills demanded of an increasingly volatile workforce.

So a convergence, even congruence, is possible between the more general mixed-discipline courses developed to meet the needs of new mass student constituencies and the synoptic skills demanded in a post-industrial society. It can even be argued that in the university of the 21st century new forms of general higher education will need to be developed. But these are likely to be very different from the old patterns of general education that preceded the descent into specialization and the emergence of reductionist science.

A clear distinction has to be made between a general education that emphasizes 'life skills' related to less competitive and more communitarian values and a general education organized round the idea of flexible transferable skills and competencies with a narrower vocational orientation. Both the National Curriculum in schools, with its emphasis on key stages, and National Vocational Qualifications (and now General NVQs) in further education will have a significant impact on the university curriculum. [. . .]

There is unlikely ever to be a revival of old-style general education – based on the élitist liberal–literary values of nineteenth-century England or even the corporatist administrative culture of the-great-and-the-good of the mid-twentieth century. Both, the former especially, are too closely associated with a generalist (and amateur?) intellectual tradition out of place in the new age of high technology. The mass media too have bred new forms of literacy, more verbal and visual and less literary. Also, the interpretative frameworks and synoptic language which will flourish in the volatile environment of a post-industrial society will be different from the old value-laden codes traditionally associated with them in the past. They may be more like computer programs – value-free patterns of thought which give a solidity to rapid knowledge flows. And they may retain only vestigial elements of those critical references to older cultural traditions. Finally, the validity of meta-languages, as of all grand narratives, is rejected by reductionist scientists, technical and professional experts and playful postmodernists alike.

The effects of massification on the university curriculum, therefore, are as difficult to predict as the wider influence of post-industrialism. But a number of shifts are likely to occur which cumulatively may transform the idea of a university over the next generation. First, mass entry may give greater emphasis to undergraduate education. Of course a straightforward distinction between undergraduate and postgraduate courses will become more difficult, certainly if conceived in sequential terms. Many of the latter may actually be 'lower level' than the former, if élite undergraduate courses are compared with mass postgraduate ones. Taught post-experience courses are likely to become an increasingly important part of the portfolio of courses offered by institutions.

Second, because student numbers will rise and unit costs fall, courses will have to be rationalized, in terms both of their organization and their delivery. Formal instruction may become a less dominant element in student learning. Greater use is also likely to be made of standardized teaching packages. The wired-up campus will open up possibilities unknown even a decade ago; the video revolution can transform the economics (and aesthetics) of large-scale lecturing as well as shrinking the gap between on-campus instruction and distance learning; interactive computer networks can stimulate 'active learning'; simulations can replace costly and time-consuming experiments.

The outcome will be a new learning economy; courses restructuring into compatible modules which can be combined into larger-scale study programmes by means of credit accumulation and transfer. The effects will be intellectual as well as organizational. By being repackaged the nature of courses will change because students will be different (with weaker allegiances to particular disciplines?) and will experience them differently (serially not cumulatively?).

Individual modules will be standardized to reduce costs. New students sucked into a mass system, less adequately or differently prepared than students in the past, without prior expectations of higher education, and likely to follow much more diverse careers subsequently, may benefit from a more closely organized curriculum. But these modules will be able to be combined much more freely and flexibly, which may suit mature students who bring a rich experience to their higher education and less-than-full-time students who need to balance study with work and family. So different groups of students, and individuals, will experience the same academic material in different ways.

Third, there will be many more mixed-discipline courses with much broader academic goals – for intellectual as much as social reasons. These courses will not be 'soft options' for less able students. Today academic 'hot spots' more often occur in the borderland between disciplines than in their heartlands. The indeterminate territory of inter- and trans-disciplinarity, therefore, may be colonized by high-flyers, among students and researchers, leaving mainstream disciplinary investigation to others. Furthermore, the traditional disciplines may lose their old power in an increasingly issue-oriented and topic-related curriculum.

The risk, of course, is that higher education will adjust only grudgingly to these new students. Institutions may try to maintain an ancient and probably mythical 'gold standard' and, as a result, see coping with mass entry in terms of devising catching-up strategies, remedial programmes, rather than as an opportunity to renegotiate the boundaries between secondary, further, adult and higher education. Similarly, there is a risk that mature students will be stigmatized as 'non-standard', even deviant. But institutions should use their growing presence to transform the curriculum at its very heart. The impact of part-time and mature students goes far beyond designing user-friendly course structures or allowing generous credit for prior or experiential learning, important as these both are.

The traditional ethos of higher education cannot remain unmoved by such a radical transformation. The idea of the university in the 21st century must undergo equally radical revision. The old intimacy of

British higher education is its peculiar charm – and special strength. It is bound up in a knot of values which remain influential in assessing quality, defining excellence and determining success. But this tradition will be difficult to sustain in a brave new world of standard packages and transferable modules, a problem-solving rather than knowledge-based curriculum and the rest.

Yet, even in its extended post-binary form, even if significant elements of further and adult education are incorporated, British higher education is still a traditional system by international standards, in qualitative more than quantitative terms. Certainly, it is still very unlike the American system in which (almost) anything goes. Demand is limited by the nature of the product as much as by its availability. Some will be relieved by the prospect of self-limiting demand; others will itch to change the product.

## RESTRUCTURING THE UNIVERSITY

The university's response to this new environment remains difficult to predict. It is unlikely to be consistent. Mass higher education remains a deeply ambiguous phenomenon, its timing problematical. In parts of British higher education, conditions close to mass access have already arrived; in others, their arrival will be indefinitely delayed. Although it is safe to assume that over the next decade the mass component of the system will grow and the élite component shrink, this shrinkage, relative rather than absolute, is likely to be accompanied by strengthening of the élite sector.

This differentiation between institutions (of which this strengthening will only be part), and also within them as teaching departments, graduate schools and research units adopt increasingly divergent missions, is likely to be far more radical in its effects than the officially sanctioned 'diversity' regarded by both politicians and higher education leaders as a necessary counter-weight to the pressures for uniformity produced by the abandonment of the binary system. 'Diversity' describes policy designed to prevent convergence; differentiation is a process of active divergence. Although differentiation is unlikely, in the short term, to be formalized into a rigid hierarchy, such as the division of all universities into research (R), mixed (X) or teaching (T) institutions proposed by the Advisory Board for the Research Councils (ABRC 1987), the centrifugal forces at work in British higher education are more powerful than 'academic drift', involving the emulation of the most prestigious.

Differentiation will apply to subjects too. Some will remain highly selective. Manpower planning will continue to predetermine the number of places in medical schools or departments of education. Mismatches between supply and demand will persist, either because of genuine failures in market intelligence or, more probably, political attempts to second-guess the market. As a result, entry to English departments will probably always be more selective than to engineering departments. Many subjects, of course, are already close to open-access for candidates with the basic entry qualifications [. . .].

This subject differentiation is likely to be as radical as differentiation between institutions. It will go far beyond mere differences of academic level or degrees of selectivity. Rather, the fundamental intentions of disciplines, and so intellectual construction, will diverge to such an extent that they become incommensurable. The difficulty of sustaining shared academic values and compatible professional structures, and maintaining common academic standards, will increase. So, in terms both of institutions and subjects, progress towards mass higher education will produce greater rather than less unevenness.

The nature of institutions is also likely to change. The most obvious difference will be scale. As British higher education moves to much higher levels of participation and takes on a post-binary form, institutions will grow in size. British universities remain exceptionally small by international standards. The largest would only be middle-sized in the rest of Europe, and below-average in the United States. An important difference between the present and previous expansions is that in the past the system grew by establishing brand-new universities or, as with the polytechnics, adding new types of institution; now, and probably in the future, the system will grow through the expansion of existing institutions. A simple logic applies: a mass system requires mass institutions.

This seems to present a formidable challenge to the idea of a university. Institutional scale is subtly but powerfully related to the academic intimacy of British higher education, which has already been discussed. This intimacy created a flexible environment in which, for example, learning packages can be negotiated. The more public, formal (and rigid?) instructional traditions, typical of higher education in continental Europe and of many institutions in the United States, perhaps offer a less congenial environment, although it can be argued they make it easier to articulate institution-wide policies on credit transfer, modularization and similar initiatives. Whatever the costs and benefits, academic intimacy, it seems, will be more difficult to maintain within the much larger institutions likely to emerge in Britain over the next decade.

On the other hand, large institutions require different styles of management. Those with up to about 5,000 FTE students, or perhaps 7,000 if their students are mainly full-time and missions uncomplicated, can be managed along collegial lines, in broad terms academic government serviced by a professional administration. Those with between 5,000–7,000 and, say, 15,000 must be managed on different terms. A cadre of senior managers drawn from both academic and administrative staffs and experts has to be developed: in their management culture, 'executive' displaces 'administrative' as the dominant ethos. It is this transition from 'collegial' to 'managerial' styles of institutional government that many British institutions have had to struggle through in the past decade. [. . .]

However, institutions with significantly more than 15,000 students probably need to be managed in a third way, closer to the pattern that prevails in large corporations. The senior management will shrink to a much smaller strategic core, concerned with guarding the institution's integrity (in terms of resources) and mission (in academic terms). Radical devolution of responsibilities to operating units will be needed that goes far beyond straightforward accountability for managing allocated budgets: instead, they should be allowed to take key decisions, establish priorities, even negotiate with external agents without frequent or detailed reference to the centre.

Operating units will need to do business directly, not only with private organizations that sponsor or buy their research and teaching services, but also research councils and even funding councils. As with large corporations, the centre's function will be not to control (and inhibit?) such bilateral negotiations, but to establish a framework in which they flourish. As a result much flatter and more flexible hierarchies will need to be created within institutions, loosely coupled networks rather than rigid line-management.

This transition from 'managerial' to 'strategic' or 'corporate' government will have a significant impact on delivery of the curriculum. The rather looser structures created by 'corporate' management will make its (over?) centralized control more difficult – with ambivalent results. On the one hand, it may be more difficult to impose binding institution-wide policies on access, modularization and similar issues; although in mass institutions the centre will have the authority to establish the general principles governing such policies, their details will have to be negotiated between operating units. On the other hand, looser structures and flatter hierarchies may help to preserve the condition in which the tradition of academic intimacy can be shielded from the pressures of mass organization. More significantly, they may allow operating units the freedom to adopt divergent missions, a key precondition of the university's ability to meet the challenges of the post-industrial age.

## THE IDEA OF THE UNIVERSITY IN THE 21ST CENTURY

The choices facing British higher education, because of the system's underdevelopment, backwardness, élitism (call it what you will), appear starker than those facing other European systems. But they are not essentially different, coalescing into a simple issue. In the second half of the 20th century all higher education systems – the American first, then continental European universities, now the British – have had to struggle with massification in organizational, managerial and funding terms. In the 21st century, not necessarily in the same order, they will all have to confront massification as an intellectual phenomenon. Indeed this encounter may be experienced first and most sharply in Britain, precisely because élite values and practices still pervade the system.

The present moment in Britain may be recalled as the time when a still inward system of higher education was irreversibly opened up, rather as America's was between 1945 and 1970, to the immeasurable benefit of all; or as the time when the ill-defined but deeply etched 'quality' of British universities and colleges was lost as irreversibly. Not that there is a choice – any more than there was at the time of the Robbins Report, or after the two world wars, or at the Victorian birth of the modern university system. Today's much prized ethos, apparently in danger of being swamped by tomorrow's mass expansion, is itself the product of earlier expansions regarded in their day as equally threatening.

Massification as a social phenomenon is irresistible because it is part of a wider democratic revolution. Access to higher education is bound up more tightly than ever in our notions of citizenship. In that sense wide-open universities are the culmination, the apotheosis, of efforts a century or more ago to create state-sponsored school systems open to all, the final stage on the long march from ignorance to enlightenment. But the categories of liberalism are inadequate to describe the full impact of massification. It has been accompanied by the commodification of higher education because, to the extent that democratic rights are now mediated through the market, the knowledge, skills and social prestige higher education makes available have become commodities.

At the end of the twentieth century the socio-economic context has been transformed; the intellectual environment arguably destabilized. Massification, therefore, becomes much more than a 'liberal' or a 'market' phenomenon. It triggers an intellectual transformation. The pattern and content of courses, and the values they silently transmit, have to be recast in the light of these changes – and to meet the needs of a new mass student constituency unaware, even impatient, of the disciplined culture of former élites. There is likely to be a significant drift away from conventional disciplines, conventional methods of course delivery and conventional patterns of research organization. Whether institutions themselves can survive in recognizable forms has become an urgent question.

The tension felt by many in higher education is generally seen as the product of the transition from élite to mass forms (Trow 1973); the emphasis is organizational. A truer description is of the contrast between integrity and pluralism, which places greater emphasis on the intellectual aspects of this transformation. In this chapter two pressure points in particular have been identified. The first is the curriculum. How to maintain its essential integrity, whether academic or professional, which students expect with the intellectual confusion and socio-economic pluralism endemic on the edge of the 21st century? Pragmatic accretion and adjustment, the half-thought pattern of the past, will no longer do. The second is the institution, most especially the university. At issue here are its values as much as its structure; the two are entwined. Once the university had clear if permeable boundaries. Now these boundaries are dissolving – physically as the interpenetration of academy, society, economy, culture becomes more intense; and intellectually as truth, reason, even science shimmer (shiver?) in a postmodern world that confusingly is a high-technology world too.

How to conjure integrity out of pluralism remains higher education's most urgent task at the end of the twentieth century. Or, better still, how to redescribe notions of excellence, referenced in the past, in terms of an integrity that is future-directed, and how to redefine a threatening confusion as a more hopeful pluralism. The idea of the university in the 21st century, therefore, is not redundant rhetoric; its definition is central to the proper organization of higher education. But, precisely for this reason, it must be rooted in the institutional constraints that shape and intellectual imperatives that drive the modern university.

# REFERENCES

Advisory Board for the Research Councils (1987) *A Strategy for the Science Base*, London: HMSO.

Archer, M. (1979) *Social Origins of Educational Systems*, London: Sage.

Barnett, R. (1991) *The Idea of Higher Education*, Buckingham: Open University Press.

Bell, D. (1973) *The Coming of Post-Industrial Society*, New York: Basic Books.

Bell, D. (1976) *The Cultural Contradictions of Capitalism*, New York: Basis Books.

Berman, M. (1982) *All That Is Solid Melts into Air*, New York:

Björklund, E. (1991) *Swedish Research on Higher Education in Perspective*, Stockholm: National Board for Universities and Colleges.

Bloom, A. (1987) *The Closing of the American Mind*, New York: Simon and Schuster.

Department for Education (1992) *Statistical Bulletin 18/92, Mature Students in Higher Education*, London: DFE.

Department of Education and Science/Scottish Education Department (1978 and 1979) *Higher Education into the 1990s*, London: HMSO and *Future Trends in Higher Education*, London: HMSO.

Giddens, A. (1990) *The Consequences of Modernity*, Cambridge: Polity.

Habermas, J. (1987) 'The idea of the university: learning processes', in *The New Conservatism: Cultural Criticism and the Historians' Debate*, Cambridge: Polity.

Habermas, J. (1990) *The Philosophical Discourse of Modernity*, Cambridge: Polity.

Jaspers, K. (1963, originally published 1946) *The Idea of the University*, London: Peter Owen.

Kerr, C. (1963) *The Uses of the University*, Cambridge, Mass.: Harvard University Press.

Leverhulme Inquiry Final Report: Blackstone, T. and Williams, G. (eds) (1983) *Excellence in Diversity*, Guildford: Society for Research into Higher Education.

Leverhulme Inquiry (seminar reports):

1 Lindley, R. (ed.) (1981) *Higher Education and the Labour Market*, Guildford: Society for Research into HIgher Education.

2 Fulton, O. (ed.) (1981) *Access to Higher Education*, Guildford: Society for Research into Higher Education.

3 Wagner, L. (ed.) (1982) *Agenda for Institutional Change in Higher Education*, Guildford: Society for Research into Higher Education.

4 Oldham, G. (ed.) (1982) *The Future of Research*, Guildford: Society for Research into Higher Education.

5 Robinson, K. (ed.) (1982) *The Arts in Higher Education*, Guildford: Society for Research into Higher Education.

6 Bligh, D. (ed.) (1982) *Professionalism and Flexibility for Learning*, Guildford: Society for Research into Higher Education.

7 Bligh, D. (ed.) (1982) *Accountability or Freedom for Teachers?*, Guildford: Society for Research into Higher Education.

8 Morris, A. and Sizer, J. (eds) (1982) *Resources and Higher Education*, Guildford: Society for Research into Higher Education.

9 Shattock, M. (ed.) (1983) *The Structure and Governance of Higher Education*, Guildford: Society for Research into Higher Education.

Lyotard, J-F. (1984) *The Postmodern Condition*, Manchester: Manchester University Press.

National Advisory Body (1984) *A Strategy for Local Authority Higher Education in the late 1980s and Beyond*, London: NAB.

Newman, J. H. (1976, originally published 1853) *The Idea of a University*, Oxford: Oxford University Press.

Oakeshott, M. (1989) 'The idea of a university' and 'The universities', in *The Voice of Liberal Learning*, New Haven: Yale University Press.

Organisation for Economic Co-operation and Development (1992) *Education at a Glance: OECD Indicators*, Paris: OECD.

Ortega, y Gasset, J. (1946) *Mission of the University*, London: Kegan Paul.

Parsons, T. and Platt, G. (1973) *The American University*, Cambridge, Mass.: Harvard University Press.

Robbins, L. (1963) *Higher Education*, London: HMSO.

Shils, E. (1989) 'The modern university and liberal democracy', *Minerva*, Winter 1989.

Shils, E. (1992) 'The service of society and the advancement of learning in the twenty-first century', *Minerva*, Summer 1992.

Trow, M. (1973) *Problems in the Transition from Elite to Mass Higher Education*, Berkeley: Carnegie Commission on Higher Education.

Universities Council for Adult and Continuing Education (1991) *The Organisation of Continuing Education in Universities*, Exeter: Department of Adult and Continuing Education.

University Grants Committee (1984) *A Strategy for Higher Education into the 1990s*, London: HMSO.

# Chapter 16

# Guidance and coherence in flexible learning

*Chris Cooper*

## LIFELONG LEARNING

Many factors make effective lifelong learning valuable for individual, organizational and national success. Lifestyles have changed. The expectation is that fewer people will have a single occupation in their lifetime, and increasingly we will have *serial* careers (a number of different occupations, one after the other, possibly with breaks between) or *portfolio careers* (as serial careers, but at times involving several contracts for work concurrently). Both of these may involve part-time working, and periods without work. A *portfolio lifestyle* includes work, learning, home, community and leisure pursuits in complex and overlapping patterns, and at its best offers the opportunity to tailor these to particular interests and priorities.

There are, additionally, many influences upon us, from changes in our personal priorities to economic and political changes, and opportunities open to us, which are at least uncertain and perhaps quite unpredictable. In this climate, the successful strategy for learning and work is *flexible planning*, in which individuals plan for a *range* of possible outcomes and a *range* of routes through which they can achieve their aims in life. This will prepare them to adapt to new priorities, to cope with set-backs and to seize new opportunities. For the organization, and for the national economy, a similar message applies. The concept of the *learning organization* which grows through recognizing new developments, learning new skills, incorporating new practices, changing direction if necessary (in much the same way that individuals do) is now established. The organization will seek to employ 'lifelong learners' in order to implement this strategy. It will recognize (as some large organizations, such as the Ford Motor Co., already do (Southee 1991)) that it is to the benefit of the organization to encourage and support learning beyond the needs of the workplace. It is a learning culture that is required, which encourages everybody to learn for *all* areas of their lives. Ball (1991: 11), working from the need for a 'world class workforce', points to the model of a *learning society,* in which we are all members and all may aspire to fulfil our own potential and achieve our proper excellence in our own time and at our own pace. The 'lifelong learner' is much more likely to be a net contributor to the economy, not simply through paid employment, but in all areas of life, as a member of the learning society.

## FLEXIBLE LEARNING

Lifelong learners, progressing through portfolio lifestyles, sometimes working for learning organizations, will find the traditional picture of learning in the workplace separated from academic study, with the constraints of the traditional academic year, and little opportunity to vary the context of fixed courses, a poor match to real learning needs. They need to build on learning already undertaken, to select the exact learning necessary, without unnecessary additions, and to fit this alongside many other activities in their portfolio lifestyles. Providers of education and training are responding by developing flexible learning opportunities.

Flexible learning is education and training offered in ways intended to make the provision more adaptable to the needs of different learners. A number of mechanisms, including modularization, accreditation of prior learning, open and distance learning, may be introduced by a single provider, perhaps within an individual course or course scheme, or a collaboration between different organizations may be necessary. Cooper (1991a) describes many of these mechanisms.

### Modularization

Modularization breaks the learning involved in longer courses into short modules of learning which may include the assessment of learning outcomes. Although it is not in itself a strictly necessary precursor of other aspects of flexible learning, it does act as an important release trigger, greatly enabling a number of features of flexible learning.

- With these modules no longer tied into the long course, they may be identified on an individual basis as appropriate to specific learning needs, and on completion the individual will achieve recognition of the learning undertaken.
- 'Personalization' of learning programmes to individual needs, which cannot be fully met by 'off-the-peg' courses, can be achieved by selection of some modules from other subject areas to improve largely predetermined courses. This allows individual interests to be reflected even where other considerations require substantial elements to be common to all learners.

- Individually negotiated programmes become possible. These represent the greatest move from a position of teacher authority, with the expertise necessary to determine the curriculum, to learner autonomy, recognizing that the individual may determine her/his own learning needs and the programme which will deliver the required learning outcomes.
- More effective responses can be made to individual circumstances, because it becomes easier to interrupt, or change mode to meet learner needs, whether unforeseen, such as illness or bereavement, or anticipated events, including childcare or career change. Learning can be planned to fit alongside such changes, rather than being disrupted or terminated as a consequence.

## Accreditation of prior learning

The accreditation of prior learning (APL) gives credit towards a qualification for learning previously achieved, including uncertificated learning and experiential learning, usually on the basis of a portfolio of evidence for that learning. The identification of the specific credit towards a new qualification for prior learning is a significant move towards increased flexibility of learning. It goes beyond the simple recognition of prior learning long undertaken as part of the admissions process when judging the suitability of mature students to undertake new studies. APL recognizes that the learning has occurred and need not be repeated, and that elements of the new course may therefore be omitted. Where modularization has occurred this process of accreditation can be more straightforward, and it helps create a culture in which it ceases to be abnormal. In the UK, fifteen Training and Enterprise Councils (TECs) and Local Enterprise Companies (LECs) are piloting a two-year initiative, Skill Choice, between 1993 and 1995, offering individuals in employment credits towards the cost of purchasing guidance and APL services. Further education colleges have been a major provider within Skill Choice, which has facilitated the development of APL practices, particularly for corporate clients, where economies of scale apply.

## Open and distance learning

Open and distance learning breaks the tyranny of the institution. Most formal learning involves attendance at an institutional location at regular set times. This presents major problems for many adult learners who cannot meet this precondition for learning, owing to work, family or other commitments. By allowing the learner to choose the timing, location and pace of study, at home, in the workplace, to suit individual preferences, employers' needs or personal circumstances, open and distance learning allows the greatest flexibility within formal learning.

At the European level, open and distance learning is increasingly recognized, and seen to deliver more cost-effective learning. Commitment to its development within Europe is enshrined in Article 126 of the Maastricht Treaty. New networks are emerging, such as the European Association of Distance Teaching Universities (EADTU), and the EU education and training programmes, such as COMETT, have been developing the delivery of open and distance learning, by supporting the production of new systems and materials, including hundreds of distance learning packages. The EU has also resourced the strengthening of network links between the Continent's open universities, including those emerging in countries without such provision. The need for language support for students studying in a foreign language are being addressed by open and distance learning institutions.

Companies large and small are benefiting from open and distance learning. Employment-based learning can be more precisely focused, and delivery standardized for all. Siemens, for example, is investing in open and distance learning to provide equality and consistency in the quality of its training throughout the world.

## Collaborative arrangements

Collaborative and accreditation arrangements can very substantially increase the flexibility of learning, in terms of location, mode, time and duration of study. These include the franchising of provision, open college networks, credit accumulation and transfer arrangements, Access consortia, accreditation of in-company training, and other formal and informal arrangements between organizations, which bring together providers in different sectors of education and training, and at different levels, enabling progression and transfer between these.

## Technological advance

Technological advance is greatly facilitating advances in flexible learning, from simple use of audio-visual packages, broadcast media including satellite transmission, telephone support services, and especially the increasing use of computer-based learning, including CD-ROM materials, interactive video, and the much-discussed Information SuperHighway. These can offer the development of a European or world-wide market in education and training and economies of scale, reducing the cost of learning (IRDAC 1994). These advances have provided access to learning for those in difficult locations or with complex lifestyles.

Together, these elements create a framework of flexible learning designed to produce learning programmes which are more closely tailored than previously possible to the learning needs of individuals and groups. They enable learners to identify their current point of development and their learning needs, and to start new learning from this point by identifying and gaining credit for old learning, and selecting learning programmes which build upon this. They are specifically chosen to achieve the desired learning outcomes, while being undertaken in ways which fit easily with the learner's personal circumstances.

## DANGERS IN FLEXIBLE LEARNING

However, Cooper (1991a) has identified a number of inherent dangers in these attempts to widen access through flexible learning systems. The very attempts to improve flexibility can restrict it. There are a number of key issues:

- the impact of complexity;
- the loss of support mechanisms;
- the loss of personal recognition;
- the 'fractioning' of the individual;
- the relationship between learning modes and social contact levels.

### The impact of complexity

Flexible learning systems, by their very nature, result in a significant increase in the number of possible learning options. In making a higher education choice, instead of the choice from a finite number of degree and diploma programmes, helpfully listed in major guides published annually, there is now the possibility of taking the modules within a programme; dropping some, adding others, taking several modules at another institution in Europe, changing the order in which modules are studied to at least some extent, and having your personally selected programme approved. Even if you only wish to take one or two modules of current relevance, attention is now focused upon the detail of each module, and its learning outcomes, rather than on broad descriptions of long courses. To take advantage of the flexibility, the learner must become much more self-aware, knowing what her/his current skills and understandings are (not as simple as it would appear) and having clear plans for development, and therefore knowing her/his individual learning needs, in order to begin selecting from this expanded offer of opportunities. Learners will also have to judge the merits of gaining credit for prior learning. Until they have engaged in the process, how will they know whether they will be given sufficient credit to warrant the work and cost involved? Will they miss the benefits of group dynamics, and of relating the prior learning to the new context, if they take credit, and do not study the modules concerned? There is therefore a considerable risk that the individual faced with this will simply feel overwhelmed and confused by the sheer complexity of it. The easy response will be to fall back on the old-style predetermined course of study. Learners will not be helped by these systems if there is no support through the complexity of decision-making. The very systems introduced for the empowerment of learners may do most to disempower them, placing them at the mercy of the educational equivalent of 'insurance salesmen'.

## The loss of support mechanisms

The intention of flexible learning is to make the learning programme more personal to the individual. The purpose of modular programmes is to allow movement between different subject areas, choice of different times of presentation, change in pace of study, breaks from study, etc. This inevitably brings frequent changes in the composition of student groupings, and the probability that an individual student will study different modules with quite different sets of fellow students. This can result in the loss of the peer support mechanisms which are more significant in our learning than many would immediately recognize. Many students find it important to share with a group, in discussion of topics studied, in sharing information about the learning programme, its structure, location of sessions, checking understanding of assessment requirements, and institutional rules and regulations, and simply under-standing the lecture/book/video, etc. This is important enough for the learning process, but the support from fellow students does not stop there. Help and advice on all aspects of life as a student, such as money, entertainment, careers and relationships – as well as learning skills – is passed between students, and whatever the professionals may feel, this is the bulk of such support, essential in ensuring that students can cope with the many changes they experience during learning, both positive and negative. However, in order for the necessary relationships between students to be established, an initial rapport must develop, and the fragmentation of learning which can accompany flexible systems can work against this. Especially isolated are students on individually negoti-ated programmes, who will have the minimum common experience.

## The loss of personal recognition

The loss of identification within a cohort of students sharing a common learning experience is not only a matter of loss of support amongst students. It has implications for the development of a sense of identity as a student. That identity is less clear. '*I am a student on an individually negotiated programme with a mix of subjects x, y and z*' is less clear than '*I am a law student*'. Indeed, while it may involve unhelpful stereotypes, many staff and students will have a fairly clear picture of 'a law student' and 'a civil engineering student'. New students can be seen to identify with, and conform to, the group norms for their subject area. The breakdown of this clarity by flexible learning systems, whereas it may support greater diversity, and be considered valuable in the long term, makes the search for identity a more difficult, possibly more painful, experience. This sense of identity, when achieved, helps to motivate the learner, and also provides the frame of reference for seeking support mechanisms within the institution.

This recognition of identity is not simply a matter for the learners themselves. It also affects the institution, and its ability to recognize the learner. The most radical flexible learning routes, which may involve APL and even movement across different institutions to achieve the required programme, have the potential not only to leave the learner feeling isolated from other students, but to have this isolation reinforced by the staff with whom she or he comes into contact, who may well have a diminished contact with, knowledge of, and sense of responsibility for a student who only attends certain modules, and is not, like others, one of the students on 'her/his course'.

## The 'fractioning' of the individual

Even when there is recognition of the learner, these changes move towards this recognition being only of the 'fraction' of the learner seen in this context. One lecturer may see the student taking geography modules. Another sees the student taking business modules. Who sees the whole person, helps the student see where the overall learning programme is going, how this fits with their future plans, what adaptations are necessary? Who takes responsibility for offering support services, for helping when the study causes difficulty at home or at work? The 'fractioning' of the learner is an inherent danger of flexible learning systems, so clearly designed to help integrate the learning into the life of the learner.

There is a real problem, when this occurs, that the learner feels less able to discuss difficulties in the student 'fraction' of the whole person, because the institution does not see her/his strengths alongside. Cooper expressed this thus:

> If I am the learner, I wish to be recognised as the whole me, with my work, my family commitments, my values, my strengths and (perhaps) my weaknesses. Only in the context of the whole me will the part

make sense, and only if you have recognised my strengths (which may lie outside this small part) will I feel able to bring my weaknesses to you.

(Cooper 1991a: 284)

If only the 'geography student' fraction is seen, and this is weak, it is much more difficult to bring this to the table than if the whole person is seen, with considerable strength on the business modules, successful involvement in the Students' Union, and dealing well with difficult family circumstances. It must be remembered that 'the student' is only one part of the whole person.

At this point, some UK opinion would argue that this reflects concepts more appropriate to social work than to the world of learning. There is a hard economic rationale in this approach. Providers of education and training are in the business of delivering the desired learning outcomes to their customers. Increasingly, they are judged and funded on their ability to deliver this. To allow non-completion to increase because attention to the full needs of learners/customers is lost in this fragmentation of the experience will result in poor performance and reduced income, whether as a result of reduced market share, or loss of core funding. This fractioning effect has a further financial implication. Employers may feel reduced or even no commitment to pay for training of individuals with portfolio lifestyles whom they employ on limited contracts. Individuals may seek guidance to minimize problems resulting from this, and to maximize benefit from what training is available, or for which they pay independently (CBI 1994).

## The relationship between learning modes and social contact levels

In employment, flexible working systems are leading to a greater variety of working practices. The development of serial careers, portfolio careers and lifestyles has added to pre-existing opportunities afforded by part-time, self-employed and 'tele-commuting' work styles. The pattern of lifelong employment is now uncertain, and the ongoing social relationships which it brought can no longer be relied upon. Social relationships in the new patterns are more transient, and some new patterns change the nature of the contact. Tele-commuting, even with a longer-term employer, can reduce the social (strictly non-work) contact to a minimum. Portfolio careers, such as consultancy work, may reduce the social contact in the same way, as this may well be undertaken from home. At the same time, the nature of contact with others is less social in its nature, in that it is focused upon contract negotiation and delivery. It does not provide the same opportunities for developing social relationships over time with those who are peers and colleagues. It should not be assumed that this applies only to senior posts, or professional-level persons. It may equally apply to an unskilled or skilled worker, hiring on a portfolio basis.

This may be intensified by flexible learning approaches. An isolated tele-worker or, to use a more traditional example, travelling sales representative (who works from the car rather than the home) may obtain only low levels of satisfying social contact from the work situation. Each of these has good reasons, when looking to undertake some formal learning, for choosing the flexibility of open or distance learning. This, however, has a strong probability of also providing a low level of social contact. Unless there is another area of life providing our examples with a high level of social interaction (perhaps living in a close village community, a busy family life, or a high-interaction leisure activity) then it may be more appropriate to choose a course involving attendance with a group of students, providing high social contact.

The introduction of flexible learning systems is progressing at a significant pace, with a very high commitment in some quarters to ensure that learning opportunities are made more accessible to a broader range of potential learners. The ability of flexible learning to do this is, however, seriously limited by the problems outlined.

## GUIDANCE

Like many terms now used in a professionally defined manner, 'guidance' has been interpreted in various ways, and uses, in a more precise way, a word which has looser, and potentially very opposed, colloquial meanings. In a British context, this is confused by the use of 'guidance' in many contexts to mean the setting of rules or parameters within which to operate, so producing constraints, being directional, representing statements from a position of power. In another context, the Marriage Guidance Council was an organization known for providing *counselling* (non-judgemental, enabling clients to find their own solutions) for those who wished to talk about their relationships, including those that were breaking down. This organization escaped the confusion through its name change to RELATE. For a substantial period in the latter half of the century, the most clearly understood area of guidance was that of *careers* guidance, most commonly that undertaken by publicly funded services, known as youth employment services and careers services, and latterly (usually as a result of broadened scope) guidance services. Increasingly, these were based upon concepts of occupational choice and progression in which guidance was a process which helped young people to make informed realistic choices and to implement them. The considerable focus of these services upon young people who have not yet achieved independent adulthood exacerbated the popular misconception that guidance would be 'directional', i.e. that the client would be told which was the most appropriate solution. This lingering misunderstanding is clearly demonstrated in Murgatroyd *et al.* (1987), comparing guidance and counselling, and believing only the latter can be client-focused and facilitative.

As new *educational guidance services for adults* developed in the 1970s and especially in the 1980s, the professional expectation that guidance was non-directive, enabling individuals to develop the skills and understanding to take control of their own lives, came to the fore:

> Educational Guidance is the process of enabling individuals to evaluate their own development, identify learning needs, and choose the most appropriate ways they can meet them, in the light of their personal circumstances; then to pursue and complete a learning programme, review this achievement, and identify future goals.
>
> (Cooper 1990: 17)

The Unit for the Development of Adult Continuing Education (UDACE) (1986) provided a definition of educational guidance in terms of the seven activities involved: informing, advising, counselling, assessing, enabling, advocating, and feeding back. It is important to understand that these defining activities do not involve doing things for the client, except where strictly necessary, but are concerned with striving to empower clients to develop skills and understanding to achieve outcomes for themselves It is also important to note that the term 'counselling' refers to the use of what many would define as 'counselling skills', and does not require accreditation as a counsellor. While expressed in relation to educational guidance, these activities have received broad acceptance, with minor modification, in relation to careers and other forms of guidance.

## Guidance and the coherent experience

Educational institutions and industrial and commercial organizations need to invest in guidance to support learning to help learners cope with the fragmentation inherent in many aspects of flexible learning and work. Faced with complex choices, difficulty in finding appropriate provision, and a range of barriers to access, pre-entry guidance can support learners in their choice and access. This helps institutions to ensure that individuals are undertaking the most appropriate learning, with the highest motivation.

During learning, guidance, sometimes manifested as tutorial activity, can be the coordinating strand in a flexible learning programme which draws upon diverse discipline modules, with some independent study and open learning modules, whether this is at college or the workplace. It will help the learner to recognize the scope for transfer of learning between different settings – a key skill for portfolio lifestyles and for less fragmented ones. It will help individuals to relate learning undertaken to current roles, including those which do not permit the extent of change anticipated (e.g. the work role remains the same, and does not allow new ideas to be implemented). It will, conversely, enable individuals to identify learning to cope with more rapid than expected change, which too frequently results in stress and poor performance in organizations. Choice may continue during the programme, when learner guidance and support will also help to maintain the greatest satisfaction with the programme, and reduce drop-out.

Help with onward progression ensures continuing planning for further development, meeting future needs. Throughout, effective guidance can help choice to be well-informed and related to need, and ensure that transitional uncertainties (both in making the transfer between roles, and in transferring learning between them) are minimized. In doing this, it helps learners, especially those undertaking flexible learning in a portfolio lifestyle, to make sense of the experience in relation to their own learning needs (which may be unclear to the provider of learning opportunities), and thus has a very significant role in achieving coherence in the learning experience. The result is efficient and effective use of the resources of the institutions and individuals involved. The argument for effective institutional guidance systems lies in this potential for bringing together the satisfaction of individual, organizational and national needs for development and innovation.

## GUIDANCE AND LEARNING

Recognition of its value has led to a growing interest in guidance within learning. UDACE and the Council for National Academic Awards (CNAA) managed a one-year project in 1991 to improve 'Guidance and Counselling in Higher Education', in which six institutions participated in a range of developments (HEQC 1994). In the further education sector, the Further Education Funding Council (FEFC 1992) has given some emphasis to guidance and counselling in its funding methodology, and the Further Education Unit (FEU 1994) has managed a project on 'Enhancing Guidance in Colleges'. The Education and Employment Department is currently funding further development work in Higher Education, exploring the theme of Guidance and Learner Autonomy.

Within the British further education sector (which includes sixth form colleges), FEU (1994) describes four main types of delivery structure for guidance:

- *the integrated model*, in which a centralized combined admissions and guidance unit has responsibility for pre-entry guidance;

- *dispersal functions*, in which a range of guidance functions exist, but operate separately. Provision pre-entry, on programme, and for exit tends to be separated, as do specialist functions (e.g. careers, counselling);
- *the informal approach*, relying on personal contact with all staff for guidance, which is not a separate provision or responsibility. This is a small-college approach which becomes difficult with larger numbers (and more so with the fragmentation effect within flexible learning);
- *tutor-led*, in which guidance on-programme is delivered through a tutorial programme, associated with recording of achievement.

Each delivery structure has relative strengths and weaknesses (discussed in the FEU report). The picture is largely one of *ad hoc* development of provision. There is a lack of policy development, and no guarantee of relevant provision at the different stages of progression through learning. The *integrated* approach focuses on pre-entry guidance, the *tutor-led* on on-programme guidance, whereas the *dispersed* and *informal* approaches do not necessarily provide a clear overview of guidance provision to enable the college to establish a coherent approach to, and management of, that provision, or to evaluate its comprehensiveness. A three-dimensional model which enables the institution, regardless of sector, to examine the totality of its guidance provision, is first described by Cooper (1991b: 12–13) and since updated (Figure 16.1). Guidance and support covering *academic options, study practices, vocational, personal or other issues, including financial and additional needs, accommodation, etc.* is identified. This guidance and support may come from within the course team, from cross-institution services (student services, registry, CATS units, counselling services, etc.) or from external agencies (including industry, especially in the form of work placement mentors) or non-professionals (family, friends, colleagues, neighbours, etc.).

An important issue is that many of these informal 'guides' and, indeed, many in a semi-formal relationship, such as line managers and personnel staff in industry, and personal tutors, course leaders, and others in educational institutions, will not perceive themselves to be in a guidance relationship. This can have an important impact upon the value of the 'intervention', as someone who sees themselves having a casual, friendly conversation with another person who is a friend, colleague or neighbour may not perceive a need to be accurate, up-to-date and impartial in what they say, while the recipient of their advice may believe they have asked for this. There may be problems about the boundaries of the relationship, confidentiality and also hierarchical issues where a formal relationship (worker/line manager, or student/tutor) exists.

Thus, a course tutor who perceives the relationship in terms of the individual's progress on the course may provide a response which is

**The stage at which the learner is within the learning programme:**
- **pre-entry and induction**     help for students before starting the course and at the point of entry
- **progression through:**     help for students during their studies
- **progression beyond:**     help about future plans

**The area of learner guidance and support activity:**
- **academic**     learning programme/course/module/option/pathway choices
- **study skills**     skills for effective learning: managing learning
- **vocational**     occupational choice, career progression, relating new skills to current employment
- **personal**     personal development, relationships, etc.
- **other support**     financial
legal
housing
special needs (disability, age, gender, race, nationality, etc.)

**The source of the learner guidance and support:**
- **within the course/scheme**     people (academic, professional and administrative staff; students in formal and informal support) and media-based support
- **within the college**     cross-college services – specialist provision, all methods and modes
- **outside the college**     public services, employers, other colleges' services; family, friends

*Figure 16.1* Learner guidance and support in an educational setting: a three-dimensional model (after Cooper (1991b))

unhelpful to an individual who has a major personal crisis not directly related to the course but which is inevitably having an impact upon the student's progression on it. A careers adviser may see the issue too specifically in occupational terms, when this is subservient to a much broader issue of the 'who am I' type, relating to overall lifestyle, motivations and values. There is therefore an issue of raising awareness amongst many persons involved about what guidance is, and their role in it, even if they are not full-time professionals. The important issue here is not to turn everyone into full-time guidance workers, but to clarify the range of involvements, so both the guider and the learner are aware of the limitations of any one interaction.

The model enables us to do this, by demonstrating how pervasive across the institution is involvement in guidance and support; by setting the contribution of each alongside the overall picture; by use of the three dimensions to identify areas in which additional provision is necessary; and drawing boundaries between different providers of guidance and support. The model specifically does not allocate functions to different professionals, as this would pre-empt the different solutions appropriate to, or preferred by, individual institutions and the learners within them.

## GUIDANCE AND TUTORING

The learner–tutor relationship is ideally seen as providing feedback on the success of learning at meetings which are both frequent and regular. At its best this will have been a relationship in which 'learning to learn' was also covered – including both generic skills and those relating to the specific subject at the appropriate level – and, in addition, the tutor would have been sensitive to the learner's personal circumstances and concerns, and their impact on learning. Too often, the relationship has, as a result of many pressures upon staff, combined with a lack of clarity about the function, degenerated into a misunderstood burden upon both parties. While there is an argument for beginning the tutoring role before entry, assisting with the transition, and discussing and providing references which relate to progression beyond the institution, the dominant focus is upon *helping the learner in her/his progression through the programme*. It is essentially concerned with provision made *within the learning programme*, rather than with a cross-college service. It is concerned very much with help in areas of academic and study skills issues, but not these alone: vocational, personal and other support is also of concern. However, the point of referral to specialists may come early for many tutors. This is partly an institutional decision, about the level of central provision for guidance, counselling, study skills, etc., partly about the subject area which may determine knowledge of specific career options, for example, and partly concerned with the individual expertise, understanding and preference of the tutor, interacting with learner preferences. Tutoring is therefore concerned with *all areas of learner guidance and support*.

Figure 16.2 outlines the major roles of the tutor as being those of the Anchor, the Mentor, and the Interpreter, for the learner (Cooper 1992). This analysis, placing the function clearly in the context of the overall model, identifies the need of the tutor to network with many others across the institution (and beyond) to undertake the roles, and also clarifies that this is a guidance function. So identifying the tutor enables the institution to understand the function, its relationship to other guidance and support provided, to identify the standards to which the work should be undertaken, and the training needs. It is also clearer that

Personal tutoring is identified as being of key importance for student progression within the learning programme. The tutor has a number of roles, which may be expressed in terms of being the **Anchor,** the **Interpreter** and the **Mentor** for a student.

(a) The **Anchor**
  - providing the student with a stable point of reference, and continuity;
  - demonstrating that the student is recognized and known personally;
  - providing a safe/secure environment where doubt/anxieties may be expressed;

(b) The **Interpreter**
  - clarifying the duties, obligation, and rights of the student and of the College;
  - being an advocate for the student to/within the institution;

(c) The **Mentor**
  - supporting the student in exploring his/her academic, personal and social development;
  - holding an overview of the student's progress.

---

The **Anchor** roles are concerned with the *well-being* of the student; the **Interpreter** roles with two-way *understanding*; and the **Mentor** roles with the *development* of the student.

The **Personal Tutor** will normally be a first point of contact, either responding directly, or through referral, in all or most areas of guidance identified in the three-dimensional model of guidance. **All academic staff** will normally be expected to undertake aspects of the Anchor, Interpreter and Mentor roles in the context of the learning opportunities for which they are responsible as part of their normal role within the College.

*Figure 16.2* Personal tutoring (after Cooper (1992: 46))

this training should be common to that of others involved in similar levels of guidance provision, such as reception guidance staff within Student Services Departments in institutions.

It is too easy to fall into a consideration of 'the tutor system', or 'the careers guidance service' (often separated from 'the careers education programme'). However, it is clear that these are part of an overall guidance system which must be examined. The questions become:

- Is there continuity of guidance from pre-entry to exit (progression beyond the programme)?
- Is there adequate provision for each *stage* of progression, and for each *area* of guidance and support activity?
- Is there an appropriate division of responsibility for provision between

those delivering the learning programme, cross-institution specialist departments, and external agencies?

- Is there coordination of this guidance system to ensure a coherent delivery to learners?
- How does this enhance the coherent student experience?

This escape from old constraints when examining guidance systems is essential if they are to be developed to meet the needs of highly flexible learning programmes. Support from both staff and fellow students, taken for granted in more traditional learning programmes, must be recreated in different ways in flexible programmes. Guidance which would not have been required must now be developed to respond to the new opportunities. For instance, guidance is needed to support potential candidates for APL, who may otherwise lack confidence that their learning (especially experiential) deserves credit, or alternatively be confused that hard-won learning has no value in the current programme. Equally, new guidance provision must result when modularization requires repeated on-programme choice. Will this be delivered within-programme, cross-college or externally? What relationships will be developed between guidance providers? Will all providers understand the inter-relationships between guidance and support in the different areas, so that choices reflect personal circumstances as well as learning needs? Responding to the complexity of flexible learning in a way which enables real advantage to be obtained from the flexibility of learning programmes will require us to analyse old approaches, identify fundamental issues, and recreate systems which maintain the best of old provision while introducing new approaches which deliver guidance and support in new, imaginative ways. Old barriers, between full-time and part-time, between college-based, work-based and home-based learning, are eroded, and guidance systems must reflect this. Learning in the workplace constitutes a major element of learning which is increasingly being brought into a more formal and equal relationship with academic learning. As lifelong learners, workers have the same support needs. The learning organization will need to ensure that personnel are provided with guidance and support, assisting choice, entry, progression through and beyond learning and work.

Continuity of guidance throughout should ensure the highest degree of success. Improved institutional provision in both education and the workplace will do much to help, but there is inevitably a need to support individuals (and small organizations) when they move beyond the scope of institutional guidance systems which, with portfolio life-styles, will only cover a proportion of the population for some elements of their portfolio, and will miss many individuals altogether. This is where a local community-based independent educational guidance service is so important, providing guidance through all phases, assisting the learner in reaching decisions, acquiring relevant skills, assessing progress, while also assisting essential networking between the institutional provision, which no institutionally based guidance provision can offer. To do so, community-based educational guidance services must be concerned with all types of learning, for the home, for the workplace, for leisure, for community involvement. Although the institutional guidance systems can encourage the concept of the learning society, it is the community-based services (currently severely threatened) which will be best placed to support learning across this broader base. The combination of institutionally-based and community-based educational guidance, supporting coherence of experience for the learner, is a critical, essential component of truly flexible learning provision.

## REFERENCES

Ball, C. (1991) *More Means Different: Widening Access to Higher Education*, London: RSA.

Confederation of British Industry (1994) *Flexible Working Contracts: Who Pays for Training?* London: CBI.

Cooper, C. (1990) 'Meeting the needs: educational guidance within higher education', *Educational Guidance News and Views*, Spring.

Cooper, C. (1991a) 'Educational guidance and flexible learning', *Adults Learning*, **2** (10).

Cooper, C. (1991b) 'Guidance in higher education', *Educational Guidance News and Views*, Summer.

Cooper, C. J. G. (1992) *Anglia Polytechnic Guidance and Counselling Project (Final Report)*, Anglia Polytechnic.

Further Education Funding Council (1992) *Funding Learning*, Coventry: FEFC.

Further Education Unit (1994) *Managing the Delivery of Guidance in Colleges*, London: FEU.

Higher Education Queen Council (1994) *Guidance and Counselling in Higher Education*, London: HEQC.

IRDAC (1994) *Quality and Relevance*, Brussels: European Commission.

Murgatroyd, Woolf and Rhys (1987)

Southee, S. (1991) 'The Ford EDAP development', Guidance in the Workplace series, *Educational Guidance News and Views*, Spring.

UDACE (1986)

# Chapter 17

# New technologies for open learning

## The superhighway to the learning society?

*Gill Kirkup and Ann Jones*

> Distance education now seems like the answer to the adult educator's ideal of lifelong learning for all.
>
> (Boyd and Dirkx 1994: 11)

> . . . the information-technology revolution is creating a new form of electronic, interactive education that should blossom into a lifelong learning system that allows almost anyone to learn almost anything from anywhere at anytime.
>
> (Halal and Liebowitz 1994: 21)

This chapter will examine the evidence for the above claims by describing the historical development of open and distance education, and reviewing the past and potential future role of information and communication technologies in developing new forms of open and distance learning that might support the development of a learning society.

## OPEN LEARNING, DISTANCE EDUCATION AND THE LEARNING SOCIETY

Open learning (OL) and distance education (DE) have become inextricably bound together and the field of non-traditional post-school education abounds with overlapping terminology. 'Open learning' is a term recently popular in the UK and becoming more widespread, although a North American educator would be more familiar with the term 'independent study', which includes the notion of both distance (independence from the teacher) and openness and flexibility (personal autonomy over studies).

Internationally, the term 'distance education' (DE) is favoured over 'independent study' (Moore 1991), especially since the use of new information and communication technologies (ICTs) stresses the possibilities of communicating across distances of time and space. OL and DE are entwined, and many writers refer to 'ODL' (Open and Distance

Learning). Where appropriate this is the term used in this chapter. Where only distance education is being referred to we refer to 'DE'.

It is the possibilities raised by new technologies in the delivery of education and training which link OL and DE to contemporary notions of the learning society. The latter entails:

> The spread of education to all people in the society and into the multiple organizations of society . . .
>
> (Cross 1981: 2)

The learning society is one in which learning takes place throughout life. Included in this idea is the notion of opening up learning to those who might not previously or otherwise have been engaged in learning, and this aspect is one that is shared with the idea of open learning. Ball explains that the process of creating a learning society is a gradual one, and comments that it will require a range of institutions:

> The key to success will be the development of learning institutions, including not only schools, colleges and universities, but also learning companies and learning organizations, in a learning city or learning community (whether defined by neighbourhood, shared work or common interest).
>
> (Ball 1993: 2)

Open and distance education is already serving many such institutions, and the advent of new technologies and the convergence of technologies brings with it the possibility of extending the range of institutions for which it can provide education, thereby extending learning opportunities to more individuals. Open learning will be a key feature if a learning society is to be realized.

'Openness' and 'distance' have not always been connected: face-to-face teaching can be 'open' in respect to entry qualifications, and most traditional adult education has been of this sort. Distance education on the other hand can be very selective in its students, in particular at university and professional level. One of the best definitions of distance education (Keegan 1988: 30) identifies the following six main elements:

- Separation of teacher and learner, which distinguishes it from face-to-face lecturing.
- Influence of an educational organization, which distinguishes it from private study.
- Use of technical media, usually print, to unite teacher and learner and carry the educational content.
- Provision of two-way communication so that the student may benefit from or even initiate dialogue.

- Possibility of occasional meetings for both didactic and socialization purposes.
- Participation in an industrialized form of education which, if accepted, contains the genus of radical separation of distance education from other forms.

This definition of DE is now changing because of ICT applications, and it will be revisited later in this chapter. First, however, it is important to establish an historical framework for DE developments, because these have always relied on communication technologies applied to educational aims. It can be argued that the success of distance education in delivering education and training across all age and social groups has been a significant spur to the development of the idea of a learning society.

## THE HISTORY OF OPEN LEARNING AND DISTANCE EDUCATION

The earliest 'modern' form of DE was 'open' in its widest sense: Isaac Pitman's 1840 course in shorthand writing. Pitman himself, and later members of his Phonographic Corresponding Society, provided tuition in shorthand, free by post, to anyone who wanted it (Elliott 1978).

In the nineteenth century the development of DE was driven by popular movements to widen the educational provision for adults. In some countries (e.g. the UK) adults were excluded from established institutions such as universities because the curriculum did not fulfil their needs and selection criteria were restrictive. In other countries widely scattered populations could not be served by face-to-face methods. Nineteenth-century development in distance education relied on the technology of a postal system (as well as cheap print) which could guarantee the regular collection and delivery of materials at very low cost, for example the UK penny post.

The main emphasis was on second-chance education for people who could not attend conventional education, but vocational education was also provided by short correspondence courses through farmers' and mechanics' institutes (Watkins 1991). In the nineteenth and early twentieth centuries it was rare in western Europe for face-to-face institutions also to offer correspondence tuition. Extension courses and adult education provision remained in evening classes. In eastern Europe, on the other hand, widespread DE was provided from the 1920s onwards by a variety of institutions, including all the major universities. In Australia and North America universities provided DE to serve widely dispersed populations. Institutions offering both face-to-face and distance education became known as 'dual mode' institutions.

Distance educators have always tried, not always successfully, to take advantage of developing communication technologies. In 1912 the University of Wisconsin began a successful association with the publishers McGraw-Hill whereby specially commissioned texts were published and sold on the open market. This meant that Wisconsin students could obtain well-produced study material cheaply and distance education texts could also be used by face-to-face institutions. It was also in Wisconsin that the first educational broadcasting took place in 1919, an experiment which failed under pressure from commercial radio. In the UK the British Broadcasting Corporation (BBC) developed an extensive educational programme for adults in the 1920s and 1930s, often tied to book publication. This was targeted at adult study groups, and included accompanying text materials. In societies with low literacy levels and erratic postal services, education through radio, especially to rural areas, has been much more successful (Dodds 1985). Educational broadcasting through television has followed a similar, but later, trajectory in industrialized countries where ownership of televisions is high. However, it is more rarely used as a specifically pedagogic medium for adult learners, partly because the cost of producing the programmes.

What is clear from this history is that the idea of the power of technology to transform education is not new. Technology applied to DE has also opened education to some students, for example, those with physical disabilities, enabling them to participate for the first time alongside able-bodied students. They could simply use DE, including a variety of different media, to study at home. Others whose disabilities involved communication, hearing, vision or speech could often get materials in alternative media, and submit assessment by the use of alternative media (Vincent 1983).

## OPEN AND DISTANCE LEARNING IN THE RANGE OF ADULT PROVISION

According to Ball's (1993) definition quoted above, the learning society in part consists of a range of learning institutions. The success of a learning society depends on the nature of these institutions and their structural positions. In this respect, ODL is not developing with the same institutional structures, uses of media and student support services everywhere across the globe. Reference has already been made to the locational and historical factors which determine the development of DE in any region. For example, with the collapse of the USSR in the early 1990s, countries that were previously part of the USSR had to redesign their educational and training systems. In the old USSR there had been generous provision of adult distance education, but this was now viewed as being of low status and low quality. It relied almost absolutely on correspondence texts because there was little money to develop educational radio and TV. Private telephone ownership was not established and privately owned personal computers were almost non-existent (Nordic Council of Ministers 1993).

Distinctions can be made between large-scale (e.g. the Open University (OUUK)) and small-scale providers of distance education; the former is usually a publicly funded system, and the latter may be public or private. A more important distinction is that made by Neil between the 'whole system control model' and systems which are 'embedded into communities of educational agencies' (quoted in Moore 1991). In the whole-system model the institution has control over its finance, examinations and accreditation, curriculum and instructional services. Globally there are now about 20 national autonomous distance teaching universities which belong in this category. It can be argued that the success of the OUUK in producing and integrating multiple media is due to this level of control. For example, the Open Learning Foundation (UK) which produces courses through consortia of face-to-face institutions which then operate as dual-mode has not been able to take advantage of these high capital cost media.

Political and economic developments in the 1980s and 1990s, in industrialized countries such as the UK, have moved away from resourcing large autonomous educational institutions towards encouraging cooperative working between institutions and sometimes private industry. This has increased the number and variety of organizations which are producing and/or delivering DE and expanding into the adult learning market. The scale of this expansion in the UK alone can be seen in the entries to the UK Open Learning Directory which concentrates on programmes and materials in vocational training and basic skills. The 1994 Directory contains 2,500 examples of OL materials and 250 UK organizations that offer a range of services to support OL. The communities of educational agencies are thereby being expanded through the development and use of ODL.

The picture world-wide is one of the expansion of ODL in adult education provision. However, evidence for the extent of take-up of these opportunities, or the extent to which learners negotiate them successfully, is less easy to come by. This is an especially important question when students are disadvantaged adults, as questions are raised about the extent of social justice within developments towards a learning society:

> If distance education is based essentially on self-learning, to what extent is it inherently accessible to the most disadvantaged sections of the public? Is self-learning not a form of education that implies a degree of independence which these sections of the population lack?
>
> (Seabright and Nickolmann 1992: 25)

The efficacy of DE courses compared with more traditional teaching methods, or of some teaching/learning media over others, is still not well researched. Van Kekerix and Andrews, reviewing the literature on the effectiveness of different media quote Clark (1983) as part of their conclusion that it is hard to find clear evidence that new media help students learn any better than less high-tech 'correspondence' text:

> media are mere vehicles that deliver instruction but do not influence student achievement any more than the truck that delivers our groceries causes changes in our nutrition.
>
> (Van Kekerix and Andrews 1991: 144)

## THE STRENGTHS AND WEAKNESS OF OPEN LEARNING AND DISTANCE EDUCATION

The previous sections have described the history of ODL as one of growth to provide for the educational needs of people who could not, or would not – for whatever reason – engage in face-to-face education. More recently, the expansion of education and training in many countries has led governments to put pressure on established educational institutions to teach more students, and a more diverse body of students, whilst incurring little, if any, increased cost. Here ODL is more of a solution to institutional problems than to students' problems. Many institutions have identified ODL as a potential way of achieving cost savings and are experimenting with combining elements of ODL with face-to-face mode in 'dual-mode' courses, but not always with the hoped-for achievements.

The success of ODL packages cannot be assumed. There is now an extensive body of critical work on the weaknesses of ODL, the most important of which are:

- its inability to offer dialogue in the way that a face-to-face, more Socratic educational ideal might;
- the inflexibility of content and study method;
- the isolation and individualization of the student;
- the reality of its 'openness'.

These have to be set against what are usually regarded as the strengths of ODL:

- flexibility in place and time of study;
- flexibility in pace of study, although if the course is assessed there may be assignment deadlines;
- in open-access systems, no prior study or qualifications required;
- modularity and flexibility of materials.

Any discussion about the use of new ICTs must include how such technologies might overcome the previous weakness of ODL without undermining its strengths.

## Limited possibilities of dialogue

One of the problems of many models of ODL is the limited possibilities for dialogue both between teachers and learners and amongst learners. How limited that dialogue is will largely depend on the range of media and technologies used. For example, programmes broadcast on radio involve one-way communication, whereas an audio teleconference allows dialogue to occur. Students need dialogue with their teachers and with other students in order to consolidate and check on their own learning. This is why, in most structured ODL systems, regular student assessment, usually in some correspondence mode, is central, to provide formative feedback to the student if not to provide summative performance assessment. Such dialogue allows students to assess their learning and develop a sense of community with other students; it allows the institution to assess how well it is achieving its teaching objectives, and allows students to give feedback on the quality and content of courses.

Evans and Nation (1989) argue for more dialogue in ODL so that adult students can play a greater part in designing the content of their own education. They assert the importance of the 'open text' in democratic education and see, as an aim, that students should become 'collaborative developers of their own courses through critical reflection'.

## Structure and packaging of learning materials

Highly structured course materials (which ODL materials usually are) are teacher-centred, allowing little flexibility for students' different educational objectives or learning styles, or for different learners' needs. The linear structure of a transmitted television programme, for example, permits very little flexibility for learners; even a programmed learning text which offers students different routes through the material is directive and presumes a limited set of routes and the same final goal for each student. An educational situation on which little structure has been imposed by the teacher and which is rich in opportunities for dialogue can encourage more flexible learning, but if there is too little structure then the unsophisticated learner, in particular, may struggle and fail. Since different learners need different amounts of support and independence, it is difficult to design a large-scale system which is optimal for all students.

## Individualization and isolation

It has been argued (Young 1988) that the move towards home-based ODL reflects and promotes a similar shift in social trends towards the individualization of society (e.g. from bus to car and from cinema to TV, and most recently from family viewing to individualized viewing as homes have multiple TV sets). This trend has also been observed by critical analysts of ICTs, one of whom describes:

> The increasingly privatised family . . . shut off from public life, turned in on itself . . . connected to the wider world only through the electronic forms of satellite/cable TV and teleshopping.
>
> (Morley 1994: 101)

However, it is more often argued that the strengths of ODL are in enabling the isolated individual to engage in a structured programme of study. In addition, ODL does not need to have as its target the individual student – it may be aimed at student or community groups, as are most of the basic literacy and core skills programmes of India and Africa. This individual focus has been criticized by those in adult and continuing education; for example Keddie (1980) considers individualism now to be the dominant ideology of adult education in the UK, and one, she argues, which promotes an abstract, fragmented view of the learner rather than giving emphasis to a social and historical context.

## Openness

> A final criticism of ODL is that, ironically, it is often not very 'open': 'every kind of openness associated with distance education seems to have its opposite side, a tendency to closure'.
>
> (Harris 1987: 3)

Harris (1987), for example, examined the OUUK and argued that the bureaucratic nature of its entrance procedures (which are in theory open to anyone) and its industrial model of course construction (which again is in theory 'open' to all kinds of intellectual input and to public scrutiny in its final form) do, in fact, lead to the rejection of some kinds of students and of some kinds of knowledge. A system in which students must register and begin studying at the same time in the year, and read and complete extensive paperwork, must lead to certain students feeling alienated from the system before they are even registered as students. The public nature of course materials means that they are checked for libellous materials in a way which does not apply in the classroom. It has also been difficult to deal with some issues, for example pornography and representation, when course materials dealing with the issue are published or broadcast, rather than restricted to a small group.

## POTENTIAL OF ICTs TO BE THE VEHICLE FOR A LEARNING SOCIETY

Two developments in particular have the potential to transform ODL from one element of adult education into the primary device of a learning society. One is the increasing availability and variety of functions of ICTs and the other is national governments' priorities for increasing adult learning while reducing government funding. Distance educators are enthusiastic about ICTs because they seem to have the potential to overcome some of the disadvantages of DE discussed previously, as well as offering new educational possibilities. Conventional educators and politicians have also seen the potential for ICTs to improve the quality and range of resources available to any student, and to help cope with an increasing number of students whilst resources decrease. This is leading to a collapse of the previously clear boundaries between conventional and distance education.

Mason and Kaye (quoted in Paulson 1992: 56), who are concerned with telematics (telecommunications plus computers) in particular, question the final element of Keegan's definition of DE (pp. 273–4) as well as adding other new possibilities, to produce a definition including the following:

- The breaking down of conceptual distinctions between distance education and place-based education.
- The changing of traditional roles of faculty, administrative and support staff, adjunct tutors.
- The provision of an opportunity, which never existed before, to create a network of scholars, 'space' for collective thinking, and access to peers for socializing and serendipitous change.

As well as telematics, other new developments, including hypertext, multimedia and desktop publishing (DTP), are also contributing to this change. Telematics, hypertext and multimedia presume some level of student and teacher access to computer equipment and electronic networks as a minimum requirement. But in many cases these media can only be exploited if a student has unlimited access in their own home. DTP on the other hand may be the invisible revolution in ODL. This chapter has argued that for many ODL providers world-wide correspondence texts remain the core teaching medium. DTP offers providers a potential revolution in the way these texts are produced, and unlike the others it is a technology which remains invisible to the student.

## Telematics

Computer-mediated communication (CMC) was seen in the 1980s as probably the most important ICT application for adult education. It has always been true that a greater degree of dialogue between teacher and learner, or amongst groups of learners, can be achieved through some media rather than others. CMC uses computers linked through the local telephone network, and internationally via satellites, to provide a new means of communication. It has the potential to allow both 'real-time' (synchronous) and time-independent (asynchronous) communication between individuals; amongst and between groups; and to organizations and databases outside education. Use of an electronic network can provide a student or group with access to information outside their immediate resources. For example, 'Compuserve' offers access to library databases, journal abstracts, news services and mail shopping as well as the facility for interpersonal communication. Telematics can therefore support individualized learning or enhance collaborative learning, and encourage a sense of community that many students look for when they study. This has been especially important for students with disabilities; for many, although not all, their disability is no barrier to CMC and they experience access and communication equal to those of their able-bodied fellow students (Coombs 1993).

Students (and teachers and sometimes non-academic subject experts) are organized, or organize themselves, into groups for *computer conferences*. These can be based round a topic, or a student characteristic, such as belonging to the 'class' of a particular tutor. Conferences can be private 'conversations' in the sense that only named individuals are able to read them or contribute to them, or they can be open to any participant. However, until recently CMC has been a text communication device, dependent on a degree of literacy (traditional as well as technological). It has been more obviously suitable to more advanced levels of education where students expect to be asked to express themselves in writing. The medium would be of little use to students in countries which are using ODL to teach basic literacy and life skills, or to populations with low literacy skills, as long as it remains a text-based medium.

The European Union (EU) has been keen to direct research funding into telematics applications, including education. One experiment, ELNET: The European 'Business and Languages' Learning Network, provided an electronic network for business studies students in some universities in the UK, France and Germany to produce cross-cultural learning in a 'virtual educational establishment' (i.e. to replicate some of the learning of an educational exchange visit) (Davies 1994). Cross-national networking is promoted in Europe as much for business and political reasons as for educational ones, and it is hoped that networking will be promoted amongst workers as well as students. Such activities are promoted as developing a learning organization, which according to Burgoyne (1992) must include inter-organization learning.

Evaluation of these projects has demonstrated that both students and teachers need to learn new skills both to interrogate distant information systems and to communicate with each other using a new medium. These skills can be regarded as another kind of literacy. In many cases educational providers have simply adapted or added some telematics to face-to-face or other DE provision, whereas what is needed is materials designed for the strengths and weaknesses of the medium (Paulson 1992).

## Hypertexts

Unlike CMC, hypertext makes use of a variety of different ways of presenting information. According to one definition, hypertext is 'a computer-based software system for organizing and storing information to be accessed nonsequentially and constructed collaboratively by authors and users' (Jonassen 1991: 83). The information referred to here is in the form of a document which can consist of text, diagrams, pictures, video sequences, sound, etc. and so is a much more flexible and less constrained medium for many teaching purposes than text alone. The information is stored non-sequentially and structured such that links are made between various items. The user navigates through the hypertext by making use of these links to move from one item to another. When the learner clicks on an 'active' word, the program calls up the item to which it has been linked. In theory, thousands of links can be made, and once the learner has moved to another screen, or diagram, via a link, he or she will then have new options for making further moves.

The development of hypertext systems has generated a great deal of excitement about their educational exploitation and potential. It was argued that their lack of linearity made them an ideal tool for learners to use to explore resources in a way that suited them, rather than in a way prescribed by a teacher. But a major criticism of early hypertexts was that many are simply rewritten textbooks and the whole point about written prose is that it is meant to be sequential, and much is lost by trying to 'chunk' it up and link it through word associations. Rather than the metaphor of a book, the metaphor that is often offered for hypertext systems is that of a museum or art gallery. The learner decides which avenues to explore and what links to make. This makes it potentially very learner centred: suited to independent learning and therefore to ODL. Hypertexts have been used to create ODL courses, often by dual-mode institutions, by converting versions of face-to-face courses.

It was, however, soon discovered that unless some navigational aids to hypertext were provided, learners could easily get lost in the complex systems, finding themselves reading about an item, or looking at a diagram, and being unsure about their original purpose or how they got there! As with many tools for independent learning, experience and expertise may be necessary to make best use of this application. Laurillard comments that:

> Browsing, or scanning, or hunting down a piece of information from an extensive resource all play a rather small part in learning academic knowledge. The learner is likely to be working on a much smaller scale, to need help with discerning the structure and through it the meaning of a particular text being studied. This is where hypertext fails to support the learner . . . it provides no feedback . . . It is not a stand-alone learning medium, it needs additional support from the teacher, just as library work does.
>
> (Laurillard 1993: 126)

## Multimedia

Developments in hypertext have led to further developments which make more use of different media, especially video and audio. The inclusion of sounds, video and photographs greatly extends the possibilities: these are often referred to as hypermedia. The term multimedia is also used to describe quite different kinds of applications and uses, but the important development here is that of devices (usually computers but not necessarily so) which combine the more traditional computer capabilities with those of other media, hence the term.

Teaching programmes and computer-assisted learning (CAL) programmes of various kinds have been available in ODL for many years, where students can access them, in study centres or at home. The educational benefits of these kinds of programmes derive mainly from the feedback that students obtain (either on their answers or their attempts to, say, carry out modelling), and the motivational power of computers themselves. Whereas hypermedia are essentially presentational – a kind of electronic encyclopaedia – multimedia applications can include teaching.

Multimedia is very expensive to produce, and few organizations, even well-resourced ones, can afford to produce them more than just experimentally. For this reason governments have encouraged consortia of educational institutions and ICT manufacturers and developers to combine to produce multimedia which would have wide use. Such cooperation between institutions provides not only a pooling of resources but also networks for sharing, promoting and supporting learning: another important element of the learning society (Morley 1994). As with earlier 'published' media, once commercial organizations which sell the product on the open market are involved, educational products also become available to those not registered as a student.

One concern about the new multimedia material is the extent to which it makes the best and most appropriate educational use of the different media. This same concern was expressed when computers were first used in teaching and learning, often by asking whether the computer is being used to do something that could not otherwise be done (or not be done as well). Much multimedia is essentially presentational without the student interactivity that early CAL provided, which is argued to be so important (e.g. Laurillard 1993). The quality of illustrations and photographs that can now be achieved is such that applications, especially when combined with sound and movement, can be very appealing. However, in some cases simple video would serve as well as a more expensive multimedia. In others the learner is exploring what is essentially a multimedia database or encyclopaedia. For example, a CD-ROM in social history can provide the learner with primary sources of material, historical maps, photographs, architectural plans and biographies. All of these could be provided on paper in facsimile form, but would be likely to be more expensive to produce and distribute in this form.

Having material electronically available therefore does not guarantee that a student can use it in that form. Educators do not yet know what is the optimum amount of text information a student can deal with on a screen. If students resort to printing out material, at what point would it have been more cost-effective for them to have used an original paper-based version? There is not enough information yet about how students engage with and use such materials; research is at an early stage. Although electronic versions of encyclopaedias can include much more information than print-based versions (and include sound and video), this in itself does not give them any more teaching and educational capabilities than any other resource or encyclopaedia.

A different example of an interactive use of multimedia is Durbridge's *Art Explorer* (Durbridge and Stratford 1995), which is in the tradition of programmes which provide an environment for learners to explore, act on and change, and to see the results of their actions. This tradition is usually found in the sciences, where learners may be exploring the laws of physics. The first activity in this package invites learners to describe paintings in terms of their own constructs, which leads them to reflect on how they perceive and categorize paintings and how this compares with experts' views. In another part of the package, where the pictures are 'live', learners can alter various features of the paintings to bring their attention to the resulting changes. Various activities follow of a more guided nature which allow the learner to experience, as if with an expert's eye, how paintings work their three-dimensional effects. Through these activities learners can engage in the 'what-if' questioning beloved of science, and get some very direct feedback from their observations which can inform their understanding about the role of various aspects of a painting. Perhaps the most important aspect of this example is that the activities arise out of Durbridge's research on the difficulties learners have in getting to grips with art history, and are ones which really could not be done in any other way; the package really does exploit the media.

The most potentially powerful application of ICTs, however, is a combination of the multimedia workstation with telematics. It could have an integral camera so that networked users can see each other and perhaps also communicate through an audio channel. But like any tool, such systems are only as good as their developers. One danger with the multimedia workstation is that people with no expertise in the different uses (and pitfalls) of various media can relatively easily put together a package which may look good, but does little for learners. For this reason, Laurillard (1993) advocates that any organization wanting to produce multimedia should set up a courseware development team which consists of people with complementary skills and knowledge. This is especially necessary in areas of ICT where developments are happening so rapidly that any individual can only keep abreast of one small area. A team keeps up to date by bringing together a number of individuals who have all been keeping updated in different, but related, areas. A similar model is the basis for the learning organization.

## Desktop publishing (DTP)

DTP is the use of computers to integrate text and graphics electronically. The power of desktop and/or personal computers combined with page layout programs and fine-quality laser printing makes it theoretically possible to produce correspondence texts with high-quality print and page design without the usual printing processes and without the skills of printing professionals. This has a number of potential benefits (Lefrere 1994): the production time of text design and costs of design are reduced, and the possibility of experimenting with layout makes it possible to improve the quality of materials, and update or revise them. For small-population courses texts can be produced 'on demand' from a laser printer. Texts can be individualized and printed for the needs of different sub-groups in the student population. DTP material can be designed to be distributed as hypertext or multimedia, as well as in printed form, allowing students with the facilities to print off the parts they choose. Properly trained practitioners could produce the text directly themselves, although it may be better to rely on the new skills of DTP professionals (Balser and Sturmer 1993). Already one of the problems with the expansion of ODL is that some conventional institutions presume that ODL texts are simply the lecture notes and reading list from conventionally taught courses, bound with assessment material and sold to students. As with multimedia packages it is now technically straightforward to produce materials; unlike multimedia it is also cheap. This has led to the production of some very poor-quality ODL, and there is a danger that thoughtless use of DTP could increase this.

## WINNERS AND LOSERS: EDUCATIONAL 'SURFING' OR RUMMAGING IN THE BARGAIN BASEMENT?

> The key to unlocking the new possibilities is to envision modern education as an omnipresent activity. As the technology for acquiring and distributing knowledge permeates home, work and all other locations, all social functions should be integrated into a seamless web of learning. Everyday living will then take place in an electronic school without walls.
>
> (Halal and Liebowitz 1994: 26)

Statements like this are increasingly common in both the popular and the educational media of the mid-1990s and certainly embody one kind of vision of a learning society. However, similar statements about the future were around in the early 1980s as the first microcomputers became available for the domestic market. In that vision children were seen as being tutored in their own home by an intelligent tutoring system as their parents tele-worked around them (Mason *et al.* 1984). But the effect of ICTs on education has been nowhere as powerful as the technological determinists predicted, and there are very good reasons for this.

We have argued that the combination of the power of small computers with their ability to be networked together makes them potentially very valuable for ODL, although teaching quality does not come automatically with the technology. This final section assesses the implications of the new ICTs for three of the actors in a learning society: the producing or delivering organization; anyone involved in producing teaching/teaching materials of any kind and/or facilitating the learning of others; and the learner.

### The providing organization

Earlier, Neil's distinction between the 'whole-system control model' and systems which are 'embedded into communities of educational agencies' was discussed and it was argued that less well resourced (and centrally organized) institutions may be at a disadvantage in making use of different media. This argument applies to ICTs too. In some countries, e.g the UK, a new mechanism has been recently introduced for ensuring 'quality' in both HE and in school education: that of competition. Laurillard (1993) argues that this produces inefficiencies as there is a limited resource to spread around and competition leads to repetition of effort. In the UK, the Government has attempted to counter the unhelpful effect of competition by special funding to HE consortia of institutions to develop courseware for free distribution to all HE institutions. Other developments, where money follows institutional assessment or status, will tend to ensure that the best-resourced institutions stay well re-sourced, whilst other stay poor. There is, therefore, differential access to ICTs by institutions, which militates against the openness of ODL and a consistent quality available to students studying with different institutions.

Many, but not all, of the organizations providing access to information and resources over the Internet at the moment do so without charge, but it is expected that in the future the most useful and popular services are likely to be by subscription only. Educational organizations will be both buyers and sellers of information services, as will students. ICTs are expensive and require certain infrastructure (such as a reliable electricity grid and telecommunications network) which some educational institu-tions in the developing world do not yet have. In a global information market the institutions of developing countries will have few information services to sell and may not be able to buy those they need. ICTs may require certain skills in their users (e.g. literacy) which tends to make their use more relevant to students in wealthy, industrial nations, thus increasing the gap in educational provision between industrialized and non-industrialized nations.

## Teachers

> . . . Apple Computer has reduced its classroom training by 75%. The corresponding savings are so vast that most corporations should soon follow suit. 'We aim to get [classroom instruction] down to zero as soon as the technology is ready' says Lucy Carter, a training director at Apple.
>
> (Halal and Liebowitz 1994: 26)

Few educators would go as far as Lucy Carter; however, CAL has been seen as a way of adding non-human resource into a classroom, hopefully at less cost than a human teacher. Where expansion is encouraged, or even required, the use of ICTs may be seen as the only response. In an ideal situation a teacher/lecturer would have the time and resources to draw on a range of commercially produced resources and, where she felt it necessary, the time and resources to produce her own with the help of a production team. However, rather than lessen the teaching load and overall burden, more use of ICTs is likely to increase it. The move to ODL requires staff time, training and, perhaps most importantly, a shift in culture. The development of educational material using ICTs will require all this and more: developments in this area are so rapid that keeping abreast of the field is a major enterprise. Resources such as international databases are very likely to remain under- or unused, and the possibilities of actually developing course materials using ICTs seem very slim indeed. Where there is an additional requirement to teach via CMC, often outside class hours, studies have shown that the extra time involved is always underestimated (e.g. Kaye 1991). Finally, some of the less interactive teaching (satellite and teleteaching) which is intended to reach mass audiences, as well as stand-alone teaching packages, pose the real threat of making the teacher redundant while not replacing her with a resource offering the same facilities.

## Learners

In terms of student access to ICTs, an opening up of opportunities for some is a closing down for others. Although some ICTs are institution-ally based, perhaps in study centres, others rely on student provision for access. However, a learning society aims for an educational system which is 'open' in the sense that its mission is to reach all classes of society, especially those people who have had less formal education than the majority, and what usually follows from this lower income. The technologies it uses must be easily accessible to these groups. The most recent UK data on the domestic ownership of information technologies demonstrate that there is still a direct relationship between access to technologies, and wealth and lifestyle (see Figure 17.1).

This figure is based on data from the UK National Household Survey carried out in 1992/3. It shows the ownership among households, with members in economically active age groups, of four major ICT devices. The ownership of computers for all employment groups remains low, and has not increased as fast as the new technology, such as audio CD. Even at the professional level only half the households have computers, and OUUK figures (Kirkwood and Jones 1994) show that access also varied by gender.

In the UK at least (and there is no evidence to show that trends are different elsewhere), there is a most obvious contradiction between the potential of ICTs for DE and the reality of their uneven distribution

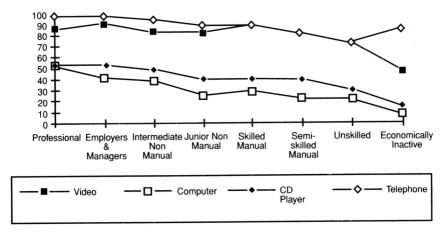

*Figure 17.1* Household ownership of information and communication technologies (ICTs) from General House Survey 1992/93

among different population groups. Access to ICTs follows a very different pattern from access to a traditional communication system such as the postal system. Here, then, is a very vivid example of Harris's statement that 'every kind of openness associated with distance education seems to have its opposite side, a tendency to closure'. To capitalize on the potential of ICTs for Open Learning, and for a learning society rather than an educated élite, implementation programmes must attempt to address inequalities caused by or reinforced by ICTs. To return to the quote from Halal and Liebowitz on the first page of this chapter, yes, the technology has the potential to provide support networks for lifelong learning. However, the applications of this new technology have not yet been proved effective enough to replace many well-established teaching and learning activities, and may never be so. Nor have the technical resources become socially ubiquitous.

## REFERENCES

Ball, C. (1993) *Making Sense of the Reform and Restructuring of Education and Training in the UK*, London: RSA, The Learning Society Exchange.

Balser, K. and Sturmer, H. (1993) *Desk Top Publishing*, Proceedings of the 1993 EDEN Conference 'East/West dialogue in distance education: changing societies, technology and quality', Berlin: 10–12 May.

Boyd, D. and Dirkx, J. M. (1994) *Realizing the Democratic Ideal in Adult Distance Learning: The Participatory Development Education Model*. Proceedings of the Distance Learning Research Conference, San Antonio, 28–29 April.

Burgoyne (1992) 'Creating a learning organization', *RSA Journal*, April, 321–330.

Clark, R. (1983) 'Reconsidering research on learning from media', *Review of Educational Research*, 53: 450.

Coombs, N. (1993) 'Global empowerment of impaired learners: data networks will transcend both distance and physical disabilities', *Education Media International*, 30 (1): 23–25.

Cross, P. K. (1981) *Adults as Learners*, San Francisco: Jossey-bass.

Davies, D. (1994) 'ELNET – the European Learning NetWork', W. C. B. Veen *et al.* (eds), *Telematics in Education: The European Case*, De Lier: Academic Book Centre, 249–259.

Dodds, T. (1985) 'The development of distance teaching: an historical perspective', reprinted in J. Jenkins and B. N. Koul (eds) (1991) *Distance Education: A Review*, Indira Ghandi National Open University and the National Extension College, 6–12.

Durbridge, N. and Stratford, M. (1995) 'Art Explorer: a multimedia prototype', Institute of Educational Technology, The Open University.

Elliott, S. (1978) 'Tuition by post: an historical perspective', *Teaching at a Distance*, 11 (May): 12–16.

Evans, T. and Nation, D. (eds) (1989) *Critical Reflection on Distance Education*, Lewes: Falmer.

Halal, W. E. and Liebowitz, J. (1994) 'Telelearning: the multimedia revolution in education', *The Futurist*, Nov–Dec, 21–26.

Harris, D. (1987) *Openness and Closure in Distance Education*, London: Falmer.

Jonassen, D. (1991) 'Hypertext as instructional design', *Educational Technology Research and Development*, 39(1): 83–92.

Kaye, A. (1991) 'Computer networking for development of distance education courses', *CITE* Report No. 146, Institute of Educational Technology, Open University.

Keddie, N. (1980) 'Adult education, an ideology of individualism', in Thompson, J. (ed.) *Adult Education for Change*, London: Hutchinson.

Keegan, D. (1988) 'On defining distance education', in D. Sewart, D. Keegan and B. Holmberg (eds), *Distance Education: International Perspectives*, London: Routledge.

Kirkwood, A. and Jones, A. (1994) 'Computing access survey 1993: Foundation Course students'. *CITE* Report No. 191, Institute of Educational Technology, Open University.

Laurillard, D. (1993) *Rethinking University Teaching: A Framework for the Effective Use of Educational Technology*, London: Routledge.

Lefrere, P. (1994) 'The technology and management of desk-top publishing', in F. Lockwood (ed.), *Materials Production in Open and Distance Teaching*, London: Paul Chapman.

Lisewsi, B. (1994) 'The open learning pilot project at the Liverpool Business School', *Open Learning*, 9(2): 12–22.

Mason, R., Jennings, L. and Evans, R. (1984) 'A day at Xanadu', *The Futurist*, February.

Moore, M. G. (1991) 'International aspects of independent study', in B. L. Watkins and S. J. Wright (eds), *The Foundations of American Distance Education*, Iowa: Kendall Hunt.

Morley, Moss-Jones, J. (1994) 'Learning organization – concepts, practices and relevance', Briefing Paper 2, NHS Training Directorate.

Nordic Council of Ministers (1993) *Distance Education in Estonia, Latvia and Lithuania*, Report and a Feasibility Study, Oslo, December.

Paulson, M. F. (1992) *From Bulletin Boards to Electronic Universities: Distance Education, Computer-Mediated Communication, and Online Education*, Research Monograph No. 7 of the American Center for the Study of Distance Education, College of Education, The Pennsylvania State University.

Seabright, V. and Friedhelm, N. (eds) (1992) *Distance Education in Europe*, Studies and Recommendations by the Council of Europe, Council of Europe, Saturn Europe's Open Learning Network.

Seabright, V. and Nickolmann, F. (1992) (eds) *Distance Education in Europe*. Studies and Recommendations by the Council of Europe, Brussels: Saturn Europe's Open Learning Network.

Van Kekerix, M. and Andrews, J. (1991) 'Electronic media and independent study', in B. L. Watkins and S. J. Wright (eds), *The Foundations of American Distance Education*, Iowa: Kendall Hunt, 135–157.

Veen, W. C. B., de Vries, P. and Vogelzang, F. (eds) (1994) *Telematics in Education: The European Case*, De Lier: Academic Book Centre.

Vincent, T. (1983) 'Home computing for the visually handicapped', *Teaching at a Distance*, 23: 24–29.

Watkins, B. L. (1991) 'A quite radical idea: the invention and elaboration of collegiate correspondence study', in B. L. Watkins and S. J. Wright (eds), *The Foundations of American Distance Education*, Iowa: Kendall Hunt.

Young, M. (1988) 'Education for the new work', in N. Paine (ed.), *Open Learning in Transition: An Agenda for Action*, Cambridge: National Extension College.

# Index